WITHDRAWN

D1490565

DESERTION DURING THE CIVIL WAR

The American Historical Association

DESERTION
DURING THE CIVIL WAR

BY

ELLA LONN, Ph.D.

PROFESSOR OF HISTORY IN
GOUCHER COLLEGE

GLOUCESTER, MASS.

PETER SMITH

1966

PREFACE

To the casual reader the knowledge of any desertion in the brave ranks of the armies engaged in the Civil War, whether conceived of as passionately devoted to the "Lost Cause" or religiously dedicated to the preservation of the Union, will come as a distinct shock; even by the historical scholar the full extent of the evil, the wide distribution through all ranks and all parts of the country, the early and continuous manifestation of disaffection, and the enormous numbers implicated on both sides may not be fully grasped. But buried in the *Official War Records* lies a perfect mine of evidence of an overwhelming amount of desertion in the Confederacy, revealing the important part this factor played in the ultimate failure of the South to achieve independence. Appalling in the Southern armies, it was even worse in the Northern regiments.

Undoubtedly, the few remaining survivors of the struggle, Northern as well as Southern, will be repelled by the very subject of this book; probably the average reader will question the worth-whileness of an exhaustive study of that which seems to record a nation's shame. But no one can peruse these pages without gaining a different outlook on the subject. For centuries it has been the fashion to glorify war, to applaud the deeds of heroism and sacrifice; men prefer to shut their eyes to the ugly and sordid sides of war, such as profiteering, mass propaganda, and the deluding of the public by government misrepresentation. Much is to be said in extenuation of the ugly phase of desertion, apparently inseparable from war, but to look it squarely in the face rather than to cover it up or to ignore it, is to see more of the truth about war and should be another step in the direction of peace. The effort to face the truth should not be condemned as muck-raking.

The reader will learn that there can be no cause so just or beloved that war in its behalf will not be attended by desertion among its defenders when a conflict waged on so high a plane as was the Civil War could not be free from it. The fires of patriotism burn more brightly at the outbreak of war than towards its close. Men at the beginning of the struggle are more oblivious of personal discomfort, less selfish than they become as the struggle progresses, and more willing to contribute in all ways to the expected victory.

The reader will perforce be impressed with the parallelism which runs through the account of defection from the armies of the antagonists. But as the Confederacy was unable to frame a constitution which was other than a slight adaptation of the old framework, so these two nations of one race and one heritage, developed the same problems during the war and evolved similar solutions.

The writer ventures the hope that by turning a search-light on a question which could scarcely have found a tolerant reading a few decades ago, a few persons will, perchance, be led to a more tolerant view in discussing and pondering the problems of our recent World War on which passions are still inflamed. The truth is here, it is hoped, impartially presented. The writer, though by accident born in the North, has not felt the slightest impulse to minimize the desertion in the Union armies nor to exaggerate that in the Confederate forces. Her audience would be the first to condemn a partisan bias. The lovers of history should be the first to apply that tolerance to contemporary history.

There remains my acknowledgment of indebtedness to the Congressional Library, the law library of the University of Chicago, and to most of the libraries in Baltimore, where unfailing courtesy in making materials available has facilitated my labors.

E. L.

Baltimore, 1928.

CONTENTS

PART I

PART II

PART I

DESERTION IN THE CONFEDERACY

CHAPTER I

Causes of Confederate Desertion

The causes of desertion from the Confederate armies are so numerous and complex that to catalogue all in detail would be to tell a considerable part of the story of the Civil War. And yet the enumeration and weighing of these elements of dissatisfaction is the understanding, in no small measure, of the ultimate failure of the effort at disunion. Hence, a brief consideration of the reasons for the manifestation of this great evil is unavoidable.

First, and probably foremost, in the minds of the Confederate leaders as an explanation of dissatisfaction stood the character of many of the privates. Some, untutored and narrow-minded, dragged from the rocky mountains of the Carolinas, Georgia, and Alabama, from the pine hills and lowlands of Louisiana, and from the swamps of Florida and Mississippi, were ignorant of the real issues at stake and were but little identified with the struggle. So ignorant were some of them that when paroled by the North after capture they actually supposed that it released them from further obligation to the Confederacy.[1] The illiterate backwoodsman, variously termed "cracker," "mossback," "kasion," "bushwhacker," or "hillbilly," according to the section in which he was located, almost cut off from the mass of his fellow-men, was little interested in the economic aspect of the war, as he could see nothing in it for himself. When dragged from his farm plot into the Southern army, he often proved a passive Union sympathizer, as he was ready to fall back into his neutrality as deserter at the first opportunity. The controlling motive with these men was frequently not love for the Union, but a determination to avoid military service. They cared little for the approbation or condemnation of their fellows, especially distant officials at Richmond. In fact, they showed a conspicuous lack of that

---

[1] The comment of a Northern officer is worth quoting: "Quite a number of deserters come in daily . . . and generally so ignorant that little reliable information can be obtained from them" (*Official War Records*, Ser. II, XXVII, pt. III, 758).

quality which we applaud as patriotism, while a few proved, as is true in every army, downright cowards. The usual stories of men maiming themselves to avoid service are to be found.[1]

Still, the fact must be recognized that some of these same ignorant mountaineers were distinctly out of sympathy with the cause of slavery as the foundation stone on which was built the prestige of their proud neighbors of the lowlands, while scattered through the States were a small number, to state the fact conservatively, who cherished a real love for the old Union. The records of conscripts who promptly deserted to the Northern armies are too numerous to be disregarded as evidence. Making all due allowance for insincerity in so explaining their defection, indubitably some spoke the truth when they declared that they did not like the cause in which they were fighting and wished to live once more under the Stars and Stripes.[2] When a deserter raised a company in border territory to enter the service of the Union, his genuineness can scarcely be questioned.[3]

The net of the conscript service, moreover, dragged in men of Northern birth and also foreigners, particularly Germans and Irishmen,[4] who knew little and cared less for the burning American question of State rights. Northern-born men were in most cases holders of considerable property or large traders for their communities. Included in this group were merchants, lumbermen, real estate dealers, bankers, doctors, and even a few planters. Many had gone into the far South recently, after 1850, so that their ties were still mainly with the North and their traditions antislavery. The reports of the Northern officers are full of instances of citizens of Northern States who had settled in the South and who had been impressed into South-

[1] Davis, *Civil War and Reconstruction in Florida*, pp. 244–246. Casler, *Four Years in the Stonewall Brigade*, p. 24.

[2] A Texan declared that he had been opposed from the commencement to the cause he was forced to defend (*O. W. R.*, Ser. I, XLVIII, pt. II, 375).

[3] The captain here alluded to had been conscripted for Confederate service while trying to escape to the North from East Tennessee. On Bragg's retreat from Tullahoma he effected his escape and immediately raised a company (*ibid.*, Ser. I, XXVI, pt. I, 654).

A group from eastern Tennessee abandoned the Confederate service within twenty-four hours after conscription, many joining General Burnside's forces (Arthur, *Western North Carolina*, p. 609). Another band of nearly 500 Tennesseeans was captured en route for Kentucky and sent to Georgia (*O. W. R.*, Ser. I, X, pt. I, 649). The cases of individuals who made this claim are countless (*ibid.*, Ser. I, XXXII, pt. III, 61).

[4] *Ibid.*, Ser. I, XXXV, pt. I, 462. Germans in Texas proposed to resist conscription (*ibid.*, Ser. I, XV, 925–929).

ern regiments. These reports are sufficiently confirmed by Confederate officers when they tersely remark, "He is a Yankee, gone to his brethren," [1] or when they allude to him openly as a Northern or Union man. Irishmen are encountered frequently who deserted from the rebels and "cheerfully took the oath of allegiance," [2] while the case of a Scotsman was noted who forsook his duties with the commissary department to join the North.

The records show clearly that Mexicans were enlisted in the Southern service but proved utterly unreliable. Starting with no particular affection for American institutions, Northern or Southern, they early passed back over the Rio Grande to take part in the difficulties which soon beset their own land.[3] Evidently the Confederacy even tried to conscript Mexicans under the laws of Texas, which at that time required residents of ten days' time to do military duty. General H. P. Bee writes from Victoria, Texas, on December 4, 1863, "When the state troops were called out and a draft ordered, the attempt to enforce it, not only failed, but caused bad feeling and a protest from the Mexican authorities, who claimed, and justly, I think, that under the Treaty of Guadaloupe de Hidalgo citizens of Mexico in that territory were not liable to forced military service." General Bee wisely suspended the Texan law.[4]

Among the recruits from Kentucky especially were a goodly number bankrupt in fortune and reputation who eagerly embraced the Southern cause, as any change offered hope of possible advantage. Evil propensities brought soldiers into trouble, whereupon, faced with the probability of execution, they fled to the foe. Men, anxious to raise companies or battalions, sought recruits in all quarters and hence sometimes enlisted genuine ruffians. Eggleston tells of some interesting characters who had found release from durance in a Richmond jail by enlistment. One, a pirate and deserter from the British navy, was the most interesting of the group, but helps us to understand the statement that "except as regarded turbulence and utter unmanageability" they proved excellent soldiers.[5] Such men would

[1] *Ibid.*, Ser. I, II, 708; IV, 567; III, 486; XXV, pt. II, 327, 414; XXIV, pt. III, 439, 952.
[2] *Ibid.*, Ser. I, XXVI, pt. I, 567. XXVII, pt. III, 163.
[3] One company is recorded as composed wholly of Mexicans, while two others, one an artillery company, were composed partly of Mexicans (*ibid.*, Ser. I, IV, 152–153; XXVI, pt. II, 549–550).
[4] *Ibid.*, Ser. I, XXVI, pt. II, 479.
[5] *A Rebel's Recollections*, pp. 171–172.

leave General Morgan's service as readily as they had entered it.[1]

Almost from the beginning many of the volunteers were mere boys, fourteen to eighteen years of age, foolish, deluded youths,[2] of whom the Confederates had no right to expect the stamina and courage of mature men. The Conscript Law after April 16, 1862, took in, with some exceptions, every male from eighteen to thirty-five years of age; the second Conscript Act of September 27 following added those between thirty-five and forty-five years; and after February 17, 1864, the draft reached lads just turned seventeen and men up to fifty, while others were liable to service in the home guard up to sixty.[3] Youths of seventeen at military schools were allowed to remain until they had attained the ripe age of eighteen on condition of being regularly drilled and of being subject to be called to the field if necessary. Every one is familiar with the part played by the youths from the Virginia Military Academy at the Battle of New Market, May 15, 1864.[4]

Obviously, men conscripted for service, or hired as substitutes, would be potential material for desertion, as their hearts were not devoted to a cause for which they had failed to volunteer. And conscription became necessary for the Confederacy in the second year of the war. Naturally, a few good soldiers entered the army as conscripts, but for the most part the men whose bodies were dragged in by force had, as Eggleston says, no spirit to bring with them, for they had already learned to brave the contumely of their neighbors for confessed cowardice.[5] But it must not be thought that conscripts

---

[1] O. W. R., Ser. II, VI, 197.

[2] Ibid., Ser. II, V, 28.

[3] American Annual Cyclopedia, 1862, p. 13. Statutes at Large of the Confederate States of America, 1862, chap. XXXI; 1864, chap. LXV.

[4] O. W. R., Ser. I, XLI, pt. IV, 1041. Wise, End of an Era, pp. 287-309. One of the most touching stories the writer has found is that of a mere lad who had been recognized as a deserter and brought in in a Union uniform before General Stuart. "He was even younger than I at first thought him— indeed, a mere boy. His complexion was fair; his hair flaxen and curling; his eyes blue, mild, and as soft in their expression as a girl's. Their expression, as they met the lowering glances of Stuart, was almost confiding. . . . The prisoner acknowledged that he was a deserter from the Southern army with the simplicity, candor, and calmness of one who saw in the fact nothing extraordinary, or calculated in any manner to affect his destiny unpleasantly. His horror when he heard Stuart's order, 'Hang him on that tree,' moved even the latter's disciplined heart to refer the case to Lee."—Cooke, Wearing the Gray, pp. 225-227.

[5] A Rebel's Recollections, pp. 49-50. O. W. R., Ser. I, X, pt. I, 432; XLII, pt. III, 177.

had any monopoly of desertion. In northeastern Georgia it was held in 1862 that one half of the men had deserted though the conscript law had not yet been enforced.

Substitutes enjoyed a reputation not much better among the soldiery. One officer reports that four fifths of his deserters were substitutes, who deserted within twenty-four hours of being received at his headquarters; and in 1863, because of the high average of desertion in this class of recruits, the War Department ordered substitutes accepted only if their moral, physical, and soldierly qualifications clearly equaled those of the soldier excused, and then only on the authority of the commanding general.[1] And in the Confederate Senate it was openly urged in 1863 that it would be no breach of contract to call on those who had furnished substitutes, as the system had excited dissatisfaction among those who had been unable thus to escape service.[2] Such action was taken by the Confederate Congress and warmly defended by Jefferson Davis.

Second in the list of causes came, undoubtedly, lack of the most ordinary necessities for the soldier—food, clothing, pay, and equipment. When men are pinched for food for three months at a stretch, at the same time that they are being subjected to protracted and arduous campaigns and constant exposure; when they have not been paid or furnished with any new clothing in from six to ten months; and when their government is not even able to put arms in their hands, the courage and enthusiasm of the bravest will ebb. The suffering of the Confederate soldier is an oft-told tale, but some further evidence rehearsed here will serve to sharpen the impression of hardships as a prime cause in the tremendous amount of desertion.

There was constantly, after the first eighteen months, complaint of a lack of proper and sufficient clothing to be at all comfortable even in the mildest weather. An adjutant general complained that there were some Louisiana troops without a particle of underclothing, while overcoats from their rarity were objects of curiosity. Summer clothing and no bedding were poor equipment for a winter campaign. In some divisions, as early as March, 1863, the men had scarcely clothing to hide their nakedness. The surgeon chief attributed much of the disease to a lamentable lack of blankets, while the destitution

---

[1] *Ibid.*, Ser. IV, II, 171; Ser. I, XXV, pt. II, 787.
[2] "Journal of the Senate of the Confederate States of America," *U. S. Sen. Doc.*, 58th Cong., 2d Sess., No. 234, III, 446.

of clothing was not compensated for by tents. During the last winter strips of old carpet were to be seen serving for blankets.[1]

But the incessant cry was for shoes. Longstreet reported over 6,000 men in his corps without shoes in November, 1862; the purchase of 5,000 pairs of shoes by private individuals in September of that year was by no means sufficient to supply the need. Possibly there is a modicum of truth in the charge made by an officer in the fall of 1862 that a number in order to be left behind threw away their shoes. But it was not long before the lack of foot-gear was no excuse.[2] One year later Longstreet reported one half of his troops without shoes, while Johnston sent a requisition for 13,000 pairs in February, 1864. Striking indeed is the following statement: "The Fifth Regiment is unable to drill for want of shoes. The Eighth Regiment will soon be unfit for duty from the same cause; and indeed, when shoes are supplied, the men will be unable to wear them for a long while, such is the horrible condition of their feet from long exposure."[3] Limping on the hard turnpikes with blistered feet, they literally traced their path with blood. Sometimes they ploughed through mud over their ankles or again they slipped on roads hard and sharp with ice so that they were falling and their guns going off all down the column. It was not unusual to require them to march under such conditions fifty miles a day.[4] As a feeble substitute for shoes, the men flocked to the cattle-pens when cattle were being butchered for food, to cut strips for moccasins before the hides were cold. But the moist, fresh skins without soles slipped about so that the wearers, constantly up and down, would finally kick them off to wrap their feet in rags or in straw or to limp along barefoot. Ragged and shoeless, clothed in a medley of garments which could not be called uniforms, they amply merited the name of "Lee's tatterdemalions."[5]

---

[1] O. W. R., Ser. I, XXI, 1098; XXXI, pt. III, 731; XXII, pt. II, 797, 1056–1057. Goss, Recollections of a Private, p. 65.

[2] O. W. R., Ser. I, XIX, pt. II, 629–630; XIX, pt. I, 144, 614.

[3] Ibid., Ser. I, XIX, pt. II, 630, 614; XXXI, pt. III, 818; XXI, 1098; XXVI, pt. II, 818; XXXII, pt. II, 697. Frequently the men could render no effective service, as they could not keep up with the column in a march.

[4] Colonel J. S. Williams writes, "and I have seen the blood in their tracks as they marched from Ivy to this place" (ibid., Ser. I, IV, 230).

[5] Jones, "The Morale of the Confederate Army," Confederate Military History, XXII, 126. Sorrel, Recollections of a Confederate Staff Officer, pp. 133–134, 219.

O. W. R., Ser. I, XXXII, pt. II, 60. The hope of a full supply of shoes from

Beginning as early as October, 1862, the pressure for food grew steadily more insistent. A ration of hominy and a quarter of a pound of beef for breakfast, a pint of rice and the same quantity of beef for dinner, and nothing for supper, the ration allowed during the fall and winter of 1863–1864, but poorly fills the "stomachs on which soldiers must fight." [1] A few months later Lee's men had the luxury of a few peas and a small amount of dried fruit. About a year later Longstreet reported that his men in Tennessee were living on half rations of meat and bread without reason to hope for better prospects. Even the beasts were limited to half rations, with hope of fresh pasturage only for the distant future.[2] The ration of one half pound of flour, provided in October, 1864, was not, according to the chief surgeon, sufficient. The beef issued was found nearly always poor, with the bone constituting most of the weight. Corn-meal and brackish water was the unvaried diet for Texan troops in September, 1863, while two deserters reported a cavalry company as living for three days on berries and persimmons.[3] To be without anything to eat one whole day was a common occurrence; a fast of two days while marching and fighting was not uncommon, while a complete lack of rations for three and four days occurred. On one march, no rations were issued to a battalion of artillery for one entire week, the men subsisting on the corn which had been intended for the battery horses, raw bacon captured from the enemy, and water from the springs and creeks. A soldier in the Army of Virginia was in rare good luck to have his flour, meat, and coffee at the same time.[4] The possible fallacy of the theory of the relation of food to health under all conditions can be no better illustrated than by a story told by Sorrel of how a certain general had loaves of good wheat flour baked for his men, but Johnny Reb preferred

tanneries at work throughout the Confederacy in January, 1864, was not fulfilled (*ibid.*). The charge that the men frequently sold their shoes as soon as issued probably had a germ of truth (*ibid.*, Ser. I, XLI, pt. IV, 1071–1072).

[1] *Ibid.*, Ser. I, XXXV, pt. I, 462. It was even less in 1864. See *American Annual Cyclopedia*, 1864, p. 32. Wise (*History of the Seventeenth Virginia Infantry*, p. 204) gives it as one third of a pound of bacon, one pound of flour, and a tablespoon of rice a day for that period of the war.

[2] *O. W. R.*, Ser. I, XXV, pt. II, 730; XXXII, pt. III, 679.

[3] *Ibid.*, Ser. I, XLI, pt. IV, 1071–1072, 1033–1034; XXVI, pt. II, 264; XXXI, 831.

[4] McCarthy, *Detailed Minutiæ of a Soldier's Life*, p. 57. When rations became scanty, a soldier was glad to cut a cord of wood for a neighboring farmer for fifty cents in money or its equivalent in food (*ibid.*, p. 57). See also Headley, *Confederate Operations in Canada and New York*, p. 68.

his flour stirred with grease in a frying-pan and cooked into a solid, hard mass, which by its indigestible qualities kept his hunger partly appeased, whereas the light, wholesome loaves were too easily digested.[1] By February, 1865, the ration issued the men every other day was so small and the men so hungry that they ate it up at one meal. It is notorious that the Confederates donned Federal uniforms, and that the Southern army often relied on the captures from the foe for supplies. General Banks was habitually called General Jackson's commissary general, and after a battle there was often double rejoicing, over a victory and over a "square meal."

It is not strange that General Price's army had to be armed in 1861 with muskets which could not be properly served and that one general reported that numbers of his men deliberately walked away during an engagement because their guns were wholly useless.[2] It is significant to find Adjutant J. P. Johnson reporting at the very close of 1863 that at least 30,000 stands of arms were needed to arm troops in the Trans-Mississippi Department, and to find General McCulloch complaining that he had not received one gun, despite applications repeated until he was ashamed to write again.[3]

The soldiers' pay—the paltry sum of eleven dollars a month in Treasury notes—was almost always delayed, and the depreciation already manifest in the fall of 1862, due to military failures, made it of little value when it did come. The lack of ready funds which kept the men unpaid for from two to eight months in 1861 was still more marked in 1864, when complaints came from all sections that pay was eleven, twelve, and fourteen months behind. Occasionally the difficulty lay in the fact that no one in a given battery, composed of illiterate mountaineers, knew how to make out a proper muster and pay-roll, while that same illiteracy led them to believe that they were being defrauded of their just pay.[4] A private's pay for a month would scarcely buy one meal for his family or a year's

[1] Sorrel, *Recollections of a Confederate Staff Officer*, p. 281. He also relates the story of a captain who carried his coat-tail full of corn while on a flag of truce mission, because he distrusted the hunger of any one to whom he might have intrusted it (*ibid.*, p. 311).

[2] *O. W. R.*, Ser. I, VIII, 425; VII, 114. They carried powder in horns, gourds, and bottles.

[3] *Ibid.*, Ser. I, XXII, pt. II, 1060; XXVI, pt. II, 405. Bragg reported on November 3, 1862, that for the first time he had to complain of a surplus of arms (*ibid.*, Ser. I, XX, pt. II, 386).

[4] *Ibid.*, Ser. I, III, 716; VII, 789–90; XXII, pt. II, 924. Eggleston, in *A Rebel's Recollections* (p. 170), tells how he secured the pay for one group in two hours and restored peace to a camp which was on the verge of mutiny.

pay buy him a pair of boots.[1] This lack of funds operated to make a soldier on leave often unable to defray the cost of reaching his command.[2] The prominence of this factor in desertion is attested by the statement of a group of officers who gave it as their opinion that the recent desertions from the regiment were mainly the result of this discontent, and that the chief causes of this state of feeling were the insufficiency of rations and the failure of the paymaster to pay the men off.[3]

The importance of attention to camp morale, so striking a feature in the recent World War, was not then recognized. The Confederate army, in the opinion of one observer, started wrong the very first winter in its neglect of cleanliness and of exercise. City men, accustomed to stated hours of business and recreation, whose minds were accustomed to the stimulus of thought and recreation, drooped under the monotony of a camp sunk knee-deep in mire, where the only relief from the tedium of long yarns spun around a feeble camp-fire was heavy sleep in a damp bed, curled up in a musty blanket—when there were blankets—in a close tent—when there were tents. And hale, sturdy countrymen, accustomed to the active life of mountain or plantation, found the change to camp life no more agreeable.[4]

And yet only a strong morale could help sustain mortal flesh through the discomforts and hardships inseparable from warfare. Drenching thunder-storms; filth and dirt, which the absence of soap turned into cutaneous diseases; long, jading marches for several days and parts of nights over stony roads, through a country almost entirely without water, were mere incidents of a campaign.[5] "Cooties" were, unfortunately, known before the World War. Cholera, measles, even smallpox, made their appearance in camp, while hospital accommodations were not even decent. The poor sufferers lay on the bare floor, wrapped in thin blankets, rarely with straw pillows under their heads. A Northern prisoner declared that he saw the sick and wounded decaying in their own filth, the death-rate

---

[1] *O. W. R.*, Ser. I, XXXI, pt. II, 342.

[2] This was the opinion of the Honorable James Phelan, a Congressman (*ibid.*, Ser. IV, III, 707). A frequent reply was that a man could not walk to his company. The lack of funds operated also to hinder the capture of deserters. Many officers found it impossible to travel in pursuit of their absentees, as they could not pay their expenses, and in many parts there was no provision for government transportation (*ibid.*, Ser. I, XLI, pt. IV, 1073).

[3] *Ibid.*, Ser. I, XLVI, pt. II, 1148.

[4] De Leon, *Four Years in Rebel Capitals*, pp. 140–141.

[5] *O. W. R.*, Ser. I, XVI, pt. I, 935; XLVI, pt. II, 1099.

mounting because of the want of medical stores.[1] A captain drew a picture of his company as being without a single cooking utensil or a bag in which to draw their rations, as cooking their pittance of a meal in the ashes without sifting, as being kept in the swamp until their systems were poisoned with miasma and malaria. So pressing were the exigencies of their position frequently, that the men had no time to cook. It was not unusual to see distributed to a company of starving men a barrel of flour, which it was utterly impossible for them to convert into bread with the means and the time allowed them. They could not procure even a piece of plank or a flour-sack upon which to work up the dough.[2]

Added to physical want and depression on the part of the soldiers were homesickness and mental anxiety concerning their families, whom they knew to be in need of the necessities of life in the face of ever-soaring prices: flour, fifty dollars a barrel; salt, sixty to seventy cents a pound; bacon, seventy-five cents a pound; and butter, twelve dollars a pound.[3] With the poor mountain whites, the margin of food supplies from a five-acre farm was always necessarily small. The men felt that their services in the army were useless and that their families required their attention, especially when their homes lap hopelessly within the Federal lines.[4] Furthermore, many a man felt himself literally forced to desert in order to defend his family from outlaws. It is small wonder, when soldiers from Arkansas and the western frontier heard of Indians scalping families living on the border, that they left camp at once, with or without leave, to turn their arms to the defense of their homes. Appeals and laments from these same families did not fail to reveal their sufferings. The most familiar tale illustrating the operation of this cause is one which appears in several sources. Such an appeal as the following could not fail to grip a father's heart:

A certain Edward Cooper was being tried by court-martial for desertion. When he was told to produce witnesses, he said his only

[1] For a full account see *O. W. R.*, Ser. I, XIX, pt. II, 8.

[2] Ibid., Ser. I, XXII, pt. II, 1032. *American Annual Cyclopedia*, 1862, p. 14.

[3] The inflated prices at Richmond even as early as 1863 are too well known to require more than a passing comment. At a private house $25 a day was demanded for lodgings (Wise, *History of the Seventeenth Virginia Infantry*, p. 173. *O. W. R.*, Ser. I, XXIII, pt. II, 95).

[4] *O. W. R.*, Ser. I, XLI, pt. II, 1054. Mr. Smith of North Carolina stated in Congress that appeals came daily from soldiers speaking of the sufferings at home (*American Annual Cyclopedia*, 1864, p. 208).

defense was a letter from his wife, which he handed to the president of the court. It read as follows:

"My dear Edward:—I have always been proud of you, and since your connection with the Confederate army, I have been prouder of you than ever before. I would not have you do anything wrong for the world, but before God, Edward, unless you come home, we must die. Last night, I was aroused by little Eddie's crying. I called and said 'What is the matter, Eddie?' and he said, 'O mamma! I am so hungry.' And Lucy, Edward, your darling Lucy; she never complains, but she is growing thinner and thinner every day. And before God, Edward, unless you come home, we must die.

"Your Mary."

The court was melted to tears, but as was their plain duty, sentenced the prisoner to death for desertion. However, Lee, reviewing the case, pardoned the prisoner.[1]

As if it were not enough to be robbed and eaten out by the contending armies, the same sections often became a prey to the arson, murder, and pillage of Tories and deserters. Often three or four families with ten or fifteen children were huddled under one roof with only the charity board between them and starvation. From deserter to Tory was not a difficult step.

The tax-in-kind law, which seized one tenth of the farmers' produce, and the impressment system roused the troops to the point where they were determined to protect their families from injustice and wrong on the part of the government, even to the abandonment of the contest. The law of March 26, 1863, required the impressment of all articles absolutely necessary for the war which could not be purchased. Since the government could regulate the prices for all such articles, and since its agents fixed them far below the market price, no one would sell to the government at one half of the price he could command of his neighbors. The inevitable consequence was that the government never could purchase, but must always impress. These agents operated under no rules—at least, observed none—and were not subject to supervision. Bad and indifferent officers impressed in the way which proved easiest for them, usually on near-by plantations or where the least resistance could be offered. Naturally, wives of absent soldiers were exactly those

---

[1] Told in Moore, *History of North Carolina* (Alfred Williams & Co., Raleigh, North Carolina), II, 237–238, and in Underwood, *Women of the Confederacy*, pp. 169–171.

least able to oppose resistance to impressment, and hence they were often called upon for more than a fair proportion. Soldiers, faced with the choice of serving the State or their families, when famine was stalking through the land, obeyed the stronger of the two obligations. The suspicion was widely entertained that the people employed by quartermasters to buy supplies for the army bought at one price and sold at an advanced figure, sharing the profit with the purchasing officer.[1]

The unredeemed promise of furloughs made at the time that the conscription law was passed was an excuse almost invariably offered by culprits when arrested, at least in North Carolina. And yet by the spring of 1863, if officers had permitted the men to go home, the armies would have been reduced to a corporal's guard, and Governor Vance frankly admitted that he did not see how that promise was to be redeemed.[2] It is interesting to see how General Pemberton "made a virtue of necessity" by proclaiming a thirty days' furlough to his army, "as they had all gone to their homes without leave." [3] The failure to extend to the troops of Georgia, Alabama, and South Carolina, when passing their homes, the same indulgence as had been granted those of Mississippi, gave much dissatisfaction and led numbers to leave the ranks en route.[4]

Another grievance which contributed to desertion was the belief that men were conscripted wrongfully into the service, that this was a "rich man's war but a poor man's fight," since the wealthy seemed to bribe their way to freedom or to comfortable posts as magistrates, overseers, or government officials. Even so important a supporter of the government as James Phelon, a prominent citizen of Mississippi, wrote President Davis on December 9, 1862: "It seems as if nine-tenths of the youngsters of the land whose relatives are conspicuous in society, wealthy, or influential, obtain some safe perch where they can doze with their heads under their wings." [5] The temporary suspension of the Conscription Bureau in 1863 was interpreted by some citizens as an evidence of the displeasure of the government with it for seizing men. Probably the wretched private

[1] Johnston, *Narrative of Military Operations,* pp. 424–425. *O. W. R.,* Ser. I, XXIII, pt. II, 696.

[2] Note the picture presented of the condition in this respect in North Carolina by Governor Vance in April, 1863 (*O. W. R.,* Ser. I, LI, pt. II, 709–710).

[3] Jones, *A Rebel War Clerk's Diary,* II, 3.

[4] *O. W. R.,* Ser. I, XLVII, pt. II, 1286.

[5] *Ibid.,* Ser. I, XVII, pt. II, 791–792.

had a quite distorted view of the dereliction of the wealthy. Jones, a clerk in the War Department, asserts repeatedly that much defection was due to a deep-seated conviction that the wealthy were enjoying comforts as usual at home.[1] The absolute necessity of exemption of farmers, manufacturers, and mechanics is perfectly obvious if the country was to be fed, clothed, and armed.

All Southern soldiers had a strong consciousness of themselves as free moral agents; they were wholly unaccustomed to acting on any other than their own motion. They were unused to control of any sort and were not disposed to obey any one except for good and sufficient reason, fully stated. Volunteers held themselves as gentlemen.[2] As free-born American citizens they resented the conscript laws. To illustrate this feeling, a story might be cited of how the death at Manassas of three officers, who while serving on a court-martial had sentenced four deserters to be shot, was interpreted by the privates as a divine judgment.[3] Some cherished also a sense of injustice in being subjected to the rigid discipline of Lee's army when bands of partisan rangers, like Mosby's or Forrest's, roamed almost at will. The dashes into enemy country, the brisk adventures, and active movement held a great fascination for all who joined the army as a frolic. So serious did Lee hold the matter that he expressed the hope that all partisan bands except Mosby's would be disbanded in his department.

Conscripts nursed as a grievance the fact that they were not even allowed certain natural rights—to select their own companies with relatives and neighbors. Governor Vance pressed on President Davis the fact that the service lost by attempting to fill up certain regiments first without respect to the wishes of the conscripts. "Large numbers actually threaten to desert before they leave camp," he wrote, "and generally make good their threats."[4] They held firmly to the belief that they were morally free to depart at or near the time of termination of their enlistment.[5] Especially did they insist that they should

---

[1] *Ibid.*, Ser. IV, II, 638. Jones, *A Rebel War Clerk's Diary*, II, 272, 277, 280, 305.

[2] General Lee's statement on this subject, made on his retreat from Gettysburg, is illuminating: "Our people are so little liable to control that it is difficult to get them to follow any course not in accordance with their inclination" (*O. W. R.*, Ser. I, XXVII, pt. III, 1048).

[3] Casler, *op. cit.*, p. 114.

[4] *O. W. R.*, Ser. IV, III, 1043.

[5] Such a case arose with some South Carolina troops (*ibid.*, Ser. I, XXXV, pt. I, 560–561); true also of the Missouri and Kentucky forces (*ibid.*, Ser. I, III, 733, and XX, pt. II, 26).

be allowed to change their service upon renewal of enlistment, as many wanted to be transferred from the infantry to the cavalry. North Carolinians, for instance, used to horseback riding in the mountains, but unaccustomed to walking long distances, felt themselves better fitted for cavalry service.[1]

Men sincerely believed that they had a kind of right to serve in certain localities—usually near their homes, and were averse to being transferred to other points. Numerous desertions followed the transfer of some troops to the Army of Virginia in 1863, and General Jones frankly admitted his doubts whether one half of the Florida troops would honor orders to leave that State.[2] As soon as it was suspected by some Kentucky troops that they were to be led from their own State, they began to desert, while other companies marched cheerfully when they supposed they were going toward Kentucky. An officer had to report bluntly to Richmond, "Our troops here will not go; they will throw down their arms first." [3] A group of Texan troops threatened to take the matter into their own hands unless they were speedily marched back to San Antonio, while other men openly admitted that they had deserted rather than cross the Mississippi.

Closely linked with the right of selecting the company in which the soldier should serve was the right of electing their own officers. Dislike of a commanding officer, dismissal of a favorite officer, absence of a commander, and the false rumor of the resignation of Lee were alleged as causes of desertion. Early in the war even corporals were elected, with, as can be readily surmised, ill results. Until December, 1861, Eggleston declared that he never knew an instance in which a captain dared offend his men by breaking a non-commissioned officer or by supporting one without submitting the matter to a vote of the company. Even in the first instance which occurred after that date the captain had to bolster himself with written authority from headquarters, whereupon followed three weeks of mingled diplomacy and discipline to quell the mutiny which resulted.[4] As late as 1862 a citizen protested to Governor Letcher of Virginia against the elective principle in the army, and especially against in-

---

[1] Casler, op. cit., p. 292. See also Jones, A Rebel War Clerk's Diary, II, 37.

[2] O. W. R., Ser. I, XXXIII, 1085–1086; XXXV, pt. I, 118.

[3] Ibid., Ser. I, XX, pt. II, 390–391, 408; XLI, pt. II, 1048.

[4] Eggleston, op. cit., p. 33. The consolidating of odds and ends of paper commands into full regiments often caused disgruntled officers and men to run away (O. W. R., Ser. I, XXXII, pt. I, 346).

clusion within the rule of the grade of field officers as fraught with the most fatal consequences.

A striking cause of defection in some instances was a want of active service. When near home, even good soldiers saw no reason why they should stay away from their families with an inactive army. Furthermore, once begun, desertion itself soon became a cause of continued and further desertion; the evil fed upon itself. At first the men feared the Argus eyes of the government agents who should send them back to their regiments and to death. But before long, impunity bred contempt until deserters actually intimidated the poorly armed, inefficient home guards.[1]

Another ground of complaint which contributed to abandonment of the government is one not often recorded in this connection. But speculation and extortion, which seem inseparable from any government in time of war, were rampant throughout the Confederacy in the months of 1863 and were resented as the cause of military disasters on the ground that the army was not adequately supplied, and that the fortified posts were not provided with requisite stores. Peculation notoriously characterized much of the hauling of cotton and the work of the military boards engaged in the purchase of arms. Discrimination by brokers and money-changers against the notes in favor of "shinplasters" aided the rampart speculators. This wrong was generally held responsible for the derangement of prices and was loudly condemned by press, public officials, and private citizens. The Columbus (Georgia) *Daily Sun* held in 1862 that speculators had done more harm than the enemy's artillery. "We have in fact two wars upon our hands at once. Whilst our brave soldiers are off battling the Abolitionists a conscienceless set of vampires are at home warring upon their indigent families and threatening them with immediate starvation." [2] Feeling rose so high that obnoxious speculators were threatened with violence. It was felt that producers and distributors

---

[1] See Vance's complaint to Secretary Seddon, August 26, 1863, *ibid.*, Ser. I, XXIX, pt. II, 676.

[2] September 2, 1862. The *Richmond Enquirer* of February 11, 1863, states that an effort was being made for an extra session of the legislature in Texas partly for the purpose of regulating by law the prices of necessities.

The exact title under which the *Enquirer* appeared varied, according, apparently, to the abundance or scarcity of paper. Early in the war, the front page bore the pompous title of *The Richmond Daily Enquirer;* when paper almost vanished from the market and the editors were reduced to a single sheet, the title shrank to *Richmond Enquirer.* For the sake of uniformity and clarity, it will be consistently referred to in this work as *Richmond Enquirer.*

of goods were entitled only to a fair price, which meant a very modest profit. A war situation, certain to provoke bitterness if no one had been to blame, was held intolerable by the soldiers when they thought it due to the greed of the very men for whom they were fighting.

From 1863 the element of discouragement and hopelessness of the struggle was added to the natural weariness from the strain of the long, bitterly fought war. Some mail bags captured by the United States officers showed already in 1863 that letters of Southern soldiers breathed but one sentiment—weariness of the war. Soldiers saw, despite desperate and heroic efforts, defeat everywhere, saw their toils and sufferings unproductive against apparently inexhaustible numbers.[1]

A Southern sergeant taken prisoner in April, 1865, voiced to a Union general very accurately the feeling of his comrades: "For six or eight months back, our men have deserted by thousands. Those who remain have been held by a sentiment of honor only. They did not wish to disgrace themselves by deserting their flag. They have done their duty to the best of their ability. As to the Southern Confederacy, although they would have liked to have seen it triumph, they lost all hope of it long since," [2] Grant gauged Southern feeling accurately when in July, 1864, he urged Lincoln to issue a call for 300,000 men as a means to increase desertion from the ranks of the foe. It was notorious that desertion received an impetus from Southern defeats such as Gettysburg and Vicksburg. Lincoln's re-election, with the consequent prospect of the continued prosecution of the war, was assigned by deserters as one ground for despair of success.

Many minor causes contributed locally to promote desertion, such as a threat of invasion of a soldier's home region by the enemy; the excessive number of details to contractors and corporations, whereby so many escaped field service that others in disgust took French leave; [3] the lack of proper discipline in the army, explicable from the manner of its organization and the necessity of bringing it into

---

[1] See also the statement of a deserter, *O. W. R.*, Ser. I, XLI, pt. III, 145.
[2] De Trobriand, *Quatre ans de campagnes à l'armée du Potomac*, II, 375. See also Gay, *Life in Dixie During the War* (1901), pp. 146–155, for a very interesting story of how a Southern ironworker deserted and joined the Union troops when Sherman took Decatur, Georgia, in July, 1864. He felt that he "could not die for a lost cause" (p. 150).
[3] *O. W. R.*, Ser. I, XXVI, pt. II, 354–355.

immediate service, but nevertheless sadly demoralizing;[1] and the promises of immunity to deserters emanating from Washington. Lee states in a letter to Secretary of War Seddon his belief that a circular from Washington authorities, promising immunity to deserters and exemption from military service, had had its due effect.[2]

But more potent than all other causes, except possibly lack of devotion to the Confederacy and personal suffering, was the state of public opinion in the civilian population among the families and neighbors of deserters. Want and suffering undermined the morale, while in some sections, notably in North Carolina, though also elsewhere, the press and some State leaders inflamed the discontent with the government and preached peace at any price, impressing the people with the hopelessness of the cause.[3] General D. H. Hill, who had command in that section, put the situation succinctly in the spring of 1863: "There is a powerful faction in the state poisoning public sentiment and looking to a reconstruction. The soldiers are induced by these traitors to believe that this is an unjust war on the part of the south and that their state soldiers and citizens have been slighted and wronged by the Confederate States Government."[4] Lee also complained of the "evil consequences resulting from crude misstatements of newspaper correspondents." In February, 1865, he charged openly that "the men are influenced by the misrepresentations of their friends at home, who appear to have become very despondent as to our success. They think the cause desperate and write to the soldiers, advising them to take care of themselves, assuring them that if they will return home the bands of deserters so far outnumber the home guards that they will be in no danger of arrest."[5] Families

---

[1] An officer attributed lack of discipline in Price's army as a chief cause, and blamed especially the familiarity between officers and men. Petty crimes went unnoticed, while the punishment for greater crimes was so slight as to do no good as an example and possibly only made the criminal resentful. He declared that no officer was held accountable for the desertion of his men (*ibid.*, Ser. I, XXII, pt. II, 1050).

[2] *Ibid.*, Ser. I, XLII, pt. II, 1175.

[3] The Raleigh *Standard* and the Raleigh *Progress* were held responsible by army officers for the condition in North Carolina. General Maury complained of the despondency due to the dark aspect of affairs at Charleston so industriously circulated by the newspapers (*ibid.*, Ser. I, XXVI, pt. II, 179). The exact titles of these two papers were, of course, *The Daily Progress* and *The North Carolina Standard*, the latter appearing as a weekly and semi-weekly paper. Both were published at Raleigh, North Carolina.

[4] *O. W. R.*, Ser. I, XVIII, 1052–1053.

[5] *Ibid.*, Ser. I, XLVI, pt. II, 1254.

and friends wrote to the soldiers, harping on the grievances of the latter, insisting that they could desert with impunity, as militia officers, for these same reasons, could not and would not do their duty. Soldiers on furlough were deterred by such arguments from carrying out their original intention of returning to their posts.

Not one of the many causes enumerated above, but all, make up the complex which explains the stupendous number of desertions.

CHAPTER II

Growth and Magnitude of the Evil

The story of the rapid development of desertion through the four years of the war, of its extent in actual numbers, of its distribution through the various armies of the Confederacy, of its prevalence among the troops from the various States, and of its manifestation in the different ranks and classes of the army is one not easy to untangle.

The determination of the number infected with the virus of desertion may be approached from two angles. We shall consider first the number of deserters entering the Federal lines. Confederates began slipping across individually or in straggling groups of two or three almost immediately after the war began. Repeated with almost wearying frequency in the Union correspondence occurs the irrefutable evidence:

"Three deserters just in from the opposite side . . ."

"Two rebel deserters report . . ."

"Two intelligent sergeants from the Ninth Alabama Regiment have just come in."

"Three men deserted the Eleventh Tennessee."

"I have the honor to report that on the night of the 24th instant a deserter from the Texas troops was brought in by our picket." [1]

The first actual report of such an entry into the Union lines which the writer has found is for June 23, 1861, when General Patterson, stationed in Maryland, commented on "Deserters from their ranks, some one or more of whom come in daily." [2] In noting the desertion from General Price's army, which was said to be so great that the army was disintegrating in December of the very first year, and from which men were coming in to General Pope to lay down their arms, it must be recalled that Price was recruiting and operating in

---

[1] *O. W. R.*, Ser. I, XXX, pt. III, 117; XXXI, pt. II, 137; XXVII, pt. II, 30; IV, 4.

[2] *Ibid.*, Ser. I, II, 717.

Missouri, where sentiment had not yet fully crystallized.[1] But by December of the next year the Union generals were making rulings on the subject of the disposition to be made of Confederate deserters. It is obvious, therefore, that the latter were surrendering themselves in sufficient numbers to present a problem.

Reports of one or more deserters presenting themselves before Union officers in increasing numbers are continued throughout 1863, until by the fall of that year General Fisk complains that he is at a loss to know what to do with the increasing multitude from Price's army thronging to his lines.[2] Though wearers of the gray still straggled in singly or in groups of two, four, and five through all the remaining months of the war, and though the records often leave the reader in doubt as to the exact number, there is evidence by this year of strongly concerted action. One fugitive reports, for instance, that sixteen of his company had agreed to make the attempt to cross to the enemy on the night of January 20, 1864, in a body.[3]

By April, 1864, General Thomas reported from the Tennessee area that he was receiving about thirty deserters from the enemy daily; General Echols in October reported large numbers from Lee's and Early's armies as entering his lines weekly. Particularly significant is the fact that by the middle of this year the defection was touching not alone the conscripts, but veterans who had served faithfully since the outbreak of the war, as Grant's comment to Secretary Seward in August attests: "Not a day passes but men come into our lines, and men, too, who have been fighting for the South for more than three years." [4]

While desertions to the enemy had been checked in general by the vigor of the Confederate authorities during the first part of 1864, a marked increase of the evil was perceptible after August 1. Men from Hill's and Longstreet's corps were coming over to Grant's army daily. Groups of sixteen, twenty, twenty-five, fifty, and seventy-five were reported from all parts of the South as the daily toll.[5] This

[1] *O. W. R.*, Ser. I, VIII, 426. The very earliest record is of May 21, 1861, concerning some Tennessee troops, but is in the form of a rumor of frequent desertions (*ibid.*, Ser. I, LI, pt. I, 384).

[2] *Ibid.*, Ser. I, XXII, pt. II, 673. We are often left in doubt as to the exact number which slipped in, for the records merely say "Some deserters," "several deserters," etc.

[3] *Ibid.*, Ser. I, XXXV, pt. I, 462.

[4] *Ibid.*, Ser. II, VII, 614. This was based on the confessions of deserters.

[5] *Ibid.*, Ser. I, XLII, pt. III, 119, 150, 161, 176, 680–681, 774, 1077; XLVI, pt. III, 10, 43.

toll seems to have been exacted in all parts: General Dodge in the middle area reported fifty deserters coming in on February 5, 1863; but Hooker held that Bragg's army further south was suffering from as many as forty desertions a day, which were reducing his force faster than it could be increased by additions from conscription; twenty-one were reported to Meade as the record in the Army of the Potomac for one forenoon; while the average at such a remote point as Soda Springs, Indian Territory, in 1863 was given as ten to fifty. Thirty-six were recorded as one day's defection to the Army of the James.[1] General Grant in a letter of August, 1865, which became famous as a campaign document in the presidential election of that fall, stated that the South was losing at least one regiment a day by desertion.[2]

By 1865 desertions were no longer counted by the score, but by the hundred; whole companies, garrisons, and even regiments decamped at a time. About twenty miles beyond Cumberland Gap, two whole Kentucky regiments, refusing to leave the State, deserted and dispersed. In February, Lee's men were going over to the number of scores a day; in March a whole brigade left *en masse*.[3] Some slight conception of the numbers making their way to the Union lines—though no complete figures are available on the subject—may be gathered from the following statistics: the oath of allegiance was administered to 1905 deserters during January and February, 1864, at Chattanooga; 5,203 were received at the Nashville and Chattanooga offices from January 21 to May 31, 1865.[4]

---

[1] *Ibid.*, Ser. I, XXIII, pt. II, 73; XXXI, pt. II, 341–342; XXII, t. II, 956; XLVI, pt. III, 19, 31.

[2] To Honorable E. B. Washburne under date of August 16, 1864: "The rebels have now in their ranks their last man. The little boys and old men are guarding prisoners, guarding railroad bridges, and forming a good part of their garrisons for entrenched positions. A man lost by them cannot be replaced. They have robbed the cradle and the grave equally to get their present force. Besides what they lose in frequent skirmishes and battles, they are now losing from desertions and other causes at least one regiment per day."—*American Annual Cyclopedia*, 1864, p. 134.

[3] *O. W. R.*, Ser. I, XLVIII, pt. II, 45; LIII, 524; XXVI, pt. II, 530; XLVIII, pt. I, 1355; XLVI, pt. II, 387; XLIX, pt. 834. See also *The Sun* (Baltimore), February 14, 1865; Baltimore *American* and *Commercial Advertiser*, March 3, 1865.

[4] *O. W. R.*, Ser. I, XLIX, pt. I, 349; XXXII, pt. I, 12–13. About 200 deserters from Lee's army reached Washington in February to take the oath of allegiance. General Price lost 400 men in one day while crossing the Red River (*ibid.*, Ser. I, XXXIV, pt. II, 519). It should be noted that the latter event extends beyond the close of the war.

But the whole story is far from told through the Union records, as for every soldier who sought the Federal lines, many boldly returned to their own homes or made their way to the mountain fastnesses of Alabama or North Carolina. Let two illustrations of the comparative numbers in this respect suffice: "Three [privates] of Ransom's and two of Wise's went to the enemy and twenty-six of Ransom's deserted to the rear, supposed to be going to North Carolina." On March 8, 1865, four desertions from a given company were reported: one to the enemy, three to the rear.[1] From both sides the testimony comes that while many deserted to the enemy, many more departed for their own homes, a fact attested to by Grant as well as by Lee. The former wrote Secretary of War Stanton in February, 1865, "Their [deserters'] testimony is that many more go to their own homes than come within our lines;" while at about the same date Lee made the following report to Breckenridge, who was then Secretary of War, "Most of these men are supposed to have gone to their homes, but a number have deserted to the enemy."[2]

The first official confession of desertion by Confederate civil authorities, although statements from various commanders appear still earlier,[3] is found in a confidential circular by Secretary of State Randolph to the governors of the States under date of July 17, 1862. "Our armies are so much weakened by desertions, and by the absence of officers and men without leave, that we are unable to reap the fruits of our victories and to invade the territory of the enemy. We have resorted to courts-martial and military executions, and we have ordered all officers employed in enrolling conscripts to arrest both deserters and absentees, and offered rewards for the former."[4] The press appealed to citizens in all parts of the South to assist in the apprehension of renegades by giving information to the authorities of the hiding-places of skulkers.[5] And by September Lee was so concerned about the matter that he wrote the following

[1] *O. W. R.,* Ser. I, XLVI, pt. 1268, 1294.

[2] *Ibid.,* 596, 1265. Sheridan corroborated the fact for an earlier period when he stated that rebel deserters were coming into his lines in small squads but that he heard of large numbers in the mountains avoiding the Union army, who were making their way home (*ibid.,* Ser. I, XXIII, pt. II, 519).

[3] General Buckner reported from Tennessee, February 8, 1862, that 300 men were supposed to have gone to Henderson (*ibid.,* Ser. I, VII, 864). Notices appeared still earlier in the newspapers. See Savannah *Daily Morning News,* May 21, 1862, under the caption, "A Hint to Deserters."

[4] *O. W. R.,* Ser. IV, II, 7.

[5] *American Annual Cyclopedia,* 1862, p. 246.

significant statement to President Davis: "Some immediate legislation, in my opinion, is required, and the most summary punishment should be authorized. It ought to be construed into desertion in the face of the enemy, and thus brought under the Rules and Articles of War. To give you an idea of its extent in some brigades, I will mention that, on the morning after the battle of the 17th, General Evans reported to me on the field, where he was holding the first position, that he had but 120 of his brigade present, and that the next brigade to his, that of General Garnett, consisted of but 100 men. General Pendleton reported that the brigades of Generals Lawton and Armisted, left to guard the ford at Shepherdstown, together contained but 600 men." [1]

A rigid investigation of the returns and muster-rolls of the Army of the Tennessee, begun in December, 1862, disclosed the fact that several thousand officers and men were absent, some without permission, and some under leaves of absence ordered by officers without legal power to grant them.

By March of the next year, Governor Vance was seriously disturbed over the situation in western North Carolina. And by June following it was apparent that the evil was not confined to that State, as the chief of the Conscript Bureau was complaining of its increase and that "it was the more difficult to deal with that the soldiers now bring with them Government arms and ammunition, banding among themselves and with evaders of conscription. The enrolling officers are sometimes shot by them and the community kept in terror. This state of things exists more or less in each of our Atlantic states especially." [2] If the authorities should fail to replenish the armies and to return absentees before the next campaign, this official declared later in the year, the cause would be lost. The War Office did not mince matters, but avowed to Secretary Seddon, "The condition of things in the mountain districts of North Carolina, South Carolina, Georgia, and Alabama menaces the existence of the Confederacy as fatally as either of the armies of the United States." [3] A large number of troops of the Army of the Tennessee, fully 5,000, according to Rosecrans, which had been cut off in 1862 in the retreat from Kentucky, were scattered through Tennessee and lower Kentucky at this time and were not trying to rejoin their commands.

[1] *O. W. R.*, Ser. I, XIX, pt. I, 143.
[2] *Ibid.*, Ser. IV, II, 607, 1022.
[3] *Ibid.*, p. 786. See also *Richmond Enquirer*, February 12, 1863.

It is of Virginia that a citizen writes about July, 1863, the oft quoted tale: "A good many deserters are passing the various road daily, and greatly increase the demoralization. These deserters almos invariably have their guns and accoutrements with them, and whe halted and asked for their furlough or their authority to be absen from their commands, they just pat their guns and defiantly say 'This is my furlough,' and even enrolling officers turn away a peaceably as possible, evidently intimidated by their defiant manner." And General E. Kirby Smith wrote of the condition in the Trans Mississippi region to one of his subordinates: "The deserters mus be arrested and brought back to their commands or exterminated Affairs have reached such a crisis that in some parts of your distric the question now is whether they or we shall control." [2] And it wa just a little later that General Moxey, in command in the India Territory, found expression for his disgust with desertion in sar casm: "The elegant example of twenty-five desertions from Hard man's regiment was magnificently eclipsed by about two hundre from De Morse's regiment a very few days after. Excelsior." [3]

While the evidence here, too, as in the Union records, indicate a steady increase in the numbers and growing boldness in leavin in ever larger groups, even early intimations show startling number Note the following statistics for 1863: thirty-two men deserted th North Carolina Volunteers on May 9; a party of 200 en route fc Arkansas decamped from one regiment in the Trans-Mississip Department; eighty-seven abandoned a Tennessee regiment withi the space of ten days; all except forty men deserted the Secon Arkansas; eighty men decamped from another company in one nigh the First Alabama lost almost a hundred; sixty members of a Texa regiment forsook their colors together. [4] Complaints of increase i the evil came from Georgia; one half of the enlisted men from th northeastern counties were said to be skulking in the mountains. [5]

---

[1] O. W. R., Ser. IV, II, 721–722. The writer differs from Rhodes, who thin that this passage refers to North Carolina (History of the United State V, 444).

[2] O. W. R., Ser. I, XXVI, pt. II, 285.

[3] Ibid., Ser. I, LIII, 964.

[4] Ibid., Ser. XXIX, pt. II, 649–650; XXX, pt. III, 307; XXXI, pt. II 828–829; XXVI, pt. II, 522; XXII, pt. II, 956; XXX, pt. IV, 181; XXXI pt. II, 634.

[5] This is the estimate recorded in the Richmond Enquirer of February 1 1863. See also a letter from Governor Brown to Secretary of State Seddc August 10, 1863 (O. W. R., Ser. IV, II, 753).

Checked though the disaffection was temporarily by harsh measures during the close of 1863 and the early months of 1864,[1] the close of the latter year saw it lifting its hydra head again menacingly in Georgia in a plot among some soldiers at Rose Dew Island to go to the interior in the hope of inducing many of the troops to follow their example and thus to "put an end to the war," and in Alabama in Clanton's brigade in the secret society for laying down arms on Christmas Day in order to achieve peace. The latter seems to have been a fully organized movement between the Northern and Southern armies, with signs, grips, passwords, and obligations. Its object was to deplete the ranks by desertion and to thwart the work of the Conscript Bureau. The password to escape from prison was "Washington" repeated four times, which procured release in twenty-four hours. When approaching a Yankee guard post, after being halted and challenged, the member was to pronounce the word "Jack"; the sentinal would reply, "All right, Jack, pass on with your goose-quills." In line of battle, the sign of membership was placing the gun against the right hip at an angle of about forty-five degrees, holding it in this position long enough to be distinguished, and then carrying it to the left shoulder in the position of shoulder-arms.[2]

But the full flood of desertion seems not to have set in until the fall of 1864, when, sweeping down all barriers, it rushed on to high-water mark during the concluding months of the war in 1865. From October 1, 1864, to February 4, 1865, a period of four months, it was stated in Richmond that nearly 72,000 had taken French leave from the Confederate armies east of the Mississippi.[3] The sad tale

[1] Comte de Paris, *History of the Civil War in America,* II, 602. For proof that Lee thought the situation improved in the fall of 1863, see *O. W. R.,* Ser. I, XXIX, pt. II, 806–807. An officer thought that the condition in a certain part of Mississippi had entirely changed, due to the energy of General Polk. See also *ibid.,* Ser. I, XLI, pt. II, 502, for improvement in Arkansas. In the improvement, as well as in the later increase of the evil, the Trans-Mississippi Department lagged behind the rest of the Confederacy (*ibid.,* Ser. I, XXII, pt. II, 1028; LIII, 1029).

[2] Details of these movements may be found in *O. W. R.,* Ser. I, XXXV, pt. I, 529–531; XXVI, pt. II, 551–552; XXXII, pt. III, 681–682. The organization had already appeared in East Tennessee in 1863.

[3] *American Annual Cyclopedia,* 1865, p. 188. See also *O. W. R.,* Ser. I, XLVI, pt. III, 1353.

During the month of September, 1864, the exchange of musketry and artillery firing went on along the Potomac front without interruption. The Confederate officers would permit only a half-hour truce daily at sundown, the time of relieving pickets on both sides. Their main object in keeping

may be read in Lee's despatches, at times almost despairing, as he saw his army, undeterred by their personal devotion to even so beloved a leader as himself, melt away before his very eyes:

(November 18, 1864) "Desertion is increasing in the army notwithstanding all my efforts to stop it."

(January 27, 1865) "I have the honor to call your attention to the alarming frequency of desertion from this army. You will perceive from the accompanying papers, that 56 deserted Hill's corps in three days."

(February 25) "Hundreds of men are deserting nightly and I cannot keep the army together unless examples are made of such cases."

(February 28, in which he reports 1,094 desertions in ten days, February 15–25) "I am convinced, as already stated to you, that it proceeds from the discouraging sentiment out of the army, which, unless it can be changed, will bring us calamity. This defection in troops who have acted so nobly and borne so much is so distressing to me that I have thought proper to give you the particulars."

(March 27) "I have the honor to report the number of desertions from the 9th to the 18th, both inclusive, 1061 [incomplete] . . . I do not know what can be done to put a stop to it." [1]

The Secretary of War, at this time J. C. Breckenridge, who had assumed office only on February 6, 1865, the last of the six men to undertake this onerous post, seems to have been even more discouraged and resourceless than Lee, for he wrote the latter on March 1: "I will continue to coöperate with you in urging the author-

up this continual firing was to stop as much as possible the desertion. So great was the drift of Florida Confederates to the army commanded by General De Trobriand for the Union that some of the latter's outposts perpetrated the joke of sending over their commander's compliments to the Florida general, with an invitation to come over to take command of his brigade (De Trobriand, *Quatre ans de campagnes à l'armée du Potomac,* II, 281).

[1] *O. W. R.,* Ser. I, XLII, pt. III, 1213; XLVI, pt. II, 1143, 1258. On Feb. 24, Lee made one last despairing effort with Governor Vance: "I think some good can be accomplished by the efforts of influential citizens to change public sentiment. . . . If they would explain to the people that the cause is not hopeless; that the situation of affairs, though critical, is critical to the enemy as well as ourselves . . . and that his defeat now would result in leaving nearly our whole territory open to us; that this great result can be accomplished if all will work diligently and zealously; and that his successes are far less valuable in fact than in appearance, I think our sorely-tried people would be induced to make one more effort to bear their sufferings a little longer and regain some of the spirit that marked the first two years."—*Ibid.,* Ser. I, XLVII, pt. II, 1270.

ities and individuals of influence in the respective states to awaken a more wholesome state of public feeling. I know of nothing else that can be added to the means already employed to remedy the evil." [1]

And as the war moved on to its inevitable end, the reports became even more hopeless. Beauregard stated as his opinion on March 9 that desertion had become an epidemic; that the men had deserted by the hundred from the cars on their way to Charlotte. Another general regretted that he had nothing to report on March 31 but "disobedience of orders, neglect of duty, demoralization of the people, and desertion of both officers and men," and from present appearances he saw no prospect of a turn for the better. And so stanch a soldier as General D. H. Hill writes despairingly, "More than half of the two advanced brigades have deserted. Can nothing be done to prevent it?" [2]

Probably the most desperate aspect of the matter was the fact that no reliance could be placed on the troops which remained, as they could not be trusted to obey orders, or be relied on to stay; when sent after deserters to bring them back, they also often deserted.

Nothing portrays the utter demoralization better than the change of attitude toward desertion. First, note the comment of General Johnson in May, 1863, "The great majority of my brigade would shoot a deserter as quick as they would a snake"; then Assistant Secretary of War Campbell's remark in March, 1865, "So common is the crime, it has in popular estimation lost the stigma which justly pertains to it, and therefore the criminals are everywhere shielded by their families and by the sympathies of many communities." [3] Even as early as August, 1863, a conscript officer in South Carolina wrote to his chief at Richmond, "It is no longer a reproach to be known as a deserter." [4]

The grand total of the desertion in bald numbers may best be told by comparative figures. The War Department at Richmond estimated the number of absentees without leave in July, 1863, at 40,000 to 50,000, though the war clerk Jones gives an estimate as high as 136,000. Pollard's estimate of one half to three fourths of the army absent would seem obviously too great, while the *Richmond Enquirer's* declaration of one half absent may be dismissed as

---

[1] *Ibid.*, Ser. I, XLVI, pt. II, 1275.
[2] *Ibid.*, Ser. I, XLIX, pt. I, 1042; XLVII, pt. III, 730.
[3] *Ibid.*, Ser. I, LI, pt. II, 1064–1065. Campbell, *Reminiscences*, p. 28.
[4] *O. W. R.*, Ser. IV, II, 769.

a wild newspaper guess.[1] The truth probably lies somewhere between the conservative figure of an interested department and a palpable exaggeration. A report submitted for 1864 implies 121,000 deserters, although the figures are admittedly defective and include absentees other than deserters; while in March of the concluding year of the war the superintendent of the Conscript Bureau computed over 100,000 deserters scattered over the million square miles of the Confederacy.[2] And doubtless an even greater total was prevented only by the fact that many faint-hearted, would-be deserters were afraid that they could not "make the trip," or failed to find a favorable opportunity, for the deserters continually insisted to Union officers that large numbers of their comrades would desert if they had the chance. Sometimes the deterrent was the vigilance of the Federal pickets and hence the danger of being fired on; while again they preferred to await capture as prisoners to facing the danger of detection and death for desertion at the hands of their own officers.[3]

Some light is shed on the question of the number of deserters by the figures of men paroled in the various armies at the surrender. When General Dick Taylor surrendered May 4, 1865, at Meridian, Mississippi, he had about 8,000 men under arms; yet about 30,000 of the 42,000 soldiers paroled in the armies of the southwest took the parole at Meridian. The obvious explanation must lie in the fact that deserters flocked in from the surrounding country in order to secure the protection of the Federal government against the probable revenge of the Confederate soldiers.[4]

In discussing the total amount of desertion, cognizance must be taken of the fact of repeated desertions. Sufficiently striking is the statement of a judge of Mississippi made to President Davis in March, 1864, "I know many deserters now in desertion for the

[1] Pollard, *Life of Jefferson Davis*, p. 326. *Richmond Enquirer*, August 12, 1863.

[2] *O. W. R.*, Ser. IV, II, 674; III, 520; Ser. I, LI, pt. II, 1065–1066. The figure of 121,000 is arrived at by subtracting those present from the total in a table compiled from returns of the Confederate army. The number is placed more precisely at 104,428 by the War Department of the United States from muster-rolls in the Archives Bureau of the Confederacy. The records are, of course, incomplete, as the muster-rolls cover two years usually (*House Ex. Doc.*, 39th Cong., 1st Sess., No. 1, IV, pt. I, p, 141). The writer has striven to be conservative in all figures.

[3] "At least half would desert if they had an opportunity" (*O. W. R.*, Ser. I, XLVI, pt. II, 387; XXIV, pt. III, 407).

[4] *Confederate Military History*, XII, 501.

fourth, fifth, and sixth times who have never been punished." [1]
General Pillow, who from his work of arresting deserters was
certainly in a position to know, declared that many deserted as often
as four times, and that Alabama soldiers could not be kept in the
army so near their own homes. Escape seems to have been too easy;
one culprit on his way from the guard-house to Atlanta, effected his
escape from the car on the way; two men were released without
punishment after their second desertion; most of a group of cavalrymen, after being dismounted for desertion, promptly deserted again.
An Irishman under sentence of death for his second desertion made
good his third escape. Bragg found deserters an encumbrance and
felt that the only way of preventing them from running off again was
to shoot them. [2] General Pitner found the situation quite hopeless,
for he wrote, "If these deserters are arrested again and sent to the
Army of Tennessee, as many of them have been a second, third, and
even fourth time, they will not stay." [3] To state the fact in proportional terms, the report of the Secretary of War made near the
close of 1863 may be cited, which put the effective force of the army
at between one half and two thirds of the number on the muster-
rolls, [4] while President Davis in a speech at Macon, Georgia, in
September, 1864, affirmed his belief that if half the men absent without leave, constituting one third of the army, would return, the
South could win. [5]

Desertion was no respecter of persons, for it invaded every
command in the South with no exceptions, so far as the writer
has been able to ascertain. It was currently stated that General Hindman lost 6,000 men in a retreat from Van Buren, Arkansas; certain
of General Hill's troops, starting from the west in January, 1865,
1,600 strong, arrived with but 900; Marmaduke's cavalry, reported
8,000 strong, probably numbered in June, 1863, actually 5,000; Van
Dorn late in 1862 acknowledged a loss of 13,000, most of which he
attributed to desertion; the army in Arkansas in the Trans-Mississippi

[1] O. W. R., Ser. I, XXXII, pt. III, 626.

[2] Ibid., Ser. I, XXX, pt. III, 188–189; XLV, pt. II, 685; XXIX, pt. II,
199; XLII pt. III, 1160–1161; Ser. IV, II, 680.

[3] Ibid., Ser. IV, II, 638.

[4] American Annual Cyclopedia, 1863, pp. 18–19. Substantially the same
estimate was made for 1865 (ibid., 1864, p. 207–208).

[5] Ibid., 1865, p. 188. Davis was certainly minimizing the evil. A Northern
report in December, 1863, insists that Confederate regiments which had
numbered 500 men two months before were able then to muster only 150 or
200 men (O. W. R., Ser. I, XXVI, pt. I, 843).

Department under General Steele was stated to have dwindled by desertion, sickness, and death from 40,000 to some 15,000 or 18,000.[1] Generals Wise, Johnston, Hood, Mahone, Pickett, Steele, Price, and Stuart all suffered, while defections from the loosely organized corps of the raiders Morgan and Forrest occurred frequently. Even so excellent a disciplinarian as Lee was not immune, as has been sufficiently indicated. Every type of command suffered: the State militia, the local defense troops, and the navy.[2]

The enormous total was rolled up by desertions from the regiments of every State [3] but especially, according to Lee from the North Carolina regiments, where it was a crying evil already in 1863 and where it became worse by 1865. Possibly defection among the Alabama and Mississippi troops should also be recorded as particularly serious, while Longstreet's complaint of Georgia troops in 1865 should not pass unnoticed.[4]

It is conspicuous that military reverses and retreats, which were only defeats under another guise, gave fresh impetus to desertion. Gettysburg, Vicksburg, Price's campaigns in Missouri, the Chattanooga campaign, all are cases in point. The results of the Battle of Gettysburg began to be reflected in the Union records of deserters slipping over to the Federal lines at once, and continued all through August and September. We scarcely need the explicit statement of a Northern general in early August that several hundred deserters from Lee's army had come in, and that hundreds were yet secreted in the mountains, awaiting an opportunity to get inside the lines.[5] Lee himself reported 20,000 killed, wounded, and missing on July 29, though undoubtedly many were stragglers who rejoined the command.[6] After the surrender of Vicksburg General Pemberton found that nearly all the troops from the Trans-Mississippi and from the State of Mississippi had deserted, and he predicted that Georgians, Alabamans, and Tennesseeans would go also as they approached their homes.[7] Johnston met the same experience after he was

[1] *O. W. R.*, Ser. I, XXII, pt. II, 34; XLVII, pt. II, 1061; XXIV, pt. III, 432; XX, pt. II, 26; XXII, pt. II, 812.

[2] *Ibid.*, Ser. I, LI, pt. I, 482; XLII, pt. III, 161.

[3] Figures as to how these men were distributed through the various States will be discussed in Chapter IV.

[4] Longstreet, *From Manassas to Appomattox*, p. 651. See Appendix, Table I.

[5] *O. W. R.*, Ser. I, XXIX, pt. II, 17.

[6] *Ibid.*, Ser. I, XXVII, pt. III, 1048.

[7] *Ibid.*, Ser. I, XXIV, pt. III, 1010. Grant reports about the same date that the paroled Confederates had to a large extent deserted and were scat-

driven from Jackson by Sherman, for as he retreated eastward, his demoralized army began by the hundreds to run to the mountains, to the pine woods, and to the enemy until his force was reduced to 10,000 men.[1] Sheridan in his *Memoirs* tells how, just after the evacuation of Corinth in 1862, he found the woods and fields around Booneville filled with several thousand Confederate soldiers.[2] Probably no more conspicuous examples of desertion consequent on retreats could be offered than the two campaigns of General Price into Missouri. A Northern woman spy stated in August, 1863, that everywhere through Arkansas deserters from his army were to be encountered along the route of travel north, "fleeing like rats from a falling house," returning to their homes in Missouri, even when they expected to use their freedom to form guerilla bands.[3] A like result followed Price's second campaign into Missouri in the fall of 1864, when, in addition to the hundreds casting in their lot with the Federals, the country was filled with thousands of men who left his ranks to go to Texas, Missouri, Mexico, and their homes. Missourians abandoned him as soon as they found that he could not hold the State.

Cowardice prompted men to desert when they knew a battle was impending, or even during the actual conflict. A report by Beauregard from Corinth, April 11, 1862, is enlightening in this respect: "I allude to the fact that some officers, non-commissioned officers, and men abandoned their colors early on the first day to pillage the captured encampments; others retired shamefully from the field on both days while the thunder of cannon and the roar and rattle

tered over the country in every direction (*ibid.*, p. 529). But it is also conspicuous that desertion fell off during apparent victory or aggressive forward movement. Note in this connection Hood's statement concerning his Tennessee campaign: "Those who have seen much service in the field during this war will at once understand why it was that desertion, which had been so frequent on the retreat from Dalton to Atlanta, almost entirely ceased as soon as the army assumed the offensive and took a step forward. I did not know of a desertion on the march from Palmetto to Dalton, or from Dalton to Florence. I am informed that the provost-marshal general of the army of Tennessee reports less than three hundred desertions during the whole Tennessee campaign. The Tennessee troops entered the state with high hopes as they approached their homes."—J. B. Hood, *Advance and Retreat* (appendix), p. 337.

[1] *O. W. R.*, Ser. I, XXVI, pt. I, 681; XXIII, pt. II, 539.

[2] Sheridan, *Personal Memoirs*, I, 148. Immediately after Atlanta fell, almost every county in the State of Alabama showed a large increase in the number of deserters (*O. W. R.*, Ser. IV, III, 880–881).

[3] *Ibid.*, Ser. I, vol. XXII, pt. II, 492.

of musketry told them that their brothers were being slaughtered by the fresh legions of the enemy." [1]

Corroborative of the conclusion drawn from detached records is the explicit charge made by General Chalmers as defense for defection from his ranks, that General Bragg's Tennesseeans always deserted him largely when he fell back from Tennessee; that General Price's Arkansans nearly all left him when he retreated from Little Rock, and that General Johnston's Mississippians abandoned him when he fell back from Jackson. "It will be remembered," he says as sufficient excuse, "that Vicksburg had fallen and the whole country was greatly depressed." [2]

The disease contaminated all classes and all ranks. The ill cannot be imputed wholly to the poor and ignorant, for some young deserters were obviously members of families of standing and influence. Southern writers are prone to insist that they were wholly of the lowest class, but the records do not substantiate this view.

The number of officers who deserted the cause is startling and, at the same time, indicative of the attitude which prevailed toward desertion. Probably the large number of officers reported absent without leave on the field return of May 28, 1862, for the Army of the Tennessee—104—[3] should not be looked upon as evidence of desertion but rather as evidence of lax discipline. But by the fall of that year the commanding officers were being awakened to the seriousness and effect on the privates of desertion by their superiors. During a raid to bring back the stragglers into the Army of Virginia, General Jones was astonished at the number of officers arrested and brought to the rendezvous. Lee was sufficiently disturbed about the regimental and company officers, particularly the latter, to suggest to Secretary of State Randolph a law to degrade officers who deserted their commands on the march or in camp, those between eighteen and forty-five to be placed immediately in the ranks.[4] A measure seems to have been promptly passed "to relieve the army of disqualified, disabled, and incompetent officers," for by the close of November of the same year examining boards were being organized for the trial of offending officers. At about the same time orders

---

[1] *O. W. R.*, Ser. I, X, pt. I, 391. One deserter quite shamelessly confessed to a Northern officer that he had left when the fighting began (*ibid.*, Ser. I, XXXII, pt. III, 11).

[2] *Ibid.*, Ser. I, XXXI, pt. III, 828–829.

[3] *Ibid.*, Ser. I, X, pt. I, 791.

[4] *Ibid.*, Ser. I, XIX, pt. II, 622, 629–630.

were issued from Richmond that the pay of such officers should be suspended until the absence was explained.[1] But evidently these boards did not function actively, for a record of the following August refers tenderly to some officers as "remaining absent" for several months at a time.[2] Moreover the statement occurs too often that a group had deserted "with their officers" for the matter to be regarded as negligible. Of a group of 100 deserting to Mexico, the statements occurs significantly that a large number were officers.[3] As with the privates, there was a perceptible increase in the number of commissioned officers who abandoned the cause after the middle of 1864.

The highest ranking officer whom the writer has found thus delinquent is a colonel who came into the Union lines during the last dark days of the war.[4] Except for a quartermaster with the rank of major, no other officer whose desertion is recorded in the *Official War Records* had rank above that of captain or lieutenant, relatively few having a rank even so high as captain where the rank is indicated.[5]

Senator Hill threatened on the floor of Congress to give the names of officers improperly absent who had by that very absence cost the South the Battle of Missionary Ridge.[6] A Texas general charged that company officers were remiss in quietly suffering those under their command to ignore military rules, as it was their duty to lose their lives in supporting discipline as much as to die on the battlefield.[7] It is possible, as a visiting Englishman charged, that some of them played politics with an eye to future preferment as they

[1] *Ibid.*, Ser. I, XX, pt. II, 427, 434.

[2] *Ibid.*, Ser. I, XXIX, pt. II, 627.

[3] *Ibid.*, Ser. I, XLI, pt. IV, 267. See also XXII, pt. II, 956, 961; XXXII, pt. II, 634; Ser. II, VII, 614; Ser. I, XLVII, pt. III, 730.

It seems indeed remarkable that such a letter as the following could be addressed to a *general:* "It has even been reported about the streets of Forth Smith that you thought that the men ought to desert if they were not brought back into Arkansas. Such reports, no matter how false, if nothing is done to counteract them, will send off many men, who will go believing that they have the good will of their officers."—*Ibid.*, Ser. I, XXII, pt. II, 970.

[4] *Ibid.*, Ser. I, XLVI, pt. II, 961. Another colonel was imprisoned for inducing a private to desert (*ibid.*, p. 1029).

[5] *Ibid.*, Ser. I, XXII, pt. II, 309; XLII, pt. II, 89, 1175, 169; XLII, pt. III, 1079; XLVIII, pt. II, 88; XLVI, pt. II, 610. The major was facetiously reported as renouncing "the world, the flesh, and the devil, and Jefferson Davis" (*ibid.*, p. 309).

[6] *American Annual Cyclopedia*, 1863, p. 231.

[7] *O. W. R.*, Ser. I, XXXII, pt. III, 878–879.

feared to make themselves unpopular by punishing their men.[1]

It is possible to give figures as to the number of officers who deserted, based on the Confederate muster-rolls, which may therefore have some claim to reliability, even though, of course, incomplete. Of the total of more than 100,000 deserters, 1,028 were reported as officers. The largest number recorded for any State is 428 for North Carolina; Tennessee stands second with 153; while Virginia ranks third with the rather surprisingly large number of eighty-four.[2]

It is important that not all the deserters belonged to the regular forces. Surgeons and chaplains were not restrained by the nature of their duties from seeking more pleasant, if not more fertile, fields for their services.[3] A signal operator and a topographical engineer of Bragg's staff were touched by the epidemic, as well as the more lowly machinist from the ordnance department and also mechanics, workers in iron, and even teamsters.[4]

The tragedy of desertion becomes almost a farce when one reads of the desertion of 1,200 slaves at Mobile after they had been made liable to impressment in February, 1864, as details for work on fortifications or on war materials in government works or in military hospitals, with the result that the enemy raised almost as many recruits from the fugitives as the rebels had secured from the impressment. In fact, the use of a negro force needing white men to guard them produced a problem of hostility on the part of the owners from whom the negroes had been impressed. The owners were said to encourage the desertions.[5]

---

[1] Freemantle, in Hart, *American History Told by Contemporaries,* IV, 285–286.

[2] *House Ex. Doc.,* 39th Cong., 1st Sess., No. 1, IV, pt. II (Report of provost marshal general). A report of the rebel deserters received at Nashville from January 21 to May 9, 1865, affords some comparative figures. Of a total of 2,751, but ninety, or somewhat more than three per cent, were officers (*O. W. R.,* Ser. I, XLIX, pt. I, 349). See Appendix, Table I.

[3] *O. W. R.,* Ser. I, XXX, pt. III, 412.

[4] *Ibid.,* Ser. I, XXVIII, pt. I, 680; XXIII, pt. II, 564; XLI, pt. IV, 307; XXIV, pt. III, 85.

The desertion of the mechanics was due to orders from the inspector general's office, directing that certain classes of mechanics, who had hitherto been exempt from military duty, be sent to the field (*ibid.,* Ser. I, XLII, pt. III, 1179).

[5] Free negroes were subject to a draft for labor in the army, while slaves, up to 20,000, could be impressed if their owners did not offer them in sufficient numbers, the latter to be paid the regular wages promised free negroes of $11 a month. They were also apparently used as teamsters, cooks, and in the engineer corps (*ibid.,* Ser. I, LI, pt. II, 1063. *Statutes at Large of*

Not the least interesting of the deserters were those from the ranks of the Confederacy's Indian allies. Unreliable when lured into an entirely different character of warfare from that to which they were accustomed, they were rendered still more unreliable because of tribal animosities. Early in the war, December, 1861, for instance, several thousand Cherokees deserted to the Federals because of their reluctance to fight their neighbors, the Creeks. On a later occasion, August, 1862, 1,000 or 1,500 Cherokees deserted the South and went over to the enemy, and early in 1863 all of General Hindman's Indian allies were reported as deserting him and desiring peace. Always a tone of uncertainty made the leaders anxious about the Indian troops.[1]

the Confederate States of America, 1864). See also *O. W. R.,* Ser. I, XXII, pt. II, 1091; XLVI, pt. II, 1031.

[1] *Ibid.,* Ser. I, VIII, 709, 719, 712; LIII, 821; XXII, pt. II, 22, 989.

CHAPTER III

MEANS OF ESCAPE AND MEASURES OF CIRCUMVENTION

The tactics followed by the soldiers to effect their escape are fairly obvious: passage from the picket line or rifle-pit to the enemy's line; dropping out from the column at the fords and ferries and while on the march; taking advantage of gaps and passes while traversing rough country, or of the presence of swamps in the vicinity of the camp or station; slipping away at railroad stations or even jumping from a moving train; failure to return from hospitals or from furloughs; use of stolen or forged passes; escape under the confusion of attacks or captures by the enemy; and escape in civilian clothes through the connivance of friends and relatives.

Desertion to the Union forces from the picket-line, stationed about 100 yards in advance of the breastworks or trenches, usually under cover of darkness, could scarcely be prevented despite all prohibitions of intercourse with the pickets of the foe. Stepping from a rifle-pit in the direction of the enemy was hazardous but not necessarily fatal. One of the commanders frankly states that escape from the picket line was the way in which most of the desertions occurred.[1]

It was encouraged by the friendliness between pickets of the opposing sides, which seems inevitable when armies are stationed close to each other for any length of time. Before long the foes, as individuals, separated often by less than 100 yards, are more given to trading newspapers and to exchanging comments than to shooting at each other, and it persists even after the authorities set their faces sternly against it.[2] It was easy for a Southerner to call over to ask if one of his comrades, who had deserted to the Union side the night before, would be forced into the Union army. It was even easier for the Union picket to shake his head in reply, whereupon the rebel picket would remark that he would himself come over.[3] It is Grant

---

[1] *Official War Records,* Ser. I, XLII, pt. III, 1179. See also XXIV, pt. III, 490; XLII, pt. II, 4, 5, 17, 683; X, 170–172.

[2] Sorrel, *Recollections of a Confederate Staff Officer,* pp. 143–144.

[3] *O. W. R.,* Ser. I, XXV, pt. 218; XXX, pt. IV, 108.

who reported during the siege of Vicksburg that one of his pickets and one of the Confederate pickets by mutual consent laid down their arms, met half-way between the lines, and held a long conversation.[1] Two opposing pickets on another occasion met in the middle of the river, shook hands, and drank to each other's health. The tale is well known of a Confederate picket transmitting to the Federal picket the request that a Northern member of the Masonic order meet a Confederate member of the order to give reliable assurance of the treatment accorded Southern deserters.[2] If a soldier were posted as a vedette or as one of two to eight scouts in front of his picket line, the act became so much easier, and he delivered himself up to the advanced cavalry pickets on the other side.[3]

Occasionally the topography favored the deserter. Two rebel deserters made their way on one occasion to within twenty-five yards of the Federal rifle-pits, where they remained concealed until time for the change of pickets. Owing to the thick corn and the tardiness of the pickets, they were not challenged until they were within ten paces of the latter. On another occasion a convenient graveyard favored the deserter so that he came directly into the redoubt without being challenged.[4]

Often the picket men were almost cut off from the army. One man had been on duty for several days and had been to the line of works but once. If a portion of a brigade were separated from the main camp, conditions were more favorable for escape to the men's homes. And so one should not be surprised to read of fifty or sixty men who deserted from what one colonel terms "my lower camp in the *Many Sinks*," when the deserters were supposed to have gone to Kentucky.[5] It should be noted that disappearance of a private on picket duty must not always be interpreted as desertion to the foe, for he often wished to create that impression in order to avoid search and detection in his home country.[6]

Naturally, most of these desertions from the picket line occurred under cover of darkness. The records indicate that men came into the enemy lines at almost any hour of the night; frequently it was sunrise or later when they reached the other side, but almost in-

[1] *Ibid.*, Ser. I, XXIV, pt. II, 426.
[2] *Ibid.*, Ser. I, XLVI, pt. II, 587.
[3] *Ibid.*, Ser. I, X, pt. II, 129; XLVI, pt. III, 53.
[4] *Ibid.*, Ser. I, XLII, pt. II, 94; pt. III, 151.
[5] *Ibid.*, Ser. I, XLIII, pt. II, 921.
[6] *Ibid.*, Ser. I, XLVI, pt. II, 1143–1144.

variably the escape from their own lines had been effected after
darkness veiled their movements.

Opportunity was offered in the confusion of a clash with the
enemy. Barron tells of how on one occasion after such a conflict with
the Federal cavalry, two of the men in his company fell back when
their comrades turned away, and entered the enemy's breastworks
to surrender.[1]

Ferries, fords, and bridges always presented opportunities until
the officials learned to post guards at such strategic points, and even
afterwards, for deserters learned to leave in bands and so to force
their passage by violence against the guards. And guards were of little
value when they too, as sometimes happened, deserted.[2] General
Johnston knew that on his retreat from Jackson, Mississippi, in 1863
his men were deserting in large numbers by the fords on Pearl River.
If the banks were too well patrolled at a well-known crossing, the
renegade merely moved along the bank until he found an unguarded
point. The absence of fords opposed no obstacle; swimming the
James, Tennessee, Appomattox, and even Rio Grande Rivers, not
to mention smaller streams, was a feat accomplished more than
once.[3]

Escape to a swamp seems to have been easier than escape from
the swamp, as one reads of men lying hidden in the reeds of Louisiana and of South Carolina for days before a Union vessel came down
to which they could deliver themselves. An Alabamian declared that
he had spent thirty days traveling through the water and grass at
the rate of twenty miles a day.[4] In South Carolina rebels would seize
a picket boat, follow a creek, and land in the marsh near the Union
outposts.

Naturally, while the troops were on the march or moving from one
place to another, favorable opportunities for dropping out of the
column presented themselves—and were embraced. One man tells
how he slipped from his command at dusk, went into some woods
and waited until the Confederates had fallen back, surrendering
himself when the Federals came up—evidently a common practice.

[1] Barron, *The Lone Star Defenders,* p. 172.
[2] *O. W. R.,* Ser. IV, II, 783; Ser. I, XXX, pt. III, 39–40; XXIX, pt. II,
403.
[3] *Ibid.,* Ser. I, XL, pt. III, 617; XXX, pt. III, 52, 350, 386; XXIV, pt. I,
200; XXVII, pt. III, 58; XXV, pt. II, 370; XLII, pt. III, 198; XLVIII,
pt. II, 1294–1295.
[4] *Ibid.,* Ser. I, XXVI, pt. I, 499; XLVIII, pt. II, 375–376; XXVIII, pt. I,
598.

"Many of them are hiding out," he declared, "and waiting for the advance of the Federal army."[1] Soldiers marching through broken country found it possible to slip from their commands at mountain gaps. Many deserted at railroad stations, and it is on record that an entire brigade of Alabama troops left the train *en masse* at Montgomery, while others, singly or in small groups, made their escape from the cars.[2] General Johnson thought that there was a communication running east from the Appomattox River among the men on the subject of desertion, under which arrangements had been perfected for men of several different brigades to meet at the intersection of a dirt road with a certain railroad on the south side of the Potomac.[3]

Furloughs and sick leaves at an hospital inevitably offered temptation, especially if, as frequently happened, patients were discharged to return to their commands without a guard. As in every army, some feigned illness or wounds, and were thus enabled to wander off. It was complained by Lee that they filled the houses of the charitable and hospitable along the line of march.[4] Discharge from the hospitals was greatly abused.

Not even the most rigid system of passes, which worked hardships innumerable on the soldiers, presented a barrier which could not be circumvented. Eggleston tells of how every soldier passing through Richmond on leave—and very few of those from the Army of the Potomac could avoid it, as Richmond was the railway center of the east for the Confederacy—lost much of his furlough in complying with the military requirements. He ran an excellent chance of being seized by a provost guard at the railway station, of being marched to some vile prison and being held there for want of a proper passport until his furlough had expired, and of then being sent as a prisoner to his command.

Even then the system was by no means effective. "A very marvel of annoying inefficiency" was the verdict of a loyal Confederate officer. More than one deserter, according to several accounts, passed through Richmond in full uniform, avoiding arrest though every corner bristled with guards and passport inspectors. Passports, bits

---

[1] *Ibid.*, Ser. I, vol. XLVI, pt. III, 1353; XLI, pt. II, 685; XXVI, pt. II, 530; XLVII, pt. III, 699; XXX, pt. III, 601, 563.
[2] *Ibid.*, Ser. I, XXIX, pt. II, 357; X, pt. II, 17; XLIX, pt. I, 834.
[3] *Ibid.*, Ser. I, XLVI, pt. II, 1261.
[4] *Ibid.*, Ser. I, XXV, pt. II, 175; XXXII, pt. II, 333; LIII, 309; XIX, pt. II, 597, 627.

of brown paper, were freely bought and sold by dealers; non-militar
men had slight difficulty in getting them at comparatively little cos
and so conducted a thriving business. It was not beyond a deserte
to forge a pass;[1] indeed one provost marshal charged that man
privates were traveling about the country on orders forged by them
selves. It was not enough that passes were forged; it appeared tha
conscript officers in Alabama gave passes to further the notoriou
peace movement in that State. And yet sharp wits could outwit eve
this network of red tape, and in a fashion so bold and simple tha
it makes one gasp. A deserting soldier would betake himself to th
station from which he wished to depart; throwing his gun ove
his shoulder, he would pace a certain section as if doing sentry dut
and would demand a passport of every soldier who appeared. Whe
his train pulled in, he boarded it, and proceeded to pass through th
train, inspecting the passes of the soldiers in order to create the im
pression that he had been assigned to such detail duty. When he ha
arrived at the station where he wished to descend, he could leave th
train without having been once challenged by a properly accredited
official.[2]

Once outside the lines, usually with arms and equipment and a
fair amount of ammunition "borrowed" from their comrades, the
runaways still had need of wile. Frequently they stole horses from
the farmers or made their way along the mountain ridges or through
the thickets which fringed the edges of creeks to remote places of
refuge. Occasionally they secured Federal uniforms and so sought
easier entry into the Union lines or capture as Federal deserters,
which would enable them to avow promptly their true character.

Precautionary measures to discourage and prevent desertion arose
as early as the first hints of the existence of the evil. The first step
was, naturally, directed against straggling, as a straggler was always
a potential deserter. While the ill-disciplined Southern soldier
straggled at his own sweet will from the first, it was in the early
months of 1862 that complaint began to be audible. By September
straggling was recognized as a serious problem demanding attention.
An alarming number of stragglers were reported after the Chicka-

---

[1] O. W. R., Ser. I, XXVIII, pt. II, 387; Ser. IV, II, 9–10.

[2] Eggleston, A Rebel's Recollections, pp. 209–214, 216, 220. Sometimes the
government was lax, as was evidenced by a soldier who was not required even
to show his pass in traveling over the New Orleans and Jackson Railroad
(O. W. R., Ser. I, XLVIII, pt. II, 168).

mauga campaign. The country for miles around the military stations was reported full of officers and soldiers, visiting, loitering, and marauding. Many quartered themselves on the people of the country, claiming entertainment as a right, preferring loafing to service in the field or camp.[1] "I have taken every means in my power from the beginning to correct this evil [straggling]," wrote Lee after his first campaign into Maryland in 1862, "which has increased instead of diminished. A great many men belonging to the army never entered Maryland at all; many returned after getting there, while others who crossed the river kept aloof. The stream has not lessened since crossing the Potomac, though the cavalry has been constantly employed in endeavoring to arrest it . . . It occasions me the greatest concern in the future operations of the army." [2] An officer tells of how staff members, to his great disgust, made sharp play with the flats of their swords on the backs of the stragglers, to the accompaniment of harsh words, to drive them up to the column on the mountain roads, which were filled with broken regiments. In a Tennessee brigade, General Joe Wheeler kept a cavalry company at work after a battle, gathering up the foot-sore and weary, whom the troopers placed on their horses, while they themselves walked at the side. Thus none were left behind except those adroit enough to leave the road and thus to avoid the guards.[3]

Guards were placed at every small town, at all the stations, fords, and bridges, and on roads leading to towns in suspected areas, usually old men or boys, who were timid by reason of fear of secret vengeance. The bridges and fords at the foot of mountains were especially well guarded to intercept the men before they had reached the hills, where they would be difficult to pursue. At strategic points, pickets were doubled and increased vigilance was exercised.[4]

As early as July, 1862, employees of railroads were requested by a general war order to examine passes and furloughs of soldiers traveling on their roads in order to arrest deserters. By November, provost guards with a detail of three men from Lee's army served daily on the main railroad lines in Virginia under orders to arrest

[1] *Ibid.*, Ser. I, XX, pt. II, 446.
[2] *Ibid.*, Ser. I, XIX, pt. I, 143.
[3] Sorrel, *op. cit.*, pp. 107–108. *O. W. R.*, Ser. I, XVI, pt. I, 899. Deserters usually took amunition in the ratio of 100 rounds per man.
[4] *Ibid.*, Ser. I, XXVII, pt. III, 1052; XXV, pt. II, 814–815; XXXI, pt. III, 129; XXX, pt. IV, 502.

all military men unable to produce passes and to turn them over to the nearest military post on the route of travel.[1]

The strictest of precautions were taken to reduce to the minimum the opportunity of escape from the camp or from the line of march. As early as 1862, rear guards under efficient and accountable officers were placed behind the brigades to prevent the men from leaving the ranks to the right, left, front, or rear. Commanding officers of regiments were required to pass frequently along the lines of the regiment to see that the ranks were closed up and that company officers were attending to the proper order of their companies. Well to the rear of the army marched a provost guard to pick up stragglers. Frequent roll-calls, sometimes every hour, became the order of the day. At reveille, roll-calls were held, each man appearing under arms, in order that the company commander might know that the arms had not been thrown aside. Responsibility for desertion was placed squarely on commanders under pain of dismissal from the army. In some commands they were required to have their men file past them at all fords or places where the column might be broken. During the last month of the war in one brigade, non-commissioned officers were required to keep moving constantly on the line, and to report every quarter of an hour to the officers on picket duty.[2]

Early likewise came the effort to remove, wherever possible, one cause of desertion in the alleged disregard of a soldier's preference as to the company and regiment with which he was to serve. Almost pitiful is the weakness indicated in one order of September 19, 1863: "You will see from these papers the importance of using gentle means to satisfy, if possible, the men referred to. If they have cause to complain and real grievances, they should be heard and their wrongs redressed. You will then proceed to the camp of Lieutenant-Colonel Burleson, and see these men and assure them of the desire of the lieutenant-general commanding to redress all past grounds of complaint, if in his power to do so."[3] Cavalry brigades in Lee's army were reduced in size in order to insure more attention on the part of the commander to individuals, while brigades which the virus of desertion had rendered unreliable were broken up and the men distributed among other regiments which were more dependable.[4]

[1] O. W. R., Ser. I, XIX, pt. II, 722.

[2] Ibid., Ser. I, 618–619, 592; XLVI, pt. II, 1261.

[3] Ibid., Ser. I, XXVI, pt. II, 240.

[4] Ibid., Ser. I, XXVII, pt. III, 1068. It was Lee's suggestion to reduce the size of the brigades (ibid., Ser. I, XXII, pt. I, 172).

The same purpose of prevention is manifest in the prohibition in October, 1863, of permits to conscripts or to former deserters to visit their homes; in the denial to subordinate commanders of the right to grant leaves; and in the transfer of regiments from their home States to remote posts of service.[1] It is certainly a commentary on the situation to read that conscripts were easily induced to enter their names if it were for regiments stationed near their homes, as they saw better opportunity for deserting. President Davis removed some 30,000 North Carolina troops from their home localities to distant parts of the Confederacy, though Seddon protested against turning Lee's army into a "Botany Bay." [2] On the other hand, liberal furloughs were granted to soldiers whose terms were about to expire or just after a hard or disastrous campaign.[3] Even earlier came the suggestion of not allowing absentees to draw their pay as a possible deterrent to unauthorized departure. A company of General Hardman's regiment, drawn from the Indian frontier, was disarmed to prevent the departure of the soldiers for their homes.[4]

Care was exercised to insure the return of the sick and wounded upon their discharge from the hospitals by sending details to the hospitals to bring them in; some corps provided their own hospitals, to which the sick were sent daily on cars under charge of a surgeon and a guard, by whom they were turned over to the commanding officer of the post, who then became responsible for them.[5]

As a measure to secure prompt apprehension of offenders, a bounty of $30 was offered for every deserter delivered to an officer, and one of $15 for each deserter lodged in jail, with allowance for expenses.[6] In April, 1865, a furlough of forty days was offered any enlisted man who detected and aided in the conviction of any one caught in the act of desertion from the Army of the Tennessee.[7]

---

[1] *Ibid.*, Ser. IV, II, 875; Ser. I, XXII, pt. II, 1078–1079; XXIII, pt. II, 964–965.

[2] *Ibid.*, Ser. I, XXXIII, 634; XXIX, pt. II, 769; Ser. IV, II, 869.

[3] Comte de Paris, *History of the Civil War in America*, III, 7. *American Annual Cyclopedia*, 1862, p. 243. Lee's furlough at the rate of one per hundred men and General Pemberton's leaves of absence just after the fall of Vicksburg are cases in point.

[4] *O. W. R.*, Ser. I, XIX, pt. II, 679; LIII, 890.

[5] *Ibid.*, Ser. I, XLI, pt. IV, 1022; XXIII, pt. II, 747–748; XXXIX, pt. II, 807.

[6] Gen. Orders, No. 52. *O. W. R.*, Ser. IV, II, 14. See also *American Annual Cyclopedia*, 1862, p. 246.

[7] *O. W. R.*, Ser. I, XLIX, pt. II, 1240. The furlough was in general thirty days. See below, p. 77.

The law to arm and enlist negroes, which was passed just on the eve of the collapse of the Confederacy, brought a pressure for commissions as rewards for having apprehended deserters.[1]

In the session of the Confederate Congress of 1863–1864, in order to silence the murmur against the men who had escaped conscription by providing substitutes, and in order to fill the thinning ranks an act was passed drafting even those who had furnished substitutes.[2]

In March, 1865, to keep the gravity of the offense before the men, and to put the fear of death in their hearts, Lee ordered the proper Article of War read to each company once a day for three days and to every regiment at dress parade once a week for a month and at other times at the discretion of the commanding officer.[3]

Dismounting became early a favorite device to use with cavalry troops for straggling and as a preventive of desertion, the horses being seized and turned over for the use of other men, while their owners were assigned to the infantry, where they could be brought under a more rigid discipline. Morgan is authority for the statement that "there is no punishment more dreaded by a cavalry-man than being dismounted and transferred to the infantry." And it was felt as a real grievance as they had bought their horses themselves at great cost.[4]

The various measures resorted to by the Confederacy to prevent and suppress desertion ran the gamut of all possible devices from beseeching appeals to a general presidential amnesty, from gently collecting stragglers to inflicting the death penalty.

One of the earliest and most common devices was brought into operation early, was utilized faithfully throughout the period of the war, and proved quite futile: appeals to the soldiers. They emanated from the various generals, governors, editors, groups of women, and civil leaders, and even from President Davis himself in the form of an amnesty. The plea made by Lee on July 26, 1863, will serve as a typical illustration of dozens of similar appeals: "The commanding general calls upon all soldiers to rejoin their respective regiments at once. To remain at home in this, the hour of our country's

---

[1] *O. W. R.,* Ser. I, XLVI, pt. III, 1367.

[2] *Ibid.,* Ser. IV, III, 69. *Confederate Statutes at Large,* chap. LXV, Sec. 4. *American Annual Cyclopedia,* 1863, p. 231.

[3] *O. W. R.,* Ser. I, XLVI, pt. III, 1357.

[4] *Ibid.,* Ser. I, XXX, pt. IV, 655, 656; XXXIX, pt. II, 678–679; XXIII, pt. II, 20, 494, 636.

eed, is unworthy the manhood of a southern soldier. While you proudly boast that you belong to the Army of Northern Virginia, let it not be said that you deserted your comrades in a contest in which everything you hold dear is at stake. The commanding general appeals to the people of the States to send forth every man able to bear arms, to aid the brave soldiers who have so often beaten back our foes to strike a decisive blow for the safety and sanctity of our homes and the independence of our country." [1]

These appeals, accompanied now by stinging rebukes, now by threats, and again by promises of amnesty issued by generals with governmental permission, designed to inspirit and cheer, were couched in every variation of phraseology until even the most severe rebuke was without effect. Though camouflaged, General Bragg was making a virtue of necessity in November, 1862, when he issued the following general orders: "Gratified beyond expression at the confident tone and fine discipline which pervades his troops and full of admiration at their fortitude and patient submission to privations . . . the general commanding is induced to publish full pardon to all soldiers absent without authority who shall within a reasonable time return to their command and report for duty. They are urged to avail themselves of this privilege before the inauguration of the new system of military courts established by law as a vigorous and prompt administration of justice to all delinquents. Hereafter no excuse will be allowed those who abandon their colors and leave their comrades to perform their duties and defend their homes. If you come voluntarily, I will be proud to receive you. I will not have you, and you need not expect to join me, if brought as prisoners." [2]

General Holmes issued an order of pardon in the Trans-Mississippi Department during the first days of 1863 with gratifying success, but General Polk awaited with impatience the expiration of the time allowed by his proclamation of amnesty in order to proceed against the deserters in his department.[3] By 1864 offers of amnesty from

[1] *Ibid.*, Ser. I, XXVII, pt. III, 1040. Officers were often, as a part of their duty, expected to use their personal influence to prevent the evil (*ibid.*, Ser. I, XXII, pt. II, 974).

[2] *Ibid.*, Ser. I, XX, pt. II, 429. The straits to which generals were reduced in their efforts to preserve a military dignity while compromising with the crime were pathetic, as when one commander pretended that the proposal to their comrades to desert was made in "jest" (*ibid.*, Ser. I, XLVI, pt. III, 1357).

[3] *Ibid.*, Ser. I, XXII, pt. II, 797. Polk, *Leonidas Polk*, II, 318-319.

generals embody the threat of no further opportunity for so effacing the crime of desertion,[1] though the mere fact of such a proclamation is a confession of weakness; pardon was accompanied at times by the promise to deserters of service near their homes, for which they would receive the compensation allowed by law to detailed men, and by promises of furloughs.[2] Certainly, it was generally understood that any deserter who returned voluntarily would be leniently dealt with. Lee indeed declared that he had never known such cases to be punished with death.[3]

Despite a just perception on the part of Davis and of Secretary Seddon of the necessity of firm discipline, the Richmond government pursued a too lenient policy, abetted in the last desperate days even by so strict a disciplinarian as General Lee. Whether a different course would under the circumstances have been possible and whether it would have altered the course of history is at best highly doubtful.

The first acknowledgment of the evil by the War Department unearthed by the writer is in Special Orders No. 107 under date of May 9, 1862, which merely ordered all absentees to rejoin their regiments forthwith, threatening in case of failure to obey the publication of their names as *deserters!*[4] July 14 brought forth an order to enrolling officers and commandants of instruction camps to arrest deserters.[5] At this time desertion by a commissioned officer entailed only being dropped from the rolls in disgrace and danger of conscription as a private!![6] Even in the face of 40,000 to 50,000 deserters in July, 1863, the tone of the War Department is weak, as Assistant Secretary Campbell urged the "accommodation of the Department to the necessity of the case as the best policy," advocating a general amnesty act and a "new departure." He found comfort for the situation from the records of the French Revolution, which showed 120,000 deserters at one time.[7]

Campbell's views must have represented the conviction of Seddon also, for in August of that year President Davis issued an appeal in the form of a presidential proclamation of pardon and general am-

---

[1] *O. W. R.*, Ser. I, XXXII, pt. III, 786; XLIV, 990.

[2] *Ibid.*, Ser. I, XXXV, pt. II, 331; XXVI, pt. II, 387.

[3] *Ibid.*, Ser. I, XXIX, pt. II, 820.

[4] *Ibid.*, Ser. IV, I, 1120.

[5] Gen. Orders, No. 49. *American Annual Cyclopedia*, 1862, p. 246.

[6] *O. W. R.*, Ser. IV, II, 214–215.

[7] Indorsed as his comment on a letter from Governor Vance to Secretary Seddon (*ibid.*, p. 674).

nesty to all absentees, except those twice convicted of desertion, who should return to their proper commands within twenty days after publication of the amnesty in the State in which the absentees might be. It is noteworthy that this step was taken, if not at Lee's suggestion, at least after the following note from him to Davis on July 27: "I do not know whether it [an appeal to the soldiers] will have much effect unless accompanied by the declaration of an amnesty . . . I doubt the policy of this, but I would respectfully submit that perhaps a general amnesty declared by your Excellency might bring many delinquents back to the different armies of the Confederacy." [1] Davis tried to fire the hearts of his fellow-countrymen by vivid if false statements of the aims of the Washington authorities, whom he represented as prompted by malignant hate, who sought the extermination of the Southern whites by servile insurrections, and he implored the women of the Confederacy to use their all-powerful influence to "add one crowning sacrifice to that which their patriotism has so freely and constantly offered on their country's altar" by sheltering none who should be on the field of service.[2]

The women of the South responded personally and collectively. Many of the Confederate newspapers, even before the President's appeal, had carried the following plea, evidently to strengthen wavering sisters: "It is impossible for us to respect a coward and every true woman who has husband, father, brother, or lover . . . had rather see him prostrate before her with death's signet on his noble brow that has never been branded by cowardice or dishonor, than have him forfeit his good name and disgrace his manhood by refusing to do his duty to his country."

By July, 1864, pressure was being exerted on the President for a second proclamation, but he felt that the repetition of such action would only increase desertion and would result in pardon to the worst class of offenders; he therefore preferred that the generals commanding the two main armies issue an order to absentees to

---

[1] *Ibid.*, Ser. I, XXVII, pt. III, 1041.

[2] *Ibid.*, Ser. IV, II, 687–688. Davis half excused the men to justify his act: "I believe that but few of those absent are actutated by unwillingness to serve their country, but that many have found it difficult to resist the temptation of a visit to their homes and loved ones from whom they have been so long separated; and that others have left for temporary attention to their affairs with the intention of returning, and then have shrunk from the consequence of the violation of duty." *Ibid.*, 685–687.

return under the promise of good offices in their behalf, a suggestion which was acted upon by the respective commanders.[1]

And yet once more, in the face of staggering defections and in
despair of success in coercing deserters back into the ranks, in the
dark month of February, 1865, Lee turned to thoughts of a second
general pardon, which was issued this time under his name as
newly made General-in-Chief of the army. President Davis, in
assenting to the proclamation, wished to have the soldiers warned
that this would be the last interposition for deserters, a suggestion
which Lee incorporated in his statement. It was skilfully drawn to
appeal to the men's honor and sense of duty and to lure them back
by the picture of victories. The pardon did not apply to men detected
in desertion to the enemy nor to second offenders, but did apply to
all deserters then under arrest.[2]

Threats of dire penalties for failure to return inspired but slight
fear when the culprits felt themselves fairly safe from the fulfilment
of the threat. "Severe punishment to all deserters deaf to this clemency" was to be meted out, according to General Gardner. "All those
who may be found with arms in their hands," he blustered in West
Florida, March 18, 1865, "will be shot without mercy. The families
of deserters and the disloyal will be sent into the interior, their
property destroyed, and all the cattle, horses, and hogs will be driven
away or shot." [3]

The results of this weakness of discipline were what might have
been expected: increase of the evil it was intended to remedy and in-
equality of treatment in different commands. One general complained
of being kept in ignorance of authority to pardon, for he was shooting deserters, while in the adjoining parishes they were being pardoned.[4] Lee reported on August 17, 1863, that, immediately upon
publication of the presidential amnesty, "many presumed upon it,
and absented themselves from their commands, choosing to place on

[1] *O. W. R.*, Ser. I, XL, pt. III, 817–818. For Lee's dignified call, see Gen.
Orders, No 54, August 10, 1864 (*ibid.*, Ser. I, XLII, pt. II, 1169).

At heart Davis and Seddon understood perfectly the importance of firm
discipline and tried to stand for it. In April, 1864, Governor Vance's request
for suspension of the conscript law in western North Carolina was refused
(*ibid.*, Ser. I, LIII, 324 ff.).

[2] *American Annual Cyclopedia*, 1865, p. 193. It did not appear in the papers
of Mississippi until March 14.

[3] *O. W. R.*, Ser. I, LIII, 320.

[4] *Ibid.*, Ser. I, XXXIV, pt. II, 901.

it a wrong interpretation." [1] *The Independent* struck the nail on the head when it said, "let all the appeals be made which may possibly do any good; but if you want soldiers, don't forget the appeal of the law." [2] The effect of former executions was thus, naturally, destroyed.

Reprieves were common and had, of course, the same effect as repeated amnesties. Pickett accounted for the presence of 100 men in the guard-house for desertion by the fact that every man in his division sentenced for this offense during the two preceding months had been reprieved. [3] Men of influence or position escaped penalty; punishments were often remitted; the very trifling penalties often inflicted by the courts only placed a premium on desertion. Another serious difficulty arose from the fact that the records of the trial were delayed in transmission to the approving officer, so that offenders who should have been disposed of at once often found opportunity for escape while awaiting execution of the court sentence. A citizen complained that it was a mockery to try to convict any soldier who had social position or friends. He related how two young men of fortune, who had been defended by able counsel, were found guilty, not of desertion, but of "absence without leave." On top of that outrage, active measures immediately secured their pardon, so that in a few days they were parading the streets, while several poor men, who could not pay for counsel, were undergoing punishment for the same offense. [4] It was a military officer who called attention to the fact that two men of the militia service had just been released without punishment for the crime of a second desertion, though they had been arrested in the act of deserting to a Federal gunboat. The natural delay in the execution of sentences of court-martial, incident to the necessity of securing the approval of the commanding officer, was often prolonged by the loss of the record. [5] The lesson taught—that a deserter could escape the penalty of his crime—was quickly learned.

Though no man understood better than Lee the danger of weak discipline, he followed up some flagrant desertions in 1864 by instituting a system of furloughs to remove "all palliation from the offense

[1] *Ibid.*, Ser. I, XXIX, pt. II, 649–650.
[2] August 15, 1863.
[3] *O. W. R.*, Ser. I, XLII, pt. III, 1213.
[4] *Ibid.*, Ser. IV, III, 709. See also Ser. I, XLVI, pt. III, 1355.
[5] *Ibid.*, Ser. I, XLII, pt. III, 1160–1161, 1251. *Lee's Despatches*, pp. 155–156.

of desertion," suspended sentence of death on seven deserters, and recommended remission of some sentences for extenuating circumstances of extreme youth, previous gallantry, or good conduct. But in general after 1863 Lee insisted on firm measures, writing sagely, "It is certain that a relaxation of the sternness of discipline as a mere act of indulgence, unsupported by good reasons, is followed by an increase of the number of the offenders. The escape of one criminal encourages others to hope for like impunity. . . ." [1] In February, 1865, he was still making a desperate effort at discipline in the face of hundreds of desertions nightly, for Lee declared to Richmond, "I cannot keep the army together unless examples are made of such cases." [2]

By June, 1863, it was apparent that there existed no agency adequate to cope with the evil. The military commanders, occupied with the enemy, were not tempted, even by the prospect of additional recruits, to spare any considerable forces to pursue deserters. [3] And so the War Department at first hoped for solution through grafting this duty on the Conscript Bureau in 1863. [3] The bureau hoped in the beginning to discharge the new duty by retaining some cavalry conscripts from the draft as patrols in each State, by recompensing citizens for their aid in pursuits with a fair price for their horses and actual expenses of travel, by enrolling small bodies of militia with the consent of governors into temporary service under the commandants of conscripts, and by calling on men from forty to forty-five years of age for this home service. [5] The bureau naturally sought and secured the coöperation of army commanders by securing from them periodical lists of absentees, giving the names, companies and regiments, where they were thought to be, and length of time and place of desertion, submitted at first monthly, later every alternate week. Details of officers and men for making arrests were assigned. [6] The adjutant and inspector general at Richmond proceeded at once to energetic measures by asking all officers charged by commanders with the duty of arresting deserters to report to

[1] *Lee's Despatches*, p. 156.
[2] *O. W. R.*, Ser. I, XLVI, pt. II, 1258.
[3] *Ibid.*, Ser. IV, III, 976; II, 607.
[4] This bureau was created in 1862 by Gen. Orders, No. 82 (*ibid.*, p. 750).
[5] Gen. Orders, No. 7 (*ibid.*, Ser. IV, II, 607–608, 618).
[6] *Ibid.*, p. 801; III, 518. Some commanders were already having such lists prepared for their own use (*ibid.*, Ser. I, XX, pt. II, 392; XXXI, pt. III, 717).

commandants of conscripts in their respective States and to coöperate generally.[1]

But the immense increase of desertion through 1863 without corresponding expansion of the bureau rendered it inadequate to discharge its new duties. General Pillow, who had been placed in charge of the Conscript Bureau in Tennessee, Alabama, and Mississippi by General Johnston in Department No. 2, had spread a complete network of organization over those States with twenty-four points of rendezvous, at each of which was stationed a field officer with subordinate officers and a supporting force of cavalry. At each of the rendezvous there was also one company of infantry, stationed as guards for the men brought in. The supernumerary branch was separate and distinct from the conscript branch, both branches acting under the same orders and on the same duty, but in different fields of labor. With this force he swept over the States in his department and returned large numbers of deserters to their commands.[2]

General Pillow devised a plan, warmly endorsed by the governors of the States concerned and by several commanding generals, for a combination of supernumerary officers, who would not be subject to local influences in performing their duty of making arrests, with the conscription organization, and for the transfer of deserters from the west to the Virginia front, a plan depending for its enforcement on a large supporting cavalry force.[3] This plan, if it had been adopted, would have probably resulted in displacing Preston, head of the Conscript Bureau in Richmond, by Pillow, for the latter proposed to extend the plan he already had working in his area over the entire Confederacy. The plan naturally awakened no enthusiasm in Preston, who thought that the evil depended for correction on the aid of the civil powers of the various States.[4]

The bureau stationed at every small town and at every station, ford, bridge, and ferry in suspected areas an officer with a small squad of men, usually old men or boys, who were miserably equipped and intimidated by threats of vengeance. A small mounted force of the same material attempted to patrol the country. Complaint was made that they were more active in annoying citizens than in arrest-

---

[1] Gen. Orders, No. 122 (*ibid.*, Ser. IV, II, 801).

[2] *Ibid.*, pp. 819–822, 638, 805–806, 680–681. General Johnston later revoked Pillow's authority and inaugurated a regular Conscript Bureau.

[3] *Ibid.*, pp. 749–751, 805–806. Pillow was commended for his work by the Legislature of Florida, Dec. 4, 1863.

[4] *Ibid.*, p. 751.

ing deserters, but their searches of houses at irregular intervals must have reached the homes of some deserters. Some conception of the paucity of forces under the control of the commandants of the Conscript Bureau may be gained from the following statement of an enrolling officer concerning the situation in South Carolina: "The only power under my control in addition to Boykin's men . . . is about forty conscripts, who are only a quasi-organization (designated a military patrol) under the instructions of the Conscript Bureau, sanctioned by the War Department, at this place; about 15 or 18 in Pickens, 6 in Anderson, about 10 in Spartanburg, and 3 in Union District, with, perhaps, in the several districts named, about 18 to 20 disabled soldiers, furloughed and assigned to duty here for the arrest of stragglers, deserters, and evaders of conscription." [1]

After September, 1864, the matter of arresting deserters was in the hands of the reserves instead of the conscription agencies. But evidently the reserves did not discharge their task efficiently, for Lee declared on February 24, 1865, that what was needed was not, as Preston thought, a new local force, but a "plan which will make the reserves understand and feel that they are engaged in military duty and liable to military punishment for its neglect." [2]

The great difficulty which had to be met before the evil of desertion could be solved lay in the practice of transfers from one branch of the service to another. And it must be clearly understood that there were three military organizations in the Confederacy: the general Confederate service, State reserves, and State militia. The reserves were composed mostly of persons liable to the general Confederate service and deserters from that service, while the State militia was also composed chiefly of deserters and persons liable to the other two branches. Deserters from the general service were enlisted in State reserves under false names and places. [3] Already in June, 1862, by General Orders No. 43 the transfers of men from the line to partisan corps was forbidden and in February, 1863, rules governing transfers of deserters in cases of reënlistment were made explicit. [4]

The records bear constant complaints of the raising of new com-

---

[1] *O. W. R.*, Ser. I, XXXII, pt. II, 747. See also the reports of General Ramsay (XLI, pt. III, 181).

[2] *Ibid.*, Ser. IV, III, 1121–1122.

[3] Such a complaint was sent to Davis November 25, 1864 (*ibid.*, Ser. I, XLV, pt. I, 1247).

[4] *Ibid.*, Ser. I, XXIX, pt. II, 845; Ser. IV, II, 401.

panies by enlistment of deserters or of soldiers about to be dismissed from hospitals, and of other practices which the generals steadily opposed, despite the pleas of lesser men, who insisted that handsome commands could be raised in the mountains by enlisting everybody—"conscripts, deserters, and all," who would do good service if properly managed.[1] General Ross, who had furldughed one half of his command to Texas to compel the return of deserters to his brigade, wrote bitterly in the winter of 1865, "I have evidence establishing the fact that Lieut. Col. O. Steele, commanding a cavalry battalion in Texas, and many other officers of similar grade, are harboring deserters from my brigade and holding them to duty with their commands. Such conduct will eventually break up the organization of troops from the Trans-Mississippi Department." [2] Longstreet complained in March, 1865, of desertions to local organizations, especially among Georgians; he felt that though the officers were limited in their recruiting to disabled men and non-conscripts, inducements were being offered to lure men from the ranks by promises of immunity from arrest.[3] Lee early cautioned his subordinates against receiving men who had deserted from other companies. "All such should," he admonished General Imboden, in February, 1863, "be arrested and returned to their proper commands. The army cannot be kept up if men are allowed to put at defiance the laws and regulations for its government . . . I hope you will as soon as practicable eradicate from the companies you now have organized all deserters and turn them over to their officers. Your brigade is too elevated in character to retain such in its ranks." [4]

Requests for the transfer of absentees to another corps or even for permission to form new companies openly from deserters continued from 1863 to the end of the war. One captain proposed organizing deserters from Mississippi troops into new companies, their former defection to be excused on the plea of their illiteracy. Trenchant and curt is Davis' endorsement: "Impossible. Deserters cannot hope for more than pardon on condition of returning to their posts." [5] Generals Lee and Johnston urged that no new organizations be re-

---

[1] The plea here alluded to came early, September, 1862 (*ibid.*, Ser. I, XIX, pt. II, 631). For recruiting from hospitals, see *Lee's Dispatches*, p. 131.

[2] *O. W. R.*, Ser. I, XLVIII, pt. I, 1395.

[3] Longstreet, *From Manassas to Appomattox*, p. 651. See especially the defense offered by Colonel Ford (*O. W. R.*, Ser. I, XLI, pt. II, 995); see also *ibid.*, LII, pt. I, 73–74.

[4] *Ibid.*, Ser. I, LI, pt. II, 677.

[5] *Ibid.*, Ser. IV, II, 708.

cruited, as abuse was almost inevitable and the action produced discontent in the regular armies. Seddon seemed to be well aware of the mischievous effects of such practices. And so by about January, 1864, the government was found revoking the outstanding permits for new companies and consistently thereafter refusing such requests on the ground of the injury to the service as a whole by subversion of discipline and the temptation to fresh desertion, although it was conceded that in certain localities it was probable that more men could be placed in the field in that way than by returning them to their commands.[1]

Especially numerous were the complaints of recruiting the cavalry from deserters from the infantry. Occasionally the appeal took the form of pleading that deserters be mounted, as the only way to lure them back. Lee complained of Louisianians, who, on their way through Richmond, joined General Morgan's command, while Johnston denounced advertising in Georgia for recruits for Forrest's and Morgan's commands, as it broke up his infantry, as well as kept conscripts and volunteers out of the infantry, "where alone they were wanted." [2] Deeply significant was General Polk's reaction to Johnston's effort to recover some deserters supposed to be in the cavalry organizations of Mississippi and west Tennessee as untimely, since they had been "so short a time with General Forrest that any attempt to detach them now would result in a general stampede." [3] The evils of irregular cavalry service assumed an insidious form when officers, recruiting ostensibly for the cavalry under Forrest or Morgan, had really no intention of completing the companies, as their object was to keep out of the infantry; or when officers allowed men to slip within the enemy's lines in order to enter them into a new organization.

So serious had the entire question of transference from one command to another become by March, 1864, that a general order from the War Office, calling attention to the Articles of War which forbade such practices, was deemed necessary. The offense was to be regarded as desertion, while an officer guilty of negligence in the

[1] *O. W. R.*, Ser. I, XXXII, pt. III, 644–646; XLII, pt. II, 1182–1183.

[2] *Ibid.*, Ser. I, XXXII, pt. II, 604. *Lee's Despatches*, p. 131. The raider Mosby was said to have an uncompromising sense of military honor and duty. He would not allow his command to become a refuge for deserters, and hence won high regard at Richmond (Scott, *Partisan Life with Colonel John S. Mosby*, p. 34).

[3] *O. W. R.*, Ser. I, XXXII, pt. II, 662–663.

matter could be cashiered.[1] The government and officers tried to discover and return all deserters recruited in other companies to their proper commands. Lists of deserters, furnished by inspectors, were handed to generals, which constituted demands upon them to turn over the men to the nearest provost marshal for delivery to their proper companies. Although complaints of the enlistment of deserters in the regular service, and particularly in local organizations, persisted to the very end, Lee tried consistently to insist on firm discipline in regard to the matter of transfers, extending his final pardon of February, 1865, only to such men as had complied with the condition of return to their original commands.[2]

The penalty for desertion under the military law of the Confederacy was in time of war death or "such other punishment as should be ordered by the sentence of a general court-martial," [3] but men were too precious to be shot or hanged if there were any possible means of saving them for the guns of the foe. Furthermore, there were times when the number gathered in—several thousand—was so great that shooting was entirely precluded. And so, in April, 1863, the article was amended so as to provide death or confinement with or without hard labor for a period of from one to five years or such other penalty as the court-martial might decree.[4]

Hence we find truly cruel and unusual modes of punishment devised, such as shaving the head, riding wooden horses, being drummed out of the service, flogging, wearing barrel-shirts, gagging, bucking, and branding. *Bucking* was the name applied to tying a soldier's hands together at the wrists and slipping them down over his knees where they were held in place by running a stick under the knees and over the arms. But one general who tried to break up straggling by administering bucking from sunrise to sunset succeeded only in causing the desertion of half the company. A barrel-shirt was, as its name implies, merely a barrel in which holes had been cut for the arms. *Gagging* was the suggestive name applied to fastening a bayonet in the mouth by tying it with a string which passed behind the neck. The ball and chain was not infrequently re-

---

[1] *Articles of War,* sec. 22. *O. W. R.,* Ser. IV, III, 255.

[2] For two excerpts illustrating how the contrasting points of view persisted to the end, see *ibid.,* pp. 1043-1044; Ser. I, XLIX, pt. I, 963. The letters were written January 30 and January 22, 1865, respectively.

[3] *Articles of War for the Armies of the Confederate States,* Art. 52.

[4] *O. W. R.,* Ser. IV, II, 496, 853-854. Pillow was embarrassed by the numbers he raked in.

sorted to.[1] Another device was to sentence a soldier to carry a rail across his shoulders for eight hours; while again the way of the transgressor was made hard by tying him up by the thumbs at headquarters all day suspended on his toes. On one occasion, a soldier of the Stonewall Brigade reports, the whole army was kept marching around in columns all day for inspection by the officers as a penalty for the action of some of its members. The newspapers printed accounts of branding with the letter *D* in the hand or on the left hip. The most severe sentence, except death, which the writer has noted was one imposed on a North Carolinian: thirty-nine lashes on the bare back every three months for the period of the war, branding in the left hand with the letter *D,* and hard labor with the ball and chain for the balance of the war.[2] One disposition was to put them at hard labor on the forts. One general ordered offenders turned over to the civil power, assured that they could render more "service to the country in the workshops of our prisons" than in the field. They were usually sent to the place of trial in irons after arrest.[3]

But at length the officers were obliged to resort to the death penalty, as the only way to check the pernicious evil by making an example of some of the deserters. By 1863, especially after the presidential pardon, commanders are found pursuing and arresting them, holding courts-martial, shooting them at sight when they resisted, and executing sentence of death upon them. In the words of one of the generals, forbearance had ceased to be a virtue and he told his men "now, and for the last time, 'The sword of justice shall fall.'" And General Crandall stated succinctly: "Every man sworn into my command is informed that we kill for stealing and deserting."[4] Generals had, of course, no authority to shoot offenders

---

[1] Casler, *Four Years in the Stonewall Brigade,* pp. 101–102. The *Richmond Enquirer* carried on January 7, 1863, the following statement, "Ninety-three deserters were sent to their regiments to be punished. Bucking, barreljackets, and stripes were the usual sentences awaiting them." The Northern army learned about January, 1864, that many Southern deserters were wearing the ball and chain (*O. W. R.,* Ser. I, XXXII, pt. II, 136).

[2] *Daily Richmond Examiner,* July 10, 1863. *Charleston Daily Courier,* February, 13, 1863.

[3] *O. W. R.,* Ser. I, XXXI, pt. III, 716.

[4] *Ibid.,* Ser. I, XXVI, pt. II, 378; XXII, pt. II, 841. See also Lee's recommendation in August, 1863, for "the rigid enforcement of the death penalty" in the future, as the only remedy for the great evil (*ibid.,* Ser. I, XXIX, pt. II, 649–650). Beauregard issued the sharp order, "If deserters are caught report so that court may try ringleaders at once and make an immediate example" (*ibid.,* Ser. I, XLVII, pt. III, 702). And General E. Kirby Smith

except to prevent their escape or if they resisted arrest, until sentence had been imposed by a court-martial. But later in the war a colonel justified his assumption of authority in the execution of a soldier, charged with repeated desertion, in the presence of his regiment, on the ground that nothing but the most severe measures could redeem the army from the curse of desertion while the uncertainty of trial by a military court was almost tantamount to immunity.[1]

While most generals shot deserters, it is clear that others executed by hanging, reserving shooting for cases of attempted escape. A conspicuous instance of hanging occurred at Kinston, North Carolina, on February 28, 1864, when twenty-two deserters from General Hoke's brigade were so executed as an example to check the crime.[2] In a hot pursuit of the Federals some days before, a number of prisoners had been captured, among whom were recognized twenty-two North Carolinians dressed in Yankee uniform who had deserted from the Confederacy. Arraigned before a court-martial, they were condemned to be hanged. General Maury evidently found this the most effective method, for he wrote, "They don't mind being taken prisoners and sent off, but they won't face the hanging." [3]

Stonewall Jackson was one grand exception to the prevailing custom of leniency. He never failed to confirm the sentence of death passed by courts-martial on deserters. A most interesting story is told of how four men were to be executed for this crime. The firing party had been ordered to parade at four o'clock in the afternoon; shortly before the appointed hour a chaplain, not noted for his tact, presented himself in the general's tent to petition for the release of the prisoners. He found Jackson pacing up and down in great agitation, with his watch in his hand. The latter listened courteously to the plea, which culminated in the words, "General, consider your responsibility before the Lord. You are sending these men's souls to hell." But to the astonishment of the worthy divine, he found him-

---

advised General Taylor in September, 1863, to dispose of deserters "as speedily as possible the several sentences of court-martial being executed at once" (*ibid.*, Ser. I, XXVI, pt. II, 241).

[1] *Ibid.*, Ser. I, XLIX, pt. I, 1016.

[2] For an interesting sermon by the Reverend Mr. John Paris, given to the brigade after the hanging, see a pamphlet, *Sermon for Brigadier General Hoke's Brigade at Kinston, North Carolina,* now preserved in the library of Duke University. For other instances, see *Daily Richmond Examiner,* September 26, 1863; and *O. W. R.,* Ser. I, XVIII, 867; XXIII, pt. II, 56; XVIII, 867.

[3] *Ibid.*, Ser. I, XXXII, pt. III, 633.

self seized by the shoulders and thrust from the tent with the words echoing in his ears, "That, sir, is my business—do you do yours!" [1]

The procedure followed in the Stonewall Brigade on one occasion might well be calculated to inspire a wholesome fear of desertion in the breasts of all observers. One company was detailed to dig the graves for the ten convicted deserters, to make the coffins, to put up the posts, and to bury them. The prisoners were, at the appointed hour, conducted from the guard-house under a heavy guard, preceded by fifers and drummers playing a death march and by the chaplains and surgeons, to the place of execution, where the entire division was drawn up in a hollow square. The ten condemned men were placed in front of the ten wooden crosses which occupied the fourth side of the square and made to kneel with their backs to the posts. Their arms were hooked over the cross-pieces, their hands were tied in front, and they were blindfolded. They were then shot before their comrades. The entire brigade was marched by the corpses in ranks in order that the warning might have its full effect. [2]

General Forrest also made short shrift with deserters and seems in one case, at least, to have committed a great injustice. As a number of his men had departed for their homes in the enemy's lines, he left guards at the various crossings of the stream. At a certain bridge, two men who had been brought in as deserters insisted that they were then on their way to their homes in Kentucky, as they were outside the conscript age, one over-age, the other too young. As they had no passes, a drumhead court-martial condemned them. The bodies were exposed by the side of the road in full view of the passing troops, while on a tree was nailed the placard, "Shot for Desertion." Unfortunately, it proved that the statements of the supposed deserters were true. [3]

The most brutal penalty imposed for desertion which the writer

---

[1] Henderson, *Stonewall Jackson,* II, 450–451.

[2] See the graphic account in Casler, *op. cit.,* 188–190. This instance occurred in 1862. The same story is told by Sorrel, *op. cit.,* p. 222.

[3] Wyeth, *Life of General Nathan Bedford Forrest,* p. 589. Possibly the reluctance with which the death penalty was inflicted cannot be better told than by the following table of the Second Army Corps, submitted February 2, 1865, for the preceding month:

"No. tried for desertion	29
"No. found guilty	6
"No. shot	1

O. W. R., Ser. I, XLVI, 354.

has encountered was crucifixion. Although the person who recounted the tale was said to be above the average in intelligence of the section where the event is said to have occurred, the writer is inclined to believe that it represents one of the wildly exaggerated tales told by the embittered Unionists of Tennessee, which spring up in every war. However, the story is recounted for what it may be worth.

A Tennessee Unionist had been forced into the Confederate army, and had twice deserted. When he was captured for the second time, he was carried off in the night and crucified, spikes being driven through his hands and feet to fasten him to a tree. Although he was gagged to stifle his cries, life persisted for over a week, when he was discovered and released, but hunger, exposure, and pain had so weakened him that he died very shortly afterward.[1]

[1] Browne, *Four Years in Secessia,* pp. 154–155.

CHAPTER IV

DESERTER COUNTRY

The specific haunts where the deserters sought refuge, their distribution through the various States, their mode of life and conduct while in hiding, and the attitude of the civilian population toward them present phases of the subject which challenge particular interest.

There is proof of the presence of deserters in every single State of the Confederacy. They seem to have congregated in various parts of the Allegheny Mountains, beginning as early as 1862, for we find them in western North Carolina, in the extreme northwestern portion of South Carolina, in the tier of northern counties of Georgia, in northeastern Alabama, in western Tennessee, and even in the mountainous section of Virginia.[1] But there were also large numbers of them in eastern and central North Carolina; in Alabama they were scattered through eleven counties of the northern portion, covering perhaps a third of the State, but were found also in the extreme southern country along the Gulf coast and in the inaccessible corner adjoining Florida and Georgia, notably, Henry, Dale, and Coffee Counties;[2] in Georgia they were not confined to the mountainous section. Groups of them infested middle Tennessee. The swamps of western Florida and the country south of the Withlacoochee River, the southwestern corner of Georgia and of southern Mississippi, alluded to by a certain Confederate general as the "deserter's own country," and the cane-bottoms of Louisiana offered unusually favorable retreats.[3] The brush and chaparral of the Ozark Mountains of Arkansas and of the remote, northern counties of Texas proved almost as valuable to the deserters of those two States.[4]

[1] Accuracy demands the statement that the writer has found no record of deserters living in bands in Virginia before 1863, though there is no reason to assume their non-existence.

[2] The counties most frequently mentioned are Marion, Walker, Fayette, Tuscaloosa, Pickens, Jefferson, and Bibb.

[3] One citizen said of Mississippi: "'The lower and middle tier of counties are vastly rotten" (O. W. R., Ser. I, XXXII, pt. III, 626).

[4] "You might as well look for a needle in a haymow as to hunt for deserters in the forest, chaparral, and mountains of Texas" (North, *Five Years in Texas*, pp. 189–190).

One should probably not be surprised to discover deserters hiding in the capital State but yet to find the viper curled in the very bosom of the Confederacy is a shock. That the State should be filled with deserters availing themselves of the opportunity of escape by their passage through the capital when on furlough or when transfers of troops were being made is to be expected, but that we should find them deliberately establishing lairs in the mountainous sections of Virginia is a distinct surprise. Yet mention of bands in Floyd, Montgomery, Franklin, Rockbridge, and Botetourt Counties occurs in the records.[1]

The following letter from a captain to the chief of staff from Harrisonburg, Virginia, illustrates how such bands originated: "I have the honor to inform you that I have received information from a rebel deserter from the Thomas (North Carolina) Legion, that there are yet about 1,000 rebel stragglers between here and Strasburg, who are many of them armed and picking up stragglers from this army and running them off into the mountains. Many are acting under the leadership of one Captain Lincoln, who commands a band of guerillas. They are every day becoming more troublesome, as they are getting better organized and armed. Their headquarters is along the base of the mountains, on the east side of the Valley." [2]

Skulkers very naturally sought refuge in the border States in that shifting area which lay between the Union and Confederate lines, and on foreign soil across the Rio Grande in Mexico. An instance of the presence of no less than 100 deserters from Kentucky regiments lurking about Newport, Kentucky, was noted in 1863 by the *Richmond Enquirer*.[3] The *Official War Records* note a similar number in Owen County of that State about the same time, unorganized men who had merely returned home for their greater comfort. But a few months earlier Union detachments had been ordered to break up organized bands in Bath and Morgan Counties. Very late in the war General Forrest complained that Kentucky recruits could not be held in the Southern army, for, though they would flock to General Johnson's standard upon his appearance in the State, as soon as he turned southward, they would scatter to attach themselves to roving band of guerillas, jayhawkers, and plunderers who preyed

[1] *O. W. R.*, Ser. I, XLIII, pt. II, 871, 889, 921.
[2] *Ibid.*, p. 250.
[3] February 12, 1863. For the Kentucky and Tennessee region, see *O. W. R.*, Ser. I, XLIX, pt. II, 1198.

upon the people.[1] The Union officers took cognizance of a band of rebel deserters in the hills of the White River in Missouri, stealing horses in the latter State to run into Arkansas, where they were exchanged for cattle to be brought back into Missouri.[2] In Calvert and the adjacent counties of Maryland, where the rebel sympathy was lively, Confederate deserters constantly appeared and were concealed, occasionally depredating upon and, in some cases, murdering the Union adherents, and causing anxiety for the railroad bridges.[3]

It should be understood that in these retreats, especially in the border country of Virginia, Kentucky, and Tennessee, were to be found cowards and evil-doers from both sides, Union and Confederate—murderers, thieves, and deserters. Western Tennessee was repeatedly declared to be filled with stragglers and deserters.[4]

Proof of escape to Mexico is far less abundant than might be expected, though instances are not wanting.[5] Especially suggestive is the protest of General Bee against allowing renegades of various sorts to reach the Rio Grande: "The deserters, refugees, etc.," he wrote from Fort Brown on October 26, 1863, "are reporting daily to the United States consul at Matamoras. On the 23rd, fourteen well armed and mounted, rode up to his office in daylight and were assigned quarters; seven swam the river last night from this vicinity.

"The prisoners of war, said to be Yankee overseers, sent by General Smith, are said to be in Matamoras; in a word, if you will consider that Matamoras is a good recruiting station for Lincolndom, I trust you will not imperil the safety of the lives and property of the people on this river by sending any more here. I believe that the offense for which *exportation* is assessed should be expiated by *death* at the place of offense and that prisoners of war should be sent to

[1] *O. W. R.*, Ser. I, XXIII, pt. II, 49–50; XX, pt. II, 63; XLIX, pt. II, 1124–1125. Reference is had to A. R. Johnson, an adjutant.

[2] *Ibid.*, Ser. I, XLI, pt. II, 10.

[3] Based on a statement made late in the war, but evidently having an earlier application (*ibid.*, XLVI, pt. III, 682).

[4] Wyeth, *Life of General Nathan Bedford Forrest*, p. 582. A Northern officer reports as early as June, 1862, of West Virginia: "The principal citizens of Charlestown called on me today, and earnestly requested I would station a force there as soon as possible, as they were being robbed by the stragglers of both armies, there being many of Jackson's army still hanging around, deserters. . . ."—*O. W. R.*, Ser. I, LI, pt. I, 660. See also Sorrel, *Recollections of a Confederate Staff officer*, p. 222; Eggleston, *A Rebel's Recollections*, p. 85.

[5] *O. W. R.*, Ser. I, IX, 689; XLVIII, pt. II, 45.

the Federal lines (not to the Rio Grande.)"[1] And the agreement of General Bee and Governor Lopez of Tamaulipas for the mutual rendition of deserters and thieves, is sufficiently suggestive of the presence of Confederate absentees on foreign soil. About a year later, a Union officer speaks of the desertion of over a hundred cavalrymen from General Drayton's command to Matamoras in a single day.[2]

Soldiers from all the different armies found their way to the mountains, swamps, or brush: Mississippians hid in western North Carolina; North Carolinians betook themselves to the shelter of the swamps of Florida; while Louisianians lagged behind the army, secure in the fastnesses of Tennessee.

Shelter was sought, naturally, in remote places, difficult of access, where escape was easy and pursuit difficult: in the gorges and cliffs of mountain retreats, in marsh and swamp, in thicket and wood, in cane-brake and tight-eye thickets,[3] in mesquite and brush, and, where no other shelter afforded, in caves hollowed out from a low hillside or even under the level soil.

The section sought in South Carolina comprised the three counties adjoining North Carolina, namely, Pickens, Greenville, and Spartanburg, which, together with parts of the adjoining States, constituted a frontier border of 140 miles, every foot mountain country, much of it almost inaccessible to a cavalryman. Pickens District was thought, about May, 1864, to have 170 deserters, while about half that number were hiding in the hill section of Greenville District. Their presence at that point caused the government great apprehension for some important iron-works and factories and for the security of the mountain passes.

The swampy section of Florida afforded natural defense, for at high tide when the dense marsh overflowed, or when heavy rains swelled the rivers, the hummocks became islands in an impassable marsh. Even in reasonable weather soldiers were obliged to make their way through water so deep as to necessitate the removal of the cartridge belts to keep the ammunition dry, as they stumbled over

---

[1] *Ibid.*, Ser. I, XXVI, pt. II, 358. This statement is confirmed by a letter of March, 1862, from the United States consul himself. He declares that he was continually being besieged by refugees and deserters, most of whom were without funds and expected him to send them north. For many he procured situations (*ibid.*, Ser. I, IX, 661).

[2] *Ibid.*, Ser. I, XXVI, pt. II, 178; XLI, pt. IV, 267.

[3] The colloquial name for thickets too dense for the eye to penetrate.

the tangled roots of the dense tropical growth in a country so wild that even a compass was inadequate and only the perfect knowledge of guides made movement possible. To locate bands of deserters, who shifted their camps in order to evade their pursuers, was practically impossible.[1] In the region between Charlotte Harbor and Lake Okeechobee was another low, wooded section where deserters and evaders of conscription bided their time until they could join the forces of the United States.[2]

While the greater number of renegades from duty tended for greater security to band together, as will be abundantly shown, it should be distinctly recognized that there were also a large number of them hiding separately in the mountains, not banded together but playing a lone hand, so to speak, preferring to trust no man. Often it was almost impossible to find them owing to the rough country and the ease of moving about.[3] Others roamed the country as jayhawkers, cotton-stealers, runners, and marauders. They attached themselves to wildcat organizations and, under a partial recognition from unauthorized authority, district headquarters, were able to baffle every attempt to return them to duty.

Lurking in their hiding places in small groups of two or three at first, it became not unnatural for them before long to come together in bands, ranging from twenty to several hundred, organized in military form under colonels, majors, and captains, well equipped with Spencer repeating rifles and with an apparent abundance of ammunition.

One of the most conspicuous of these semi-military bodies was the "Independent Union Rangers" of Taylor County, Florida. The band drew up a constitution and signed it, including among its provisions allegiance to the United States, absolute obedience to its own officers, complete secrecy concerning operations, and equal distribution by officers of all booty. It is amusing to read above the signatures of men who had deserted the Confederacy the pledge to "punish by

[1] See the interesting report of Lieutenant Colonel Capers (*O. W. R.*, Ser. I, LIII, 316–318).
[2] This was not an idle threat with rebel soldiers in Florida. From Key West it was reported on December 14, 1863, that nineteen refugees had enlisted in the Union service and as many more would enlist under the understanding that their first service would be in Florida (*ibid.*, Ser. I, XXVI, pt. I, 855). On desertion in this State, see also *The New York Herald*, April 30, 1864; *New York Tribune*, September 6, 1864.
[3] *O. W. R.*, Ser. I, XXXII, pt. III, 859.

death any person who may *desert* or entice others to do so or shall treat with contempt his superior officers." [1]

Another region conspicuous for disloyalty lay in Floyd County in the western mountains of Virginia, which received the name of "Sisson's Kingdom," taking its name from a large family which resided in that locality. Many of the clan had volunteered for the Confederate service, and had then deserted. They held complete sway, invited other runaways to join them, and openly resisted all control of Confederate authority. So vindictive was the feud feeling that relatives lay in wait for and shot at officers who had captured deserters, as chance brought the latter back into the infested country.[2] The people in Floyd and Montgomery Counties went so far as to elect what they called a "brigadier-general of deserters" and other officers, and organized what they called a "State government," even electing a separate governor.[3] Great numbers of deserters were located in the Valley of Virginia, where they concealed themselves successfully from the small squads sent in search of them.

Certainly the bands took on the appearance of outlaws when in Arkansas a hybrid group of deserters, negroes, women, and Federals banded themselves together under a notorious criminal; when in Tennessee the same bands showed deserters, jayhawkers, and Indians; or when in Florida deserters, occupying the country held for many years by the Seminole Indians, gathered runaway slave bands to commit depredations upon the plantations and crops of Southern loyalists and to run off their slaves, even threatening the cities of Tallahassee, Madison, and Marianna.[4] In places they made weekly, often daily, incursions from their camps to a distance of fifteen or twenty miles.

General Pillow declared them to be as "vicious as copperheads" in Alabama.[5] Occasionally we read of their making a sort of fortress as at a point near Greenville, South Carolina, where a log house was provided with loopholes for defense. They pillaged, plundered, and stole horses and cattle and hogs by the hundred, not only at night but in open day,[6] taking whatever property was of use to them, of

[1] Davis, *The Civil War and Reconstruction in Florida,* p. 259. *O. W. R.,* Ser. I, LIII, 318–319.
[2] Wise, *The End of an Era,* pp. 385–391.
[3] *O. W. R.,* Ser. I, XLIII, pt. II, 907.
[4] *Ibid.,* Ser. I, XXXV, pt. II, 607.
[5] *Ibid.,* Ser. IV, II, 680.
[6] It was this arbitrary blackmail which furnished the government its first chance of assistance from the neighborhood in getting at the deserters.

government as well as private ownership. One complaint states that they frequently "hang a man by the neck till he is almost lifeless to make him tell where his money and valuables are."[1] Arson was not beyond them, for we read of their burning several court-houses and jails as well as the property of those who condemned their course of conduct;[2] they also burned bridges and sank ferry-boats. A shocking number of murders were attributed to them, and in some parts of the country, notably Louisiana, Mississippi, Alabama, and North Carolina, it was dangerous for a man suspected of guard service to travel abroad. Men were shot down at their labor in the fields. Discipline was administered by the cane, the rope, the torch, or exile. Men were shot in cold blood on their own door-sills. Sometimes disguised as Union soldiers, they committed the most horrible atrocities and barbarous inhumanities. A tale is told of how in one case they visited an old man near Florence, Alabama, and, when he refused to reveal the hiding place of some money which they were convinced he had, stripped his back, tied him face down on a table, piled on his bare back leaves torn from a Bible, and burned him to death. Not content with this barbarity, in their disappointment at failure in their quest for gold, they shot his nephew, left a grandson for dead, and finally dispatched an overseer who, unfortunately for him, came up just then.[3] One of the most offensive stories is one told by Fleming of these "Destroying Angels," as they named themselves. As they were taking all the food from a certain home, the mother remonstrated only to receive the reply, "Starve and be d—d." After carrying off or destroying everything of value, including the gin-house, the cotton-press, the corn-cribs, the stables, negro cabins, and farm implements, they prepared to burn the dwelling. The only response to the mother's appeal to leave a shelter at least for her children was this brutal remark: "You may thank your good fortune, Madame, that we have left you and your d—d brats with their heads to be sheltered."[4] A judge of an Alabama circuit

[1] *O. W. R.*, Ser. I, XXXII, pt. III, 747. For cases in North Carolina, see Arthur, *Western North Carolina*, p. 611.

[2] The court-houses of Coffee County, Alabama, and of Green County, Mississippi, may be cited (*O. W. R.*, Ser. IV, III, 1043; Ser. I, XXXII, pt. III, 711–713).

[3] *Ibid.*, Ser. I, XXXII, pt. III, 711; Ser. IV, III, 1043. See also a tale in Barron, *The Lone Star Defenders*, pp. 245–247, and see Fleming, *Civil War and Reconstruction in Alabama*, p. 119.

[4] Fleming, *Civil War and Reconstruction in Alabama*, p. 120. For several other revolting tales, see pp. 119–120, also Arthur, *op. cit.*, p. 612.

refused to hold the court unless he had a military escort to protect him against the deserters and skulkers.[1] It is no exaggeration to say than in the sections most usurped by the deserters the majority of good citizens were either driven away or murdered, and that little less than a reign of terror prevailed under the leadership of men, desperate and bad, though bold and skilful leaders. In South Carolina it was stated that there was a region sixty by forty miles in area completely in the possession of deserters.

From nearly every State came complaints of the running-off of sheriffs and Confederate agents from their homes; of the driving-away of bodies of cavalry which came to attack them; and of their coercing to their terms or killing enrolling officers and regulars. In Virginia a notice was placed on the court-house door admonishing the enrolling officer and guard to leave the country at once.[2] From Rapides Parish, Louisiana, for instance, came complaint in 1864 that two officers, one of whom was severely wounded, had been attacked by a party; from Jones County, Alabama, of the slaying of the conscript officer and of the capture of his force.[3] An enrolling officer was made to wade out into the river only to be a target for shooters from the shore.[4] Deserters hiding in North Carolina sent menacing messages to the militia officers, threatening death to the most obnoxious of them and to all who assisted them. They quickly visited the penalty of their wrath upon citizens who were willing to point out the rendezvous and hiding places of the outlaws, so that it became difficult for the military authorities to secure the aid of men who knew the local topography. So completely intimidated were the enrolling officers that one can read the following astounding report from an inspector's pen: "Many deserters have been for months in this place without molestation from him [Lieutenant Johns, the enrolling officer for Marshall County]. Charles Smith, a private of the Thirty-fourth Mississippi Regiment, a brother-in-law of Lieutenant John's clerk, notoriously a deserter, has been repeatedly in the conscript office without molestation . . . Conscripts and deserters are daily seen on the streets of the town." [5] This antagonism held over after the war had closed, for in June, 1865, a mob hung two men at

[1] *O. W. R.*, Ser. IV, III, 1044.
[2] *Ibid.*, Ser. I, XLIII, pt. II, 919.
[3] *Ibid.*, Ser. I, XXXII, pt. II, 580.
[4] Fleming, *op. cit.*, p. 119.
[5] *O. W. R.*, Ser. I, XLIX, pt. I, 950.

Columbiana, Alabama, who had been actively engaged during the war in arresting deserters.[1]

The deserters utterly defied the government. Probably insolence could go no farther than to scatter through the swamps 150 head of cattle which the quartermaster had collected for government use or to notify an agent to desist from collecting the tithe and to distribute his existing store to their families, as happened in Mississippi;[2] or to declare, as they did in Washington Parish, Louisiana, that they had a government of their own in opposition to the Confederacy.[3] Governor Milton, in a letter to Secretary Mallory of May, 1864, stated that 10,000 blankets and 6,000 pairs of shoes intended for State troops had been captured by deserters.[4] Of the same character was the rescue of some six or seven conscripts by a superior force of deserters in Mississippi in August, 1864, and the surprise and capture of a camp of conscripts. In Randolph County, Alabama, some deserters were arrested and impressed, but an armed mob compelled the jailer to surrender the keys and set the men free.[5] The constant reports of an abundance of ammunition lend credibility to the report that they were supplied by furloughed soldiers. But there must have been a number among them who had been engaged in the powder mills and who could hence teach the rest to make a home brand of powder and cartridges sufficiently deadly for protection. Their boldness reached a climax in a plot by deserters in west and middle Florida to capture the governor himself, but he was warned in time to prevent its consummation.[6] Mississippi offered the remarkable spectacle of deserters presenting themselves at the polls in armed bodies, exercising the privileges though denying the duties of citizens.[7] In Florida the military officials found it impossible to secure an interview with the band in the Middle District of Florida to discuss with them the general amnesty of August 1, 1863,

---

[1] *O. W. R.*, Ser. I, XLIX, pt. II, 963.

[2] *Ibid.*, Ser. I, XXXII, pt. III, 727. In October, 1864, a citizen complained of Montgomery County, Virginia, that unless something were done no cattle would be left for the soldiers, as deserters were using three to four a week (*ibid.*, Ser. I, XLIII, pt. II, 890).

[3] *Ibid.*, Ser. I, XXXII, pt. III, 755.

[4] Found in the *Milton Papers*, "Letter of Milton to Mallory," May 23, 1864.

[5] Rhodes, *History of the United States*, V, 432. *O. W. R.*, Ser. IV, II, 258. This occurred as early as 1862.

[6] Davis, *The Civil War and Reconstruction in Florida*, p. 261.

[7] *O. W. R.*, Ser. IV, III, 707.

with a view to their return to companies in their own State.[1]

The size of the assembled bands naturally varied. In Texas the largest group was near Bonham, where there were at three camps, within a radius of ten miles, from 200 to 400 men, all of whom could be concentrated within two hours, though the general estimated not less than 1,000 deserters in the sub-district.[2] In North Carolina they took possession of a town in 1863, drilled regularly, and intrenched themselves in a camp. They were determined to kill, not only to prevent capture, but even in revenge of the capture of each other. A band of 1,000 Missourians who refused to cross the Arkansas River with Price were joined by all the guerillas in that part of the State. A citizen's careful estimate placed the number of deserters in Mississippi in 1864 at not less than 7,000; Pillow's estimate of 8,000 to 10,000 in Alabama, with an average of 300 for a typical county in the northern section of the State, such as Jones County, is well known, while General Allen expressed to Seddon his belief that there were 8,000 in Louisiana. Some 2,800 had collected in the woods and brush of the northern district of Texas by the fall of 1863. A rough calculation of 700 to 800 for the mountain counties of South Carolina was probably not far from correct. One thousand or 1,500 was thought to be the number concentrated in Chefinokee Swamp in Georgia.

Mississippi, with its pine-lands in the east and its marshy river counties in the northwest, was unquestionably one of the worst States. A judge pictured it to President Davis in early 1864 thus: "Mississippi is almost a Sodom and Gomorrah; the pacifying element is with you, and the day of our salvation, if neglected for a day, is forever gone. I am no alarmist, but tremble in view of a just comprehension and full knowledge of the extent, depth, and magnitude of these evils." [3]

Piteous appeals went up from the few loyal, law-abiding citizens that the situation was desperate and that they would soon be "gone up." They pleaded for discipline and for men who would shoot marauders, if necessary, for their protection. The report of a captain on conditions in Greene County, Mississippi, presents a sufficiently vivid portrayal: ". . . the whole southern and southeastern section

[1] *Ibid.*, Ser. I, XXVIII, pt. II, 402.
[2] *Ibid.*, Ser. I, XXVI, pt. II, 344.
[3] *Ibid.*, Ser. I, XXII, pt. II, 608, 1030; Ser. IV, III, 880-881, 976; Ser. I, LIII, 901; XXVIII, pt. II, 411; XXXII, pt. III, 626; Ser. IV, II, 680.

of Mississippi is in a most deplorable condition, and unless succor is sent speedily the country is utterly ruined, and every loyal citizen will be driven from it." [1]

Very similar is the following report of a captain of the condition in northern Alabama: "These counties are almost, if not wholly abandoned by any military force, and are filled up by deserters and disloyal men who are avoiding the service. They have, a large number of them, banded themselves together in a sort of banditti association for the double purpose of opposition to the Government and resistance to the laws, and for harassing, robbing, and sometimes murdering the good and loyal citizens. They make weekly, in fact almost daily, incursions from their headquarters, above Pikesville, Marion County, into the adjacent counties, and rob all good citizens in their course of their horses, arms, money, provisions, clothing, bed clothing, and all else that can be of any use to them, and not unfrequently carry off as captives the males of the families. They never fail to do this if they find a man who has been prominent in the support of the Government and in aiding to send to the army deserters and others who are of our service. They are taken off ruthlessly from the bosom of their families, and are never heard of afterward and there is little doubt that they are cruelly and brutally murdered. They are organized and their numbers daily increasing, and they growing more bold and extending their incursions farther and farther." [2]

Another conspicuous feature of the organization of deserters was the means of communication between the various bands for their common protection. The mere act of congregating was in itself a menace, as it encouraged desertion by the promise of protection thus held out. And so the marauding outlaws raided from one county into another and bands came in from adjacent counties to help whip the cavalry. Furthermore, they often acted in concert with Union soldiers in the neighborhood and threatened to return with Yankee reënforcements.

Their actual manner of living, of eluding detection and capture by the Confederate regulars, of providing themselves with shelter and foods, holds all the interest of the dramatic, while it reveals the ingenuity and cunning which pursuit brings out in the pursued—

[1] O. W. R., Ser. I, XXXII, pt. III, 711. Not less than 1,000 were estimated to be living in the three southern counties of Harrison, Hancock, and Jackson (ibid., Ser. I, LII, pt. II, 493).

[2] Ibid., 746–747.

whether man or beast. During the first year of desertion, namely, 1862–1863, the absentee had little occasion for fear, if he merely did not parade himself in public places. He stayed at home, tended his crops and stock, living his old life much as before the war, as he always had ample warning of danger. Every road leading to a camp, when the men were living in groups, whether in North Carolina or in Texas, was so well picketed that not a man, woman, or child could come near them unheralded. All bands had spies and an elaborate system of signals to indicate the approach of danger. A quilt hung on the fence in varying positions, or quilts of different colors, conveyed a variety of messages to the deserter hiding within sight of his mountain cabin; hog-calling was practiced through such a range of tones that it was exalted almost into an art; or songs, apparently caroled on the way to the spring, conveyed a warning. Horns and cow-bells were also made to serve the same purpose.

While the mountainous counties of western North Carolina were filled with deserters, burning, robbing, and murdering so that the Tar-Heel State gave the authorities of the Confederacy grave cause for anxiety, it is the story of the cave life in the central portion of the State to which brief space will be given here.

As the story has already been told in considerable detail, let it suffice here to recall that the underground homes were burrowed in some low hillside to avoid moisture, or hollowed below the flat earth, if necessary. The entrance to the burrow was effected by means of a trap-door in the roof, which was cunningly concealed by boughs, dirt, and leaves most carefully arranged to look as if they had never been disturbed. The telltale freshly turned red clay from the excavation (usually six by eight feet, though often larger) was first thrown into a bed quilt, and then carried away in buckets and piggins by the faithful hands of old men, women, and children, to be thrown into a running stream near by, which obligingly carried away the evidence which would have betrayed the fugitive. A fallen log or mass of carelessly strewn stones formed a pathway to the entrance so as to render impossible the wearing of a path, while a charred tree stump or dead tree, apparently still smoking, placed ingeniously just at the mouth of the chimney, would arouse no suspicion of a fire below the surface of the earth and so awaken no dangerous question in the mind of a passing guard, alert for the presence of deserters. Much more reasonable was it to attribute the smoke to a recent negro possum-hunt. The damp cave was made habitable by a fireplace cut into the earthen wall, by a carpet of pine-needles, and by a bed of pine boughs spread on a pole frame erected on trestles of forked stakes. Occasionally there was even a cupboard cut into the earthen wall. Except for the fact that the caves were merely places of refuge during a search, life in their chilly, grave-like recesses would have been intolerable, and so for the most part their occupants used the caves only as sleeping places, and ventured out into the woods in daytime, trusting to their sharp eyes and swift legs to escape capture even if detected. For greater safety, a band would have several caves in different places to which they could make progressive brief visits. An onion or odorous herb, rubbed on the soles of the feet, was quite adequate to confuse the dogs when set on their trail. The fugitive was fed by his wife or by some female member of the family. As the latter were soon suspected by the officers and their movements watched, they became very adept smugglers in concealing provisions about their persons.

The tedium of cave life—for the charm of the comparative freedom of fishing, hunting and loafing after the rigors of camp and army life must ultimately pall—was broken by practical jokes which the men played upon each other. One trick was for several deserters to don the uniforms of Confederate soldiers, proceed to the vicinity where a cave was known to be located, prod and beat the ground systematically to locate the cave, finally triumphantly pull open the trapdoor, and sternly order out the deserter. It was sometimes part of the game to chase the poor victim around his haunts for several days before the hoax was revealed. The negro's native instinct for woodcraft was often a great help to the master through cunning suggestions, while his innocent responses to the guard usually threw the latter off the right scent. He even helped to keep his master well provisioned. One home-loving man burrowed under his hen-house within a few feet of his dwelling, the smoke going up the chimney of the house. Under such conditions, it is conceivable how men eluded capture for a year, eighteen months, or even two years.[1]

The chief points of rendezvous in South Carolina were found at the mouths of certain creeks and in certain mountain passes. "Almost every intermediate pass and valley, however, is occupied by a deserter's cabin, who on the approach of a stranger flies to the rocks and ravines where, taking his perch, he sees and observes all that is

[1] See Dodge, "Cave Dwelling of the Confederacy," *Atlantic Monthly*, October, 1891, LXVIII, pp. 514–521, for a full account.

going on, safe from the eye of his pursuer (if pursued) until a call or halloo from wife or child assures him of safety . . . In Spartanburg they seem to have no special rendezvous in the mountains, but occupy their farmhouses in the valleys and on the hills, and by a well-arranged system of signals give warning of the approach of danger. On an island in Broad River, just where Spartanburg and Union unite, contiguous to York, it is alleged that some [six] or more occupy it each night." [1]

In some places their usual vocations were plied with a boldness and immunity which seems almost incredible. In northwestern South Carolina and in Mississippi groups of forty to fifty men would stack their arms, set out a picket guard, and with traveling threshing-machines work their farms in common; they congregated at still-yards, where they distilled quantities of liquor, cut and rolled logs, and repaired their fences, and swore vengeance against any one who approached with the intention of molesting them. [2] One band of about a hundred men engaged in a profitable trade of chopping wood for the Federal boats which ran on the Mississippi. [3]

The marauding bands which preyed upon neighbors or raided government stores were self-sustaining and strong enough to terrorize civilians from rendering aid in their betrayal. But it goes without saying that deserters who tarried at ease at home, or burrowed underground, or fled to the sterile brush, foraging at night, could survive only with the aid of their families and the connivance of friends. Many an interesting tale has undoubtedly been told in the mountain cabins of North Carolina by a deserter's wife of how she cultivated the crops by day, prepared food at dusk, and when darkness veiled her movements, slipped out with the supplies somehow concealed under her limp homespun; of how by devious paths she eluded the spies set to watch her movements, of how she occasionally trapped them into beds of quicksand whence she later at her convenience rescued them; and of how she turned virago when guards were on her husband's heels and saved him by a bucket of hot water dashed into the faces of his pursuers. Men thus aided by their families in the mountainous sections of North and South Carolina or in the swamps of Florida, probably did not suffer, but those brought out of the brush in Texas

---

[1] O. W. R., Ser. IV, II, 772.
[2] Ibid., Ser. I, XXXII, pt. III, 712. See XXIII, pt. II, 951, for similar boldness in North Carolina.
[3] Ibid., Ser. I, XXII, pt. II, 954.

were reported as sadly in need of clothing, shoes, and blankets.[1] Some measure of sympathy must go out to these firm-willed resourceful women, for besides their heavy burden of work, they faced almost daily in 1864 armed men carrying death to their deserter husbands.

The criticism of the civilian population for their attitude towards deserters was almost universal. In South Carolina all in the northwest portion of the State were said to be ready to encourage the efforts of those avoiding duty, indeed to counsel desertion, and to refuse information which would lead to arrests; in Virginia there was not moral force enough in 1863 to get their own deserters out into the field, while those from other States were fed as they straggled by; in North Carolina the disaffected fed them from sympathy, the loyal from fear, and there seemed a determination "generally to do no more service in the cause." In Texas General McCullough grew vehement against men "who harbor deserters and spout treason," [2] against the abundance of sympathizers who gave information and fed them on the sly, while President Davis was informed that many of the men and almost all the women of Mississippi were openly at work to procure desertion.

[1] *O. W. R.*, Ser. I, XXVI, pt. II, 387. Young children, eight to ten years of age, naturally secretive and discreet, could stand guard as pickets (Browne, *Four Years in Secessia*, p. 378).

[2] *O. W. R.*, Ser. IV, II, 258, 769–770, 721–722, 783–785; Ser. I, XXXIV, pt. II, 942, 945.

CHAPTER V

Deserter-Hunting

The methods pursued for hunting down deserters ranged from spy-work to bloodhounds. The most conspicuous recorded case of resort to the use of spies in the Confederacy which the writer has encountered was in Louisiana in the fall of 1863. The famous guerilla Quantrill sent several of his more reliable men to the rendezvous of some deserters, to pretend that they also had deserted, and to mingle freely with the outlaws in order to learn their plans. The latter, lured into believing that Captain Quantrill himself was not loyal to the Confederacy, fully disclosed their plan to surrender themselves to General McCullough simply in order to get a supply of arms and ammunition with the secret purpose of going north in the spring.[1]

A variation of the spy method and one which may not therefore have been productive of any important results was the holding-out of inducements to soldiers to betray comrades caught in the act. The duty of questioning and arresting every suspect whom they might meet was laid upon every soldier as well as officer; but later a reward of thirty days' furlough and promotion was offered for bringing in a deserter. That the offers were not entirely barren is proved by a recommendation by General Longstreet of several privates for promotion for arresting a deserter and for exposing a plot for desertion.[2]

Early in the pursuit surprise attacks were mildly successful. Patrols sent out by the conscript guard were able to capture a few prisoners by surprise, but they were obliged to follow circuitous routes to avoid arrangements made to intercept them by superior forces of the deserters or of their abettors. Often during the first two years the captain of the home guard merely blustered with his small force through the suspected neighborhood, while all the de-

[1] *O. W. R.*, Ser. I, XXVI, pt. II, 430.
[2] *Ibid.*, Ser. I, XLVI, pt. III, 1367; XLVIII, pt. II, 87; XXXII, pt. III, 876.

serter needed to do was to keep out of sight for perhaps an hour.

When the pursuit became serious in 1863, a different and more thorough procedure was followed. The provost guards, mounted and unmounted, placed pickets at the ferries, fords, bridges, highway crossings, railroad stations, and along the front line of the enemy so as to cover all probable points of escape. Every road leading to the mountains of Alabama was vigilantly picketed in April, 1864, in every direction from Decatur. Patrols overran the whole Confederacy.[1]

There was a wide difference of opinion as to which arm of the army was the better tool for the work—the cavalry or the infantry, dependent possibly on the character of the country in which the chase had to be made. Sometimes a cavalry troop was requested, alone or in combination with the infantry. Some officers felt that infantry could operate better than cavalry because of the lack of forage or because of the roughness of the country. There were places, it was declared, where it was impossible for a cavalryman to approach, cliffs so abrupt that nothing but a mountain-goat could attempt to scale them. It was the opinion of General Polk, for instance, that infantry was much more effective than cavalry for this work. But it is apparent that cavalry was extensively used.[2] Still another general desired the aid of a light battery, though in some localities, artillery was held to be of no service. We read also of a battalion of sharpshooters and a section of horse artillery dispatched into Jones County, Mississippi, which bodies discharged their duty with vigor and success.[3] One general felt that the only way to accomplish anything was by a command which could remain in the deserter country long enough to learn the hiding places of the deserters from the inhabitants. Expeditions for short periods could accomplish nothing, as they were easily avoided in rugged country.[4]

The size of the force dispatched to hunt deserters is interesting, though necessarily varied and inconclusive. Five companies were ordered by General Smith to clear out Jackson and Winn Parishes in Louisiana; McCulloch operated in Texas with two mounted companies, though only slightly later two picked regiments of cavalry were placed at the disposal of a Colonel Danley.[5] Another officer ex-

---

[1] Comte de Paris, *History of the Civil War in America,* III, 7.

[2] *O. W. R.,* Ser. I, XXXII, pt. III, 859, 824–825, 853.

[3] *Ibid.,* Ser. I, LIII, 345; XXXII, pt. III, 632.

[4] *Ibid.,* Ser. I, XXXII, pt. III, 859.

[5] *Ibid.,* Ser. I, XXVI, pt. II, 194, 369; XXII, pt. II, 1057–1058.

pected to achieve results in South Carolina with two or three companies, whereas he, it would appear, regarded several regiments as necessary to clear out North Carolina.

As stated earlier, when commanders found the efforts of the Conscript Bureau too feeble and desertion growing rather than diminishing, they took the problem in hand.[1] Such power on the part of commanding generals to employ their forces to arrest deserters and stragglers was freely recognized by the War Department at Richmond.[2] General Polk's method was to organize against the absentees by sending out detachments all over his department. Ringleaders in arms who offered resistance were summarily disposed of, with the result that many of their followers surrendered or betook themselves to other commands. To prevent their return to their hiding places and to complete the work of routing them out, he divided his department into military districts of a covenient size, over which he placed disabled officers to whom companies raised for local defense were assigned.[3] Orders were everywhere stringent during these pursuits not to hesitate to kill on the spot offenders resisting arrest. General Smith, citing the forcing-in of 400 men in Louisiana after four had been shot, added tersely, "This is the argument which must be used in your district if milder measures will not secure the desired end."[4]

As early as January, 1863, six companies of cavalry were already scouring the mountains of east Tennessee for deserters, while a body of whites and Indians were operating in Madison County, North Carolina, at about the same time under rigid orders to clear the counties adjacent to the mountains before they returned to their command.[5] By September of the same year, Lee had dispatched several regiments of North Carolina troops and a squadron of cavalry to rid Wilkes County, North Carolina, of its organization of deserters. Only slightly later in the fall, Generals Magruder and McCulloch were engaging in the hunt for deserters in Texas.[6]

---

[1] See General Polk's frank statement to Secretary Seddon of December 28, 1863, asking that the officers charged with the collection of deserters report directly to his headquarters, as he must know the needs of his department better than they could be known at Richmond (*ibid.,* Ser. I, XXXI, pt. III, 876).

[2] *Ibid.,* Ser. IV, III, 294.

[3] *Ibid.,* Ser. I, XXXII, pt. III, 837; 855–856.

[4] *Ibid.,* Ser. I, XXII, pt. II, 1057–1058.

[5] *Ibid.,* Ser. I, XVIII, 811.

[6] *Ibid.,* Ser. I, XXVI, pt. II, 373–374, 398; XXII, pt. II, 1065–1066.

By 1864 the orders read sharply to collect all stragglers and deserters, irrespective of the commands to which they might belong.[1] Aggressive pursuit continued to the bitter end, for as late as February 27, 1865, we read that the Seventh North Carolina, about 200 strong, left for that State to arrest deserters, while on March 20, a Colonel O'Neal was ordered to northern Alabama on a similar service.[2]

Local bodies, whether termed home guards, militia, State reserves, or minute-men, as in Texas, were utilized for the pursuit and arrest of deserters. General Magruder in the fall of 1863 directed that one fourth of each company of minute men should be placed on duty for one week in their respective counties at prominent points to arrest stragglers and deserters, transmitting to his headquarters the evidence and testimony connected with each arrest. At length, however, an adequate force detached from the regular army was found the only effective body to cope with the problem. Local defense bodies, composed of all loyal citizens not liable to conscription, were useful for coöperation on occasion. It was felt that such permanent bodies could do more toward restraining the deserters and returning them to their commands than occasional visits of squads of cavalry unacquainted with the locality.[3] In the next to the last month of the war, a general order emanating from Richmond ordered all reserves, men over fifty years of age, not already specially detailed, on active duty to be employed vigorously in arresting deserters—a duty which seems to have been prosecuted with some slight success.[4]

A favorite method was to build stockades in various portions of the suspected country, and then to send out scouting parties to sweep or scour a wide stretch of woods or country with the troops deployed as if in pursuit of game.[5] The following order for a *drive* in Mississippi gives a succinct picture of the methods pursued: "I am instructed by him [General Polk] to say that he desires you to push your operations down Pearl River toward its mouth, to deploy your troops so as to move upon Honey Island and clear it out, driving such men as may have sought refuge there over into

---

[1] *O. W. R.*, Ser. I, XLI, pt. IV, 1020, 1024–1025.

[2] *Ibid.*, Ser. I, XLVI, pt. II, 720; XLIX, pt. II, 1134.

[3] *Ibid.*, Ser. I, XXIX, pt. II, 645; XXXII, pt. III, 837.

[4] Gen. Orders, No. 8, Feb. 23, 1865 (*ibid.*, Ser. IV, pt. III, 1113. See also Ser. I, XLVII, pt. II, 1382).

[5] *Ibid.*, Ser. I, XLIX, pt. I, 1057–1058; XXXII, pt. III, 826. To *breast* the country is an expression which also occurs (XXXII, pt. III, 616–617).

Louisiana. You will enter upon a new campaign against all absentees and conscripts found in East Louisiana and Southwestern Mississippi. In this campaign you will have the coöperation of all the cavalry force under the command of Colonel John S. Scott, commanding that district, and the desire of the lieutenant-general is that you make such thorough work in your operations as not to require them to be repeated. The lieutenant-general's orders to Colonel Scott are that he direct Colonel Dumonteil, commanding cavalry regiment, now in Copiah, to move eastward to Pearl River and to deploy it down that river so as to cover all the crossings as low down as the head of Honey Island, which will be about the point at which your right will rest after crossing that river . . . He will, at the same time, post three companies of the Ninth Louisiana Cavalry Battalion, under Captain Amacker, near the mouth of the river, extending across it from Shieldsborough to Mandeville. These companies will prevent escape to Fort Pike on the lake shore . . . A cordon of pickets will thus be established down Pearl River to its mouth; thence along the lake shore to within a short distance of the Mississippi River; thence northward of that river to the Homo Chitto. This cordon will prevent the escape either to New Orleans or west of the Mississippi. After crossing the Pearl River with your command you will deploy your troops so as, in conjunction with the cavalry which will close in and coöperate with you, to drive the men you are pursuing northward and make their escape impossible. You will give instructions to arrest every man capable of bearing arms from seventeen to fifty, and to concentrate them at Jackson for organization and distribution. As you pass on up the river you will keep well on to the Mississippi, so as to clear out the bottoms and as far as possible the villages along its banks." [1]

General Pillow, operating in Mississippi with about 2,000 men, established rendezvous and outposts. Infantry companies in some localities sent out scouting parties from stockades to drive the woods daily. Cavalry, a battalion of sharpshooters, and a section of horse artillery were used to good effect to break up the organized bands in Jones County, Alabama.[2] In Texas the troops, after locating with great difficulty the homes of the deserters, forced the men in out of the brush by impressing all the provisions of the section for the

---

[1] *Ibid.*, 821. For descriptions of similar drives, see *ibid.*, 633, 825, for Alabama; for Virginia, XXIX, pt. II, 809.
[2] *Ibid.*, Ser. I, XXXII, pt. III, 632.

pursuing soldiers and their horses, deferring payment until surrender should be made.[1] Sometimes a detachment was scattered about the country in small squads. But everywhere the homes of renegades were watched and searched. In the swamps it was found necessary to take possession of the horses of deserters in order to imprison them in the swamps and literally to starve them out.

Naturally, one difficulty was that pursuit simply drove the skulkers from one county to another, which problem was often anticipated by simultaneous drives. When hard pressed, the deserters only moved deeper into the mountains, the cane-brakes, or the swampy bottoms, for on the whole they seldom showed fight to the soldiery. One account relates that the men were so panic-stricken, that though their leaders twice got them in position to ambush the opposing Confederate colonel, they broke and fled both times to the swamps.[2] As soon as the force was withdrawn, they descended again upon the settlements to plunder and to lay waste the crops. The camps of the defiant outlaws were usually destroyed, but in certain sections the bands of outlaws were never wholly crushed or dispersed during the war. Sometimes a body of cavalry would chase them rapidly for days with only the result of wearing out their own horses.

Guides, who knew the difficult country, were obviously highly desirable, and difficult to secure in a terrorized country. It was easy for a commander to direct subordinates to supply competent guides, familiar with the haunts of the deserters, or to put him in communication with those who could supply such guides, but the task was harder to discharge. Neighbors would not direct them to the locality nor point out the homes of renegades. Loyal citizens could be found willing to furnish the requisite mounts, and occasionally men whose homes had been burned or whose families had been insulted by the deserters, actuated by a spirit of revenge, were anxious to guide government troops to those whom they regarded as personal foes.[3]

It was counted a gain when terror struck into the hearts of the women-folk of the deserters. Colonel Maury reported after a drive along Leaf River in Alabama that the women were working hard

---

[1] O. W. R., Ser. I, XXVI, pt. II, 455–456.

[2] Ibid., Ser. I, XXXII, pt. III, 633. As intimated earlier, they did fight the home guards and usually routed them (Browne, Four Years in Secessia, pp. 353, 384).

[3] O. W. R., Ser. I, XXXII, pt. II, 689.

to get their men to come in instead of encouraging them to take to the woods, as they had done before.[1]

Probably it is not to be wondered at that the old method of tracking down slaves with bloodhounds should have been used against deserters. These dogs were kept at all the prisons, picket posts, and guard stations to chase escaped prisoners, Union or Confederate; especially were they to be found at the ferries and fords. To kill a bloodhound on one's track was death under military law as resistance to capture. Apparently some officers at the beginning of deserter-hunting in 1863, were loath to use dogs, but there seems to have been slight repugnance as the hunt grew more pressing, for requests for dogs became frequent.[2] In Florida a record tells of a woman and her two children being torn to pieces by dogs for refusing to betray the whereabouts of her deserter husband. Probably Colonel Capers was correct when he said, in assuming command in central Florida, "The only practical way of hunting them will be with dogs and mounted men under the command of an experienced woodsman who is familiar with the country."[3]

The disposition made of deserters, once in the hands of the military guards sent out to secure them, followed natural lines. At first, when they were euphemistically termed "stragglers," as soon as a large enough party had been gathered to justify it, they were sent under a guard to the nearest command of the army in which they were properly enrolled. As the pursuit became hotter and the evil was recognized for what it was, they were sent to their commanding officers for trial, often in irons to prevent further escape.[4] After reaching their commands, they were closely watched in the guard-houses before they were brought up before the court-martial for trial. But often it proved necessary to lodge them in the local jails for safe-keeping against the endeavors of friends to rescue them. Sometimes complaint went out that the jails of certain counties were filled and an officer scarcely knew what to do with his deserter pris-

---

[1] *Ibid.*, Ser. I, XXXII, pt. III, 633.

[2] *Soldiers' Letters*, 92. *O. W. R.*, Ser. I, XLVIII, pt. II, 399; XXVI, pt. II, 455–456; vol. XXXV, pt. II, 478.

[3] *Ibid.*, Ser. I, XXXV, pt. II, 64; LIII, 318. It is almost amusing to read of the indignation of an officer over a bushwhacker who kept a gang of bloodhounds in the swamp to chase off conscripts (*ibid.*, Ser. I, XLI, pt. I, 862–863)

[4] *Ibid.*, Ser. I, XXIV, pt. III, 619; XXVI, pt. II, 551–552.

oners.[1] Toward the close of the war, temporary camps were established and the men collected were assigned to temporary organizations where they served until they could be returned to their proper commands.[2] Occasionally even after a commander succeeded in driving the deserters out of their hiding places, he was powerless to force them to join their companies. General McCullough, for instance, did force a number of men out of the brush in Texas, but when they refused to obey his orders to go to the coast, he did not have the requisite military force to coerce them or to send them to their commands. Any gesture at feeble coercion would only have driven them back into the brush, and so he temporized with them, trying in various ways to cull out the dependable from the unreliable men.[3]

A double motive may have prompted the less excusable harshness toward deserters' families: punishment for abetting desertion, and desire to reach the renegades through injury to their wives and children. The early years of the war saw, naturally, faith in appeals to the honor of citizens to assist in the apprehension of deserters by furnishing information as to places of "refuge of these creatures."[4] But appeals fell on deaf ears. Southern generals in early years allowed to pass to the enemy's lines, as undesirables or nonproducers, families of deserters, who often were permitted to sell their property and give up their employment; but it was felt later that no more permits of that character could be granted, as it induced desertion which family ties might otherwise have prevented.[5]

As might be expected with Anglo-Saxons, recourse was had to legislation, and so Congress passed some time before September, 1863, a law which imposed a fine of $300 and imprisonment for one year for enticing a soldier to desert or for purchasing his arms, clothing, or equipment. Apparently arms were freely bought by citizens, so that the matter presented a real menace. Arrests had, however, occurred earlier than this, evidently under State law. When these penalties failed to deter citizens from aiding desertion, the only remedy suggested was a heavier penalty of the same kind, and so the fine was increased in January, 1864, to $1,000 and imprison-

[1] O. W. R., Ser. I, XXXII, pt. III, 672, 853; XLIII, pt. II, 907.
[2] Ibid., Ser. I, XLIX, pt. II, 1151; XLVII, pt. II, 1321–1322.
[3] Ibid., Ser. I, LIII, 923–924.
[4] American Annual Cyclopedia, 1862, p. 246.
[5] O. W. R., Ser. I, XXXV, pt. II, 540, 616; XXVI, pt II, 258 (allowed up to August, 1864).

ment up to two years.[1] Less than one month later at the solicitation of the president, Congress for the second time suspended the habeas corpus in certain cases in order to deprive deserters of its protection.[2] How baffling and grave was this problem of abetting desertion is indicated in the terse remark of General McCullough, "If the true men of this country would swear what they know, I could send several hundred men to the penitentiary for treason." [3] Another officer reported his conviction that there were men engaged in reporting lies and in withholding supplies in order to provoke soldiers' families to disloyalty and that families assisted the men in the actual escape. A case of flagrant connivance by a father-in-law, for instance, was reported to Governor Milton.[4]

The most stringent measures against wives and children in an effort to reach the absent men seem to have been used in Florida. The colonel in command reported concerning his operations against the deserters' camp as follows: "Under these circumstances I found it impracticable to picket the road from the Natural Bridge to the bridge over the lower ferry of the Enconfina River, as directed in the orders referred to, and decided to make a reconnaisance of the country in force to the Gulf coast and attack the enemy's camp wherever found. With this object in view I ordered the detachment of cavalry, under command of Major Confield, to proceed from this point down the east bank of the Enconfina River and to co-operate with the Twelfth Battalion in an attack upon the enemy's camp upon Snyder's Island. Moving with the Twelfth Georgia Battalion from Gamble's farm to the Natural Bridge, and through the swamp on the east bank of the Ancilla River, I passed entirely through the country occupied by the disaffected citizens and deserters, and reached the camp of the enemy at daylight on the morning of the 24th instant. Here I found nothing but the deserted huts of the deserters, and no traces of any camp regularly organized by

---

[1] *Ibid.*, Ser. IV, II, 801; III, 189; Ser. I, XLVIII, pt. I, 1323. *Statutes at Large of the Confederate States,* 1864, chap. XI. *See Daily Richmond Examiner,* July 4, 1863, for a case of arrest. *U. S. Sen. Doc.,* 58th Cong., 2d Sess., No. 234, 514.

[2] *O. W. R.,* Ser. IV, III, 67, 203. Power to suspend the writ had been given the president by act of February 27, 1862, and again on October 13, 1862. The act of 1864 differed from the earlier acts in that Congress itself suspended the writ instead of empowering the president to do so. This act suspended the writ in cases of desertion or of harboring or encouraging deserters.

[3] *Ibid.*, Ser. I, XXXIV, pt. II, 941–943.

[4] *Ibid.*, Ser. I, XXXV, pt. I, 565.

the enemy." [1] The inaccessible character of the retreat, the fact that they were not organized in a camp but were concealed near their homes determined him to destroy every house on both banks of the Enconfina and Fenhalloway Rivers belonging to these people in addition to removing the families under guard to a refugee camp as directed in his orders.

The expedition was so successful that the leader, one Strickland offered to leave the swamps and to serve the Confederacy by raising stock, if he and his men were given an exemption from military service—an offer which was rejected. This offer to the colonel is so illuminating as to the type of men concerned that it seems justifiable to quote it *in extenso:* "I got your letter that you left with Mr. Johnson the 26th. I am anxious to hear from you, and you from me, for I cannot control my men since they saw you fire our house I cannot control them any longer. I ain't accountable for what they do now. As for myself, I will do anything that any half white man ever done, only to go into the Confederate war any more, though when I was in it I done my duty, I reckon. Ask Colonel Smith if I was not as good a soldier as long as he was captain, and would have been yet if Mr. Smith had of staid captain, but now I have went on the other side and tried what we call United States of Taylor, but I find it is like the Confederate men—more wind than work. As for myself, I ain't agoing in for any order, only to stay with Mr. Johnson and help him tend to his stock, and I will help him to pen or drive cattle for you, but my oath will not permit me to fight any more. If you will send and get me an exemption and my men that have taken the oath to stay in Taylor and raise stock for you, they will do so but they will not go into war if you had as many again men and dogs for our title is Florida Royals, and if we can't get a furlough from Mr. Jeff Davis during the war you will find our title right for a while; so I remain a flea until I get a furlough from headquarters and when you put your thumb on me and then raise it up I will be gone. I give you my respects for the good attention you paid to my wife, for it was not her notion for me to do as I was doing. Just see me and my men free from the war and we will try with leave to get corn till we can make. If not, you can go to moving the steers out of the adjoining three counties. So here is my love for the good atten

[1] *O. W. R.*, Ser. I, LIII, 316–317.

tions for my wife and child. If the war lasts long enough and you will raise him to be a soldier he will show the spunk of his daddy." [1] The Confederacy had the "spunk" to reject the offer.

These harsh measures brought forth from the governor of the State a sharp protest, as such methods would inevitably bring injustice to relatives of soldiers who were faithfully serving the country, and would render dependent on the State women and children who had previously been self-supporting; it had only served to increase the number of deserters and to excite the vindictive purpose to avenge the wrongs inflicted and to liberate the women and children. "While I believe deserters and skulkers no longer entitled to mercy, yet I am unwilling that any of the women and children of the State shall be deprived of legal protection and denied humane consideration. I cannot approve of a warfare upon women and children. Is it not unworthy of our arms and the cause in which we are engaged?" he wrote indignantly to General Anderson.[2] About six weeks later he addressed Secretary Seddon for redress. "Such lawless and cruel violence increased the number of deserters and prevented many from returning to their commands who otherwise would have availed themselves of an offer of pardon which had been published and distributed in the disaffected region. The unoffending and loyal citizens who have thus been wronged have a just claim upon the Confederate Government for indemnity, and their losses should be promptly and legally ascertained and established by commissioners appointed for the purpose by the Confederate Government." [3]

The fact that they had taken the oath of allegiance to the United States, so that it was difficult to discriminate between them and Northern foes; the fact that there was found at the home of the leader a muster-roll, 2,000 rounds of ammunition, and several barrels of flour from the United States Subsistence Department, evidencing the regularity of their communication with the Federal gunboats, perhaps gave Strickland and his renegades the status of rebels rather than that of deserters and justified, from a military point of view, such harsh measures. Such severity had, according to

---

[1] *Ibid.*, p. 319.

[2] *Ibid.*, p. 352.

[3] June 30, 1864. *Ibid.*, p. 350. Though General Anderson stated on May that steps had been taken to secure an inventory of the property destroyed *ibid.*, p. 353), there is no evidence of any restitution by the government.

Governor Milton, in other States, had the effect of inducing deserters to return to their command.[1]

In contrast with this severity we find instances of remarkable
leniency toward the families of deserters. For instance, in June, 1864,
we find the same Governor Milton objecting to some arrangements
by a military officer whereby families of some deserters were to be
placed on the vessel of the enemy to be transported to their husbands and fathers. He could not credit the rumor that they were
to be allowed to depart, and felt that there was no legal authority
to drive them out. The better part, in his judgment, was to make
them good citizens.[2] It is indisputable that fathers, mothers, and
families of deserters, who were non-producers and not liable to
military duty, were passed through the lines as a comfortable way
to get rid of consumers who constituted a drain without being any
help to the Confederacy.[3]

The acid test of any method is its success. Tested then by results, it is only possible to claim partial success for the Confederate
methods, even during the period of utmost endeavor. Lee's offer of
amnesty of about February, 1863, to some Georgian troops near Atlanta where he had gone to quiet some disturbances in north-eastern
Georgia, seems to have met with considerable results, for the *Richmond Enquirer* says that soldiers came in "by dozens, scores, and
hundreds." [4] Many returned in consequence of the presidential proclamation of amnesty, though others took advantage of it. Somewhat
effective also, without doubt, was the premium of furloughs offered
soldiers for capturing renegades: twenty days for arresting a desert-

[1] *O. W. R.*, Ser. I, LIII, p. 343. The only comparable case which the writer
has found is a report from Virginia where several families were sent outside
the Confederate lines for bad conduct and their homes were destroyed. The
officer in charge declared his intention of sending all who would not surrender
under his amnesty or who were not killed by him outside the lines and of destroying their nests (*ibid.*, Ser. I, XLIII, pt. II, 918). General E. Kirby Smith
had early urged that any one who encouraged desertion should be sent to the
enemy where "he belongs" (*ibid.*, Ser. I, XXXVI, pt. II, 258).

[2] *Ibid.*, Ser. I, LIII, 344.

[3] *Ibid.*, Ser. I, XLIII, pt. II, 889.

[4] February 12, 1863. This newspaper statement, meant to encourage, must
be taken with the proverbial grain of salt. In actual numbers it gives 60
as sent back to their regiments. The same issue states in connection with
Georgia that they were coming in voluntarily in groups of five, ten, and
twenty daily. The vigor of any general produced results (*O. W. R.*, Ser.
XXIII, pt. II, 632; XXXII, pt. III, 668).

ing soldier, thirty days for shooting one.[1] The increased severity after August, 1863, was held productive of results, for General Lee said that by the executions which took place after the proclamation of amnesty a stop was put to the spirit which threatened the very existence of the army.[2]

But the first tangible results recorded officially are those of Colonel Pillow for September and October, 1863, in Alabama and Mississippi, where he estimated that he had restored over 17,000 men to the army.[3] Allowing for exaggeration and error, it is clear that many thousands were forced back into the service. In Texas, reports indicate some 300 forced out of the brush near Bonham at the close of 1863, with an additional 335 coming out voluntarily through the influence of leading men of the section—a negligible number, of course.[4]

Through the months of 1864 there are many references which indicate success in gathering in deserters: thirty collected in two days in the mountains of South Carolina; 200 arrested in Virginia; 1,000 moved out of the retreats of Mississippi; "a vast stream forced in from the swamps and over the hills of Arkansas." [5] The brutal method of burning down homes and tracking by dogs succeeded in restoring only 220 deserters in Florida to the ranks. The meager results of efforts in Alabama in 1864 indicate either that Pillow had completed the work in the preceding fall or that rumors had greatly exaggerated the number of deserters in that State, probably the former. General Polk moved out more than a thousand men from the northern counties of Mississippi and put into the field 5,000 men who had been lost to the Confederacy; Lockhart reported the return of 4,323 of the 7,994 who had deserted since April 1, 1864.[6]

[1] Wise thought this method effective (*History of the Seventeenth Virginia Infantry*, p. 204).

[2] *O. W. R.*, Ser. I, XXIX, pt. II, 806.

[3] *Ibid.*, Ser. IV, II, 963. One single rendezvous, that of Selma, Alabama, reported 1,344 men returned to the army by September, though the work had just gone into operation (*ibid.*, pp. 805–806).

[4] *Ibid.*, Ser. I, XXVI, pt. II, 401. General McCulloch admitted meager results from his pacific policy (*ibid.*, p. 303).

[5] *Ibid.*, Ser. I, XXVI, pt. II, 401; XXXV, pt. II, 478; XXXIII, 1063; XXXIV, pt. I, 928; XXXII, pt. III, 860.

[6] *Ibid.*, pp. 729, 826; Ser. IV, III, 880. See General Polk's letter to a member of his family of June 11, 1864, where he expresses the belief in a better moral tone in the army than at any time since the early period of the war (Polk, *Leonidas Polk*, II, 339). *O. W. R.*, Ser. I, XXXII, pt. III, 729.

Forrest met with marked success in Tennessee as well as in Mississippi, 600 being accounted to his credit in March alone of 1865. General Duke filled the jails of Floyd and Montgomery Counties in Virginia during a drive in October of 1864; General Pickett had lodged about 100 from his command in the guard-house from the drive of November, 1864; General Jones in early service sent back 5,000 to 6,000 to the army; and over 6,000 were returned to the army through Camp Holmes, near Raleigh, North Carolina.[1]

By the middle of 1864 the records would indicate that in Mississippi, east Tennessee, Arkansas and Virginia, absenteeism had almost entirely disappeared and that the commands were increasing daily by the addition of deserters. Even in the closing black, hopeless days, when desertion was flowing over the Confederacy like a flood, men were being hunted vigorously in Mississippi, while arrests from North Carolina were also reported. As late as January, 1865, one officer had complete confidence that Mississippi could be thoroughly cleaned of deserters.[2]

The total number of deserters returned to the army by the Conscript Bureau, according to the figures of the War Department, was 33,056, but the figures are admitted to be incomplete. It should be recalled also that many surrendered voluntarily, many were stragglers overstaying their furloughs, and still others were seized on their way to their respective commands. Indubitably the number returned to the ranks during the war by all agencies was much larger.[3]

Some criticism there was of the troops which did the hunting: their work was belittled, and they were accused of gaming, drinking, horse-racing, marrying, and stealing and so constituting a nui-

[1] O. W. R., Ser. I, XLIX, pt. I, 1032; XLII, pt. III, 1213; XIX, pt. II, 629-630; Ser. IV, III, 490.

[2] Ibid., Ser. I, XXXII, pt. III, 729; XII, pt. II, 658; XXXIV, pt. I, 947; XLIX, pt. I, 944.

[3] The figure given is arrived at through a table prepared by Preston, Superintendent of the Bureau of Conscription, about February 19, 1865, in response to a call for information on a different matter by the Confederate House of Representatives. It is not clear whether Preston had compiled his statistics for the entire period of the war for those States where the date is not specified, or merely since the date of the resolution assigning the duty of desertion to the Bureau, April 16, 1862. It does not show the number returned by other means. See Appendix, Table II, based on House Ex. Doc., 39th Cong., 1st Sess., No. 1, IV, pt. I, 139. Attention is called to a clerical error in the addition of the factors, duly corrected in the number given in the text (O. W. R., Ser. IV, III, 1109).

sance to the country.[1] There were obviously features of discouragement when citizens arrested for harboring deserters were released
by the provost marshals despite indubitable proof of guilt.

But the total rolled up, 33,000, by the agencies of conscription
alone after April, 1862, is impressive—so long as we forget the
fresh desertion going on almost as fast as absentees were being
returned. Lee's figures early in 1863 are illuminating: he shows that
421 had been conscripted and 287 returned from desertion, as opposed to 1,878 lost by death, discharge, and desertion.[2] The comment of one of the witnesses of the executions in the Stonewall
Brigade is deeply significant. "It cast a gloom over the entire army,
for we had never seen so many executed at one time before. But
we knew it would never stop desertion in the army; for I believe
the more they shot the more deserted; and when they did desert
they would go over to the enemy, where they knew they would not
be found."[3] Some of the cases which this witness cites demonstrate
the fact that there were deserters who on the second desertion remained North until after the close of the war.

[1] This report declares that the cavalry sent among them to arrest deserters
has been a "nuisance to the cause and country in a large degree" (*ibid.,* Ser.
I, XXXII, pt. II, 626).

[2] *Ibid.,* Ser. I, LI, pt. II, 680.

[3] Casler, *Four Years in the Stonewall Brigade,* p. 190.

CHAPTER VI

Deserter Johnny Reb as an Asset to the North

During the earliest manifestation of desertion of the Southern cause by Confederate soldiers, the Northern commanders were called upon to deal with it individually, each according to his best judgment and on his own responsibility. The result was a halting and inconsistent policy, with considerable differences in the various commands.

The question of the treatment of Confederate deserters seems to have presented itself as a problem first in the West. The very earliest hint of the problem which the writer has encountered was in Missouri, where General Curtis directed on December 28, 1861, that persons deserting from the retreating Confederate army might be received by the officers of his army and discharged upon taking the oath of allegiance to the United States and obligating themselves to forfeit their lives, property, and honor if they returned to the rebel army or betrayed the Union in any way.[1]

In July, 1862, we find General Halleck at Corinth, Tennessee, directing Major General Thomas to release deserters on an oath of allegiance and to put them on parole.[2] An order emanating the same month from headquarters for the District of the Mississippi required that Southern deserters turn over their arms to the nearest Union officer.[3] By November the idea of insisting on a bond with proper security for fidelity to the oath of allegiance was appearing.[4] The requirement that deserters must be taken at once to the headquarters of the nearest commanding general prevailed in the armies of both the East and the West, and was according to regular war procedure.[5] Considerable opposition manifested itself to treating them

[1] *O. W. R.*, Ser. I, VIII, 473.
[2] *Ibid.*, Ser. II, IV, 150.
[3] *Ibid.*, p. 286.
[4] Gen. Orders No. 49 in the Army of the Ohio, *ibid.*, Ser. I, XX, pt. II, 4-5.
[5] *Ibid.*, Ser. I, LIII, pt. I, 315.

as prisoners of war, which procedure seems to have been first contemplated in Washington, judging from an order from the office of the commissary-general of prisoners to. send them to Camp Chase at Columbus, Ohio, as it was felt that such action would discourage desertion, promote the formation of guerilla bands,[1] and impose a heavy expense on the government, to say nothing of the injustice to individuals.

The policy followed in general by the commanders may be summed up as a desire to treat Confederate deserters with all the leniency compatible with safety and to weaken the enemy as much as possible by the encouragement of desertion. Hence, the practice was to permit the deserter to return to his home on an oath of allegiance with proper bonds for the observance of his parole as a prisoner of war, the amount of the bond being left to the discretion of the district commander and made dependent on the financial condition of the deserter. He himself was not subject to exchange unless he violated his promises. In cases of doubt as to the reliability of the individual, he was sent to Camp Chase as a political prisoner or promptly returned south across the rebel lines.[2] Usually, all persons entering Union territory from the rebel lines were required to report at once to the nearest commanding officer or to be subject to arrest as spies.[3] Men were frequently sent further north with the recommendation that they be released there in order to shift the responsibility from one general to another.[4] By the close of the year 1862, uniformity of practice seems to have been fairly well achieved, since we find almost identical directions from many generals in various parts to conduct deserters to the nearest division commander with all possible dispatch and to provide employment in the quartermaster, engineer, subsistence, or medical departments, whenever practicable, on the same terms as to other employees, or to provide transportation north.[5] Of course, the officers had no evidence as to sincerity of

[1] Exactly this outcome did follow Bragg's retreat from Tennessee (*ibid.*, Ser. II, VI, 207). Colonel Hoffman, Commissary-General of Prisoners, some time before November 30 telegraphed to Kentucky to send them as prisoners to Camp Chase (*ibid.*, Ser, II, V, 28).

[2] *Ibid.*, Ser. II, V, 299; IV, 745–6. See also Rosecrans's order No. 31 (*ibid.*, Ser. I, XX, pt. II, 122).

[3] *Ibid.*, Ser. I, vol. XXIII, pt. II, 328.

[4] Sending troops from Tennessee to Kentucky to be paroled is a case in point (*ibid.*, Ser. II, VI, 197).

[5] *Ibid.*, Ser. III, IV, 52. There was naturally some variation. In Missouri, for instance, the commander required deserting rebels to live in the counties

intention other than the statements of the deserters themselves. It was fondly hoped that officers could discriminate between the deserters, and would hold unworthy men as prisoners until the close of the war.

The policy in Washington itself was wavering and uncertain. The government moved only slowly toward a fixed, definite policy. The earliest official opinion which the writer has encountered from the office of Colonel William Hoffman, Commissary-General of Prisoners, that of December 3, 1862, ruled that deserters could not be considered prisoners of war, but should be required to take the oath of allegiance under penalty of death for its violation.[1] Precautions were taken by means of careful examinations to guard against the possibility of spies' posing as deserters. By May of the next year, Secretary of War Stanton was giving the question personal consideration, for he ordered the release of all deserters at Camp Chase on the usual condition of an oath of allegiance.[2] About two months later he decreed that such deserters at Fort Monroe as were safe might be permitted to go north after subscribing to the oath of allegiance.[3]

But within another month the commissary-general of prisoners was requesting of the War Department the formulation of a uniform policy on the question. "In the West and Southwest," he wrote, "where their numbers are very large, it would be attended with much inconvenience and expense to hold them as prisoners of war until an inquiry could be made in each case and a report submitted before ordering a discharge, and to parole them places them in a very doubtful position, in which they certainly are not for us and may be against us." He recommended the requirement of the oath of allegiance in order to place squarely on each deserter the responsibilities of citizenship and the transmission to his office of the military history of each man in order to detect violations of the oath.[4] The reply of Stanton directed that permanent disposition of rebel deserters be placed at the discretion of the commander of each

---

in which their former homes lay; i.e., in prescribed limits or to reside in another State for a probationary period, if it were deemed that their loyalty would be tempted (*O. W. R.*, Ser. I, XXII, pt. II, 720; XX, pt. II, 97).

[1] *Ibid.*, Ser. II, V, 19. Apparently he based his decision on the opinion of the Commissioner for Exchange of Prisoners (*ibid.*, Ser. II, IV, 746).

[2] *Ibid.*, Ser. II, V, 593.

[3] *Ibid.*, Ser. II, VI, 91.

[4] *Ibid.*, p. 228.

department and approved the filing of a descriptive list in Washington.[1]

President Lincoln in his *Proclamation of Pardon and Amnesty* of December 8, 1863, clearly put a premium upon desertion for all Confederate privates and officers under the rank of colonel by an offer of amnesty in return for an oath to support the constitution of the United States and to abide by the Union legislation and proclamations concerning slavery.[2]

On December 12, 1863, Grant issued his General Orders No. 10 from the headquarters of the Military Division of the Mississippi, providing that deserters would be permitted to remain at large, if their homes were within the Union lines, and would be employed at fair wages when practicable in the engineer and quartermaster's departments. Passes over military railroads and government steamboats to their homes, together with rations, were allowable. And they were to be exempted from military service for the United States.[3]

It was not until February 18, 1864, that practice had crystallized into a definite policy in General Orders No. 64, issuing from the War Office, which was virtually an adoption of Grant's policy. It prescribed that deserters coming into a Union camp or post should be examined immediately by the provost marshal in order to determine the sincerity of their renunciation of the Confederacy; it must be explained to them that they would not be imprisoned nor forced into the Northern army to fight against the Confederacy; the proclamation of December 8, 1863, must then be read to them and the oath administered; if they expressed a desire for employment, they should, if possible, be employed on government works with proper compensation.[4] Transportation and subsistence, if their homes lay within the lines of Federal occupation, or to any point in the North, if their homes lay without such lines, seems to have been the rule in the eastern army after 1863.[5] One copy of the oath was given to the deserter and one forwarded to the provost marshal general

---

[1] *Ibid.*, pp. 239–240. A notice to that effect was sent to all the commanding generals. The necessity for such discretion appears clearly at Vicksburg where Grant on July 3 forbade acceptance of any more deserters coming out from Vicksburg, and directed that all should be regarded as prisoners of war (*ibid.*, Ser. I, LII, pt. I, 387).

[2] *Ibid.*, Ser. II, VI, 680–682.

[3] *Ibid.*, Ser. I, XXXI, pt. III, 396. The usual oath was required.

[4] *Ibid.*, Ser. III, IV, 118.

[5] *Ibid.*, Ser. I, XLVI, pt. II, 828–829. Certainly early in 1863 Southern deserters had had to provide for all their own necessities.

of the department. This remained the policy to the end of the war.

During 1864 the leniency of the government was so abused by deserters violating their oath that a greater stringency is, however, observable, which, in its turn, brought injustices. Judge Galloway, Special Commissioner for Camp Chase, reported to President Lincoln on February 25 and June 11, 1864, concerning the presence at that camp of many Confederate deserters, who had given themselves up in good faith, but who had been held as prisoners of war for from three to six months. Although he felt that at least three fourths could establish the loyalty of their purposes, the government felt that so many had been released under false representations that none should be permitted to leave except upon indisputable proof of integrity of purpose.[1] Officers learned that they were being imposed upon by men who had deserted from the Union lines previous to entering Confederate service. It was revealed that prisoners of war and deserters, after taking the oath, enlisted as substitutes for Union drafted men in order to draw the bounty and also in order to effect their easy return South where they slipped back into the Confederate ranks. Hence, deserters were declared not acceptable as substitutes or recruits for service against the Confederacy. If doubt existed as to the true character of the professing deserter, he was held as a spy or prisoner of war, or sent beyond the limits of the command, though not into the rebel lines. Early in 1865, when the number of deserters became enormous, distrust was keen, and we find General Halleck directing that they be held as prisoners during a forced retreat; or, if paroled, that it be a particular locality.[2]

Very bitter complaints were heard from northern Alabama because deserters were promptly clapped into the Huntsville jail for some days and then sent to Nashville under guard where after a further period of prison life they were forwarded to be exchanged as prisoners of war or paroled under an amnesty oath. The result of this treatment was greatly to discourage desertions and the surrender of men lurking about Alabama and to drive them to bushwhacking.[3] But the rule of paroling them only at Nashville was not relaxed. Deserters surrendering themselves during a forced retreat were regularly treated as prisoners of war or, at most, paroled to a given locality. Toward the close of the war, a fresh registra-

[1] *O. W. R.*, Ser. II, VII, 225–226; VI, 943, 988.
[2] *Ibid.*, Ser. I, XLV, pt. II, 506–507.
[3] *Ibid.*, Ser. I, XLIX, pt. I, 720–721.

tion within thirty days of all deserters in Tennessee was required of those who desired to secure the military protection of the Union forces. This strict requirement was made in the face of a renewed effort on the part of the Confederacy to recruit in that State under the threatened penalty of betrayal to the Federal authorities, who were represented as treating all Southerners as outlaws and guerillas.[1]

The problem of the proper and best disposition of these Southerners was indeed difficult to solve. General Thomas saw very clearly the dangers of merely paroling them to their old homes. "I do not think it to the interest of the Government," he wrote to Governor Brough of Ohio in April, 1864, "that they should remain in Tennessee or Kentucky, as I believe many of them return to the enemy after recruiting their health and strength, because they are rebels by nature; others because of family influence, and others, like the drunkard to his bottle, because they have not sufficient moral firmness to resist the natural depravity of their hearts."[2]

The question as to the requirement of military service from these Southern renegades vexed Washington. It was decided definitely by June 13, 1863, that while they should be enrolled subject to the draft as any other citizen of the United States, service against fellow Confederates would not be required of them, as that would subject them, if captured, to the danger of death for desertion.[3] They could, of course, enroll for voluntary service against the Confederacy, and there is evidence that such service was rendered to a slight extent.[4] An entire regiment, for instance, was collected from deserters and Tories in 1863 within the borders of North Carolina. But they were not satisfactory in this service. Complaint was made, for instance, that no dependence could be placed on the First Texas Cavalry, as they deserted at every opportunity, taking with them their horses and accoutrements.[5] On the other hand, Grant had letters constantly from rebel deserters who, in the absence of other employment, had

---

[1] *Ibid.*, p. 771. This problem of the treatment of Confederate deserters did not cease even with the war, for all through May, 1865, the question of whether rebel deserters sent to Baltimore were entitled to transportation to their homes in Georgia, Missouri, etc., kept arising to torment the War Department (*ibid.*, Ser. I, XLVI, pt. III, 1080; XLVIII, pt. II, 448).

[2] *Ibid.*, Ser. I, XXXII, pt. III, 288.

[3] This decision came from the provost marshal general's office (*ibid.*, Ser. III, III, 353).

[4] *Ibid.*, Ser. I, XXII, 138, 447. The Union officials tried to use normal cau-
[5] *Ibid.*, Ser. I, XLI, pt. II, 532. It must not be assumed that this company
tion as to the men thus trusted.
was necessarily composed entirely of deserters.

enlisted and then found themselves confronting their old regiments and so wished to be transferred.[1]

A satisfactory solution for their service seemed to have been found when they were dispatched to the Northwest Department to fight the Indians, where their presence would release Union troops for service in the South.[2] A regiment of 1,000, composed of rebel deserters and prisoners, who thus avoided prison camp, and won the questionable title of Galvanized Yankees,[3] was sent from Norfolk by Grant in August, 1864, to General Pope, who was required to release an equal number of men to General Sherman.[4] Although Pope praised them as well organized and, to his surprise he confessed well disciplined, when they reached him at Milwaukee, where he kept them for service during the impending draft, General Sibley deemed it best, when they reached him at St. Paul in early October, to scatter the companies at several different forts, as he found them "desperate characters, given to open boasts of their secession proclivities," [5] who could be controlled only by "the strong hand." He reported that some of them did not hesitate at any crime or outrage and deserted whenever they had a chance and so he feared that they could not be trusted in the peculiar service in that district which required numerous small parties rather than large garrisons. He requested that no more be sent him as it required an equal force of other men to guard and keep order among them. Company A lived up to its unenviable reputation by pillaging one of the wagons containing commissary stores, which it had been detailed to guard on the way from one fort to another and by constantly deserting and committing depredations.[6]

---

[1] *O. W. R.,* Ser. I, XLII, pt. III, 842.

[2] The decision to use the ex-rebels on the frontier seems to have been reached as early as September 12, 1863, for on that date the War Department notified the provost marshal general that all rebel deserters drafted into the service would be sent to Camp Chase to be distributed among regiments in the northwest (*ibid.,* Ser. III, III, 791).

[3] Fleming, *Civil War and Reconstruction in Alabama,* pp. 118–119.

[4] *O. W. R.,* Ser. I, XLI, pt. II, 619.

[5] *Ibid.,* 831; pt. IV, 261. General Pope later changed his mind and reported them untrustworthy.

[6] *Ibid.,* pt. III, 677. Colonel Pfander reported October 27 as follows: "Matters in Company A seem to be quite loose, and I have made another experience, that a great many of the men in the companies of ex-rebels cannot be depended upon, as the two prisoners of that company confined in the guardhouse got away last evening, and, as appears by the preliminary investigation had, through the aid of some of their men on guard. Company F of the same regiment, coming up and since here, have committed depredations which

Even after the close of the war squads of 100 or more continued to arrive at St. Paul, despite General Sibley's renewed protest, because, as the adjutant general frankly admitted, he did not know what else to do with them.[1] After June these ex-rebels ceased to be a thorn in the flesh to the officers of the Northwest, as the companies so recruited were ordered mustered out of service as soon as their places could be supplied by other troops. It was perhaps a concession to save the face of the government, for they were fast mustering themselves out by desertion.[2]

Meanwhile the Union sought, in every practicable way, to encourage and promote desertion among the rebel forces. It understood and tried to correct the impression which certainly was current among many of the Confederate soldiers that they would be forced to take up arms against their former friends and relatives.[3] Some ingenious suggestions were put forth on methods to spread in the Confederate armies knowledge of the treatment accorded to Southern deserters in order to counteract the lies of harsh treatment. One was to scatter from signal stations in a high wind Grant's orders on the subject, printed on very thin paper. The device was tried, but failed to result in any great increase of desertion.[4] President Lincoln's amnesty proclamation and Grant's General Orders No. 10 were freely circulated within the rebel lines as well as announcements of Union victories which were sent into the Southern lines by cavalry men, scouts, and spies in such numbers that they could not be suppressed.[5] A still greater premium was placed on desertion by the offer to pay the highest current prices for arms, horses, mules, or other property delivered up by deserters, while the benefits of the offer were extended to railroad employees, telegraph operators, mechanics, and other civilians.[6] Military forces were even disposed at strategic points so as to aid deserters coming from the enemy.

made me fear that there would be trouble if the men were stationed in an inhabited portion of the frontier."—*Ibid.*, pt. IV, 292. See also *ibid.*, Ser. I, XLVIII, pt. II, 647.

[1] *Ibid.*, pp. 288, 317.

[2] *Ibid.*, pp. 751, 766.

[3] The writer ventures no opinion as to whether the Confederate authorities made this statement to the men, though it is probable (*ibid.*, Ser. I, LI, pt. I, 896; XLVI, pt. II, 587; XXIX, pt. II, 590).

[4] *Ibid.*, Ser. I, XLII, pt. III, 1083, 1085.

[5] *Ibid.*, Ser. I, XLVI, pt. II, 186; XXXII, pt. I, 7.

[6] Special Orders No. 3 (*ibid.*, Ser. I, XLVI, pt. II, 829). The South was well aware that agents from the North were tampering with their men at every opportunity and persuading them to desert.

Emissaries were sent into the South in the secret service to convince the Confederates of the error of their ways and of the hopelessness of their cause. Arrangements were made with men loyal to the Union or with men greedy of gain to ferry the deserters over streams or otherwise to facilitate their passage through the lines.[1] The conduct of the army was often conciliatory, as the persons and property of the civilian population were respected, negro slaves were sent back to their owners, and passes were given with generosity. In a word, the army was bidding very strongly for Union sentiment.[2]

In view of the activity in the North of such organizations as the Knights of the Golden Circle, promoted as they were by Southern agents, the existence of similar groups of Northern loyalists in the South should not pass unnoted. The secret society which became revealed by the plot for an open mutiny in Clanton's brigade [3] was by no means confined to Alabama, but had been organized between the two armies with the object of depleting the Southern ranks by desertion. It would appear likely, though difficult to prove, that it was the same organization which appeared about the same time in southwestern Virginia under the title Heroes of America, though with different signs and passwords. The latter organization was supposed to have been originally formed at the suggestion of Yankee authorities; its object was to encourage and facilitate desertion from the Confederate army, to protect deserters and to aid them in avoiding detection and arrest, to give information to Federal troops of all facts which might help in the field, to warn them of attacks, to guide the enemy in its march through the country, to point out for destruction the property of Southern loyalists—in a word to do everything which might contribute to the success of the Federal and to the defeat of the Confederate cause except for its adherents to take up arms. It seems indisputable that Federal agents were at work in that country promoting defection.[4]

---

[1] *O. W. R.*, Ser. I, XXXII, pt. III, 390. An amusing story is told of what a simple bribe was thought by Confederate officers efficacious. One man reports to his commander: "The streets [Memphis] are full of deserters. I saw a Yankee officer bring one in the barber shop and pay his bill for a shave and hair-cut, and when once they get in there they can't get out." See also for secret agents, *ibid.*, Ser. I, XXII, pt. II, 108; Maury, *Recollections of a Virginian,* p. 195.

[2] The instance specifically referred to is in Florida (*O. W. R.,* Ser. I, LIII, 309).

[3] See Chapter II, p. 27.

[4] For a full account of this order see *O. W. R.,* Ser. IV, III, 802–816.

The Northern army officials did not place restrictions on the wives of deserters who wished to join their husbands; on the contrary, expeditions were sent out expressly to bring in the families of rebel deserters, obviously to conciliate and to make more easy the transfer of allegiance.[1]

The attitude toward the rebel deserter was colored, naturally, by the way in which he could be made useful to the Union cause, and not the least valuable part of his usefulness was the information which he could and might contribute. The amount, kind, and importance of that information merits close attention.

Much of it was general in character, as is indicated by such excerpts as the following:

"Some deserters, who left the vicinity of Hudson's Branch late yesterday evening, report that Longstreet has been heavily reinforced from Lee's army, by troops under General A. P. Hill."

"They state . . . that General Bragg and staff crossed the Mississippi at Point Coupée a few evenings since, and are now in Alexandria; that he is in command." (January 28, 1864.)

"Deserters say that the subject of evacuating Virginia was discussed among the officers." (September 19, 1863.) [2]

Knowledge that Lee's army had gone south and southwest meant advance or retreat; and the fact that fifteen days' rations had been issued on a certain day was adequate notice of a movement of some sort.[3] Again, the report that all the roads leading back from Dalton, Tennessee, had been put into good repair was logically interpreted to indicate a retrograde movement. The importance of the Federal presidential election of 1864 to the Confederacy in the outcome of the war was revealed when a deserter insisted that it was openly avowed in the streets of Savannah that if Lincoln were reëlected, the South would have to yield at once.[4]

Knowledge as to the spirit and morale in the enemy's army would not directly reveal the spots at which to strike and therefore contribute to a military victory, but it was information of the first importance in that it inspired the Northern soldiers with the hope that the end was not distant, while the commanders definitely trafficked

[1] *Ibid.*, Ser. I, XXIX, pt. I, 979; Ser. II, VII, 1016.
[2] *Ibid.*, Ser. I, XXXII, pt. II, 149; XXXIV, pt. II, 172; XXX, pt. III, 745. The last bit was held of such importance that it was transmitted to Halleck by wire.
[3] *Ibid.*, Ser. I, XXXIII, 1022–1023.
[4] *Ibid.*, Ser. I, XXXV, pt. II, 307.

on their knowledge of the waning of Southern confidence. This encouragement was theirs in abundance from 1863 on. Again and again it was reported that a large number of the Confederate army would desert at the first favorable opportunity,[1] that the soldiers were watched very closely to prevent their leaving, and that the mountains of the South were full of deserters and the whole army demoralized. There was much comfort for the North in the following statement of a deserter: "The army is not increasing rapidly; the desertions amount to more or as much as the new recruits . . . The troops for special service or home defense may be regarded as a failure in East Tennessee, but it is said a large force has been organized in Georgia. It is not probable that Bragg's army will be materially strengthened, unless a large portion of the new recruits are given him which is not probable, because the army under General Joseph E. Johnston is being very much weakened by desertion . . . The feeling of the people of the northern counties of Georgia, bordering on Tennessee, has undergone some change, and is softening down. There is a strong Union sentiment in those counties, but it is suppressed and kept down. It will manifest itself at the first favorable opportunity. The feelings of the mass of secessionists in East Tennessee are abating, and would entirely disappear in the presence of a Union army." [2]

The full significance of open defiance as uncovered in the report that two divisions of the Trans-Mississippi Army, which, when ordered to cross the Mississippi, positively refused to do so,[3] would hardly be lost on the better disciplined troops of the North.

Much concrete information as to the commanders in charge,[4] the exact location of certain regiments, the numbers of men at given points, and specific actions was conveyed by the Confederate renegades. Stanton hurried on to Grant late one night the information so

[1] *O. W. R.*, Ser. I, XLI, pt. II, 787. Such direct testimony was given the Union officers as the following from the lips of a captain deserter: "In my brigade the privates talk frequently and boldly about going home; numbers are deserting daily. Leading officers think the contest will be ended by May, 1864; that they will be whipped by that time" (*ibid.*, Ser. I, XXXII, pt. II, 141). A year earlier, in October, 1863, the talk had been that the old Union would be restored by the 25th of December of that year.

[2] *Ibid.*, Ser. I, XXX, pt. III, 48–49.

[3] *Ibid.*, Ser. I, XLI, pt. III, 338–339.

[4] Unusually interesting as an illustration of this type of concrete information was that conveyed by a Confederate deserter to Colonel T. A. Davies after the first Battle of Bull Run that his old class-mate at West Point, Robert E. Lee, commanded the enemy's forces opposed to him at Blackburn's Fort (*ibid.*, Ser. I, II, 432).

gained that Longstreet was between Emersonville and Warrenton Junction, that he had two divisions of his own and that he had been recently reinforced by a division of Polk's corps and a brigade from Pickett's division.[1] While the figures given by deserters were probably usually mere guesses, their value lay in the fact that they gave an idea of the relative strength of opposing forces. In one case several deserters estimated the rebel force at three brigades;[2] in another instance, a clerk who had just left the quartermaster's department estimated Bragg's army at 60,000 fighting men, which fact gave warning that the struggle for Tennessee would be fought out at Chattanooga.[3] No Union officer serving in Tennessee in August, 1863, on the eve of a battle would despise the information of just where Polk's and Hill's corps were located—Polk's in and about Chattanooga, Hill's at Harrison and along the river in that vicinity.[4] It certainly was desirable for Rosecrans to know as soon as possible in an important campaign that a part of Bragg's army was reinforcing Lee. Such negative information as that there had been considerable shifting of position and of troops in the Confederate lines prevented reliance on reports which had by virtue of such changes become obsolete. The timely warning of the presence of seven steamboats on the Ouachita River in Arkansas may have made all the difference between victory and defeat.[5]

But information much more specific as to military maneuvres was conveyed. Two rebel deserters reported that Bragg's army had crossed the Chickamauga River and had formed in battle line six miles from Missionary Ridge at a critical moment in the struggle for those heights.[6] Shortly before Gettysburg Halleck was informed of the exact location of Longstreet's corps and of the fact that it was "coming on."[7] The exact number of guns and the size of several forts near Fort Clifton, with a statement of the location of the field works, was grist supplied to the Northern mill by Southern disloyalists.[8] Unusually specific was the betrayal of Lee's plan on the eve of the Wilderness campaign April 30, 1864: "Lee's army

[1] *Ibid.*, Ser. I, XXXIII, 1022–1023.
[2] *Ibid.*, Ser. I, XXXVI, pt. II, 559.
[3] *Ibid.*, Ser. I, XXX, pt. III, 412.
[4] *Ibid.*, p. 163.
[5] *Ibid.*, Ser. I, XXXIV, pt. II, 519.
[6] *Ibid.*, Ser. I, XXXI, pt. II, 137. See also Dana, *Recollections of the Civil War*, p. 136.
[7] *O. W. R.*, Ser. I, XXVII, pt. II, 30.
[8] *Ibid.*, Ser. I, XXXVI, pt. III, 280.

is to be divided into three columns (A. P. Hill's, Ewell's, and Long-street's). Longstreet takes the mountain road over blue ridge, via Sperryville, either to make a flank movement through the Shenandoah Valley or to reinforce Lee, in case of necessity. A. P. Hill (50,000 strong, says this officer) is to try to force your [Grant's] right from Culpepper, and for that purpose will move by way of New Baltimore, and at Warrenton to make a junction with Ewell's corps, which is to be left behind to guard the Rapidan. As soon as Hill gains the rear of our army Ewell is to advance." [1]

Information as to the resources—or rather lack of resources—of the Confederacy was so much gain. Things were blacker for Richmond in July, 1864, in that the North learned that there were only six months' supplies in Richmond; that all badly wounded soldiers were being sent to hospitals farther south, many receiving thirty, forty, and sixty day furloughs, which fact was interpreted as a desire to get rid of all possible consumers.[2] Reports are continuous that the rebels were poorly clothed, that there was a lack of horses and arms, that the soldiers were on very short rations—but, indeed the starving and tattered condition of the deserters and prisoners was sufficient evidence of that fact.

There was valuable information, both concrete and general, in the following omnibus report sent by General Thomas for Grant's information in December, 1862: "What two deserters say: Polk's Wither's, Cheatham's, and Breckinridge's divisions at Murfees-borough; estimate their force at 50,000; provisions short; flour and meat issued, but no salt; supply of clothing pretty good; boots and shoes short. No troops at Lebanon; troops expected there. Rebels well supplied with artillery; no siege guns. They think they have selected their ground between Murfreesborough and their pickets. Desertions frequent. Do not know of Bragg's whereabouts. Johnston expected there Sunday evening. No troops except conscripts and sick at Knoxville. Cars run out 5 miles toward Nashville. Heard an officer say they would fight at Murfreesborough, if the force brought against them was not too large. All disgusted with the Kentucky campaign." [3]

The actual value of the information thus acquired in advancing the Union cause is hard to estimate since evidence is not available

---

[1] O. W. R., Ser. I, XXXIII, 1023.
[2] Ibid., Ser. I, XL, pt. III, 7.
[3] Ibid., Ser. I, XX, pt. II, 156.

to check up each bit of information and the consequences resulting from it, not to mention the questionable value of the labor involved. Probably the safest way to weigh it, in the absence of such a checking-up system, is to judge the items as the Federals did then: where the statements were corroborated by several deserters, examined separately, or by spies, contrabands, refugees, or by reconnoitering parties of Union men, they were held probably correct, and this the records show so often to have been the case that the value of the information betrayed by rebel deserters must have manifestly been great.

CHAPTER VII

STATE AID

The various State governments lent aid to check the evil of desertion as best they could, though in one case, at least, that of North Carolina, the Secretary of War reproached the State for tolerating desertion.

The governors were, in the main, loyal; and several of them, notably Vance of North Carolina, Brown of Georgia, and Bonham of South Carolina, despite a disposition seriously to criticize the general government and a certain querulousness of tone in the general relations, were active in well-intentioned, if not always successful, efforts. Vance condemned as treason in the most vehement language public threats of combined resistance against conscription and against collection of the taxes, especially the tax-in-kind. As soon as absenteeism became at all serious, as it did in the fall of 1862, he ordered on his own authority the State militia, a raw and inexperienced body, to arrest deserters in order to spare the citizens "the disagreeable spectacle of Confederate soldiers traversing the country to gather up delinquent conscripts, deserters and absentees from the Army without leave." [1] In general the officers gathered up absentees with zeal and efficiency without antagonizing the citizenry, though they were defied by some skulkers.

Since desertion was not an offense under the common law, and since aiding and abetting desertion was not, therefore, punishable in North Carolina courts, and since the matter was covered by no express enactment, Vance in November of that year recommended to the assembly the passage of a law granting authority to arrest deserters and of a law penalizing the harboring or aiding of deserters.[2] The legislature refused to pass such acts, insisting that Congress should provide means to execute its own laws. And so the executive issued almost the first of the amnesty proclamations to

[1] *O. W. R.*, Ser. IV, II, 186; for the order see *ibid.*, Ser. I, XVIII, 753. It applied at first to the militia of North Carolina only.
[2] *Ibid.*, Ser. IV, II, 186.

deserters of North Carolina on January 26, 1863, which met with some measure of success.[1] When, unfortunately, two of his State officers were killed in a clash with some deserters and the slayers arrested, the chief justice of the State dismissed the latter on a writ of habeas corpus on the ground that the governor was acting without authority, since the power of seizing deserters was not granted by express law and since the power of handling desertion was a function of the central power alone. Then, when finally the governor's efforts to secure Confederate legislative action through North Carolina representatives failed, he felt obliged to substitute for his orders to arrest deserters a command merely that the militia assist Confederate officers as a posse when so requested. Desertion thereupon flourished more than ever in the State, especially since the chief justice's decision was interpreted in the army as a declaration of the unconstitutionality of the national conscript law. Vance refused to coerce the courts, as he felt that the State was in danger in any case of being overborne by the central power.[2]

When Secretary Seddon and several generals besought Governor Vance to take steps against the serious menace of desertion, he reissued on May 11, 1863, his orders to the militia, calling out considerable bodies to guard the roads and ferries, and took, as he declared, "every imaginable step to insure activity and obedience," though his State was the only one at that time to employ her militia in the arrest of conscripts and deserters.[3] He had by July raised some 800 men for local defense and also some five or six small companies along the Tennessee border for protection of the citizens against the swarm of Tories and deserters in the mountains.[4]

Vance was fertile in suggestions for expedients: he sought to secure validity for his action in using the militia to arrest deserters by asking President Davis as commander-in-chief of the army to

[1] It was declared that hundreds were thereby induced to return to their colors, that the reasonable expectation as to its effect was fully realized (*ibid.*, Ser. I, XVIII, 860–861, 928).

[2] Schwab, *The Confederate States of America*, pp. 190–191.

[3] The disaffection in North Carolina has been so greatly stressed that it is but just to call attention to Vance's defense in 1863 that his State had fuller regiments in the field than any other Confederate State (*O. W. R.*, Ser. I, LI, pt. II, 109–110, 715; *ibid.*, Ser. I, XXV, pt. II, 746).

[4] *Ibid.*, Ser. IV, II, 619. In January, 1865, Generals Beauregard and Taylor besought Governor Brown of Georgia and Governor Clark of Mississippi to so employ their militia (*ibid.*, Ser. I, XLIX, pt. I, 941). The governor of Florida felt that he could not employ the militia for that purpose (*ibid.*, Ser. I, XLVII, pt. III, 819).

requisition State militia for this service; he indorsed the plea of General Edney for suspension of the conscript law in the counties of North Carolina west of the Blue Ridge,[1] a plan which was not however approved at Richmond; and he moved to form local bands of militia or home guards, who were, however, poorly armed, inefficient, and timid to act against deserters.[2]

Evidence is not lacking of anxiety and coöperation from the other State executives in the effort to curb desertion. Governor Bonham of South Carolina promptly tendered to the commissioner of conscripts a company of mounted men, which had been in service as State troops for a year, to coöperate against skulkers in the northwestern part of the State and sought coöperation of action from Governor Vance to suppress them.[3] Governor Clark of Mississippi and Governor Moore of Louisiana loaned the State militia and reserves of their respective States to a commanding officer when under the orders of Lee he was driving deserters from the swamps of those two States.[4] Governor Letcher consented to a general war order, directing all sheriffs and constables of Virginia to arrest deserters wherever they might be found and to deliver them to an army officer or to lodge them in jail.[5]

The appeal of President Davis in a circular letter of November 26, 1862, to the governors for assistance in the return of deserters as well as in securing recruits, supplies, and labor won a prompt response in the form of addresses to the legislatures or to the people. Many of them recommended to their respective assemblies a grant for the use of the whole State constabulary for arresting conscripts and deserters and for the punishment of the persons harboring them. Especially vigorous were the recommendations of Governors Vance, Pettus of Mississippi, and Shorter of Alabama.

Governor Pettus urged upon his legislature disfranchisement of deserters. "As it is a matter of necessity to the safety of the State and the successful prosecution of the war to fill up our regiments now in the field and to return to the Army the hundreds who are

---

[1] *O. W. R.*, Ser. IV, II, 460–461. The War Department in turn suggested the formation of local defense corps of loyal citizens not liable to conscription but liable to be called when occasion demanded.

[2] *Ibid.*, Ser. I, XXIX, pt. II, 676.

[3] *Ibid.*, Ser. IV, II, 741, 765.

[4] *Ibid.*, Ser. I, XXXIX, pt. II, 807.

[5] *Ibid.*, Ser. IV, I, 1151. Only a few months later Seddon was looking to the governors for all possible assistance and for a proclamation (*ibid.*, Ser. I, XIX, pt. II, 590).

absent without leave, or on expired furloughs, or have recovered from disability and are now able to return to duty, I suggest the importance of requiring the sheriffs, magistrates, and constables to aid the military authorities of the State and of the Confederate States to enroll, and if necessary to arrest, conscripts and send them to the proper camps, and to arrest and send to their commands all who owe service to the country and either neglect or refuse to perform it. The prompt and faithful performance of this duty should be enforced by heavy penalties, extending to even the dismissal from office for wilfully failing or refusing to give the required aid in arresting and sending back to duty those who seek to avoid it. I recommend that the Legislature pass an act disfranchising every citizen who shall be convicted of evading or refusing to perform the military duties required of him by law, either by leaving the State, or hiding out from home, or otherwise. Such are not fit to associate on terms of equality with the loyal and brave who return with honorable scars from the battle for independence." [1]

Governor Shorter appealed to the people of his State, calling upon every community to drive the skulkers "by the withering punishment of public scorn to their proper places. I call upon all the officers, civil and military, of the State, and upon all good and patriotic citizens, to give all their influence, personal or official, to constrain those persons into the path of duty and patriotism; and I especially invoke them to give their aid to the proper officers in arresting and coercing those who yield to no gentler means. It may be a disagreeable task, but the evil is great and ruinous to our country's cause, and it is the part of the patriot now to shrink from no task, however disagreeable or dangerous it may be, when the country calls. It is the pride of Alabama that her soldiers never falter upon the battle-field. Let us hope that none will be permitted to hide under cover of home from their appropriate duty." [2]

The efforts of the governors to arouse the citizens of their respective States to their own treason in aiding desertion were unflagging. Each State was besought repeatedly by its chief executive to preserve the fair honor of its name. Probably no pleas of the entire period were more stirring than those of Governor Brown and of Governor Vance. The former, speaking in January, 1863, expressed his determination not only to do all in his power as the chief executive of

[1] *Ibid.*, Ser. IV, II, 249.
[2] *Ibid.*, p. 255.

Georgia in time of war as in time to peace to maintain her rights, but also to exercise all the authority vested in him to cause the citizens to perform their full duty to the Confederacy and to "the people of the sovereign States of which it is composed," and to respond promptly to every call for even more than her just quota of men and means to carry on the war. He commanded all deserters to return immediately to their respective commands, invoking for them the pardon of the central authority; and he called upon the good people of the State at the same time to bring to bear the powerful influence of a just public opinion in condemnation of all deserters and stragglers, no matter what might be their position, wealth, or influence. He commanded all militia officers, sheriffs, and constables to be vigilant in arresting all soldiers absent illegally from their commands; and he solemnly warned all disloyal citizens who were harboring or encouraging deserters that he would strictly enforce the law of treason against them, as he was determined to rid the State of all deserters who disgraced her soil.[1]

Vance seems to have dipped his pen into vitriol when he issued his proclamation of May 11, 1863. "Certainly no crime could be greater, no cowardice more abject, no treason more base," he wrote, "than for a citizen of the State, enjoying its privileges and protection without sharing its dangers, to persuade those who have had the courage to go forth in defense of their country vilely to desert the colors which they have sworn to uphold, when a miserable death or a vile and ignominious existence must be the inevitable consequence. No plea can excuse it. The father or the brother who does it should be shot instead of his deluded victim, for he deliberately destroys the soul and manhood of his own flesh and blood. And the same is done by him who harbors and conceals the deserter, for who can respect either the one or the other? What honest man will ever wish or permit his own brave sons or patriotic daughters, who bore their parts with credit in this great struggle for independence, to associate, even to the third and fourth generations, with the vile wretch who skulked in the woods, or the still viler coward who aided him, while his bleeding country was calling in vain for his help? . . .

"And woe unto you, deserters, and your aiders and abettors, when, peace being made and independence secured, these brave comrades whom ye have deserted in the hour of their trial shall return

[1] *O. W. R.*, Ser. IV, II, pp. 360–361.

honored and triumphant to their homes! Ye that hide your guilty faces by day and prowl like outlaws about by night, robbing the wives and mothers of your noble defenders of their little means while they are far away facing the enemy, do you think ye can escape a just and damning vengeance when the day of reckoning comes? And ye that shelter, conceal, and feed these miserable depredators and stimulate them to their deeds, think you that ye will be spared? Nay! Rest assured, observing and never-failing eyes have marked you, every one. And when the overjoyed wife welcomes once more her brave and honored husband to his home, and tells him how, in the long years of his absence, in the lonely hours of the night, ye who had been his comrades rudely entered her house, robbed her and her children of their bread, and heaped insult and indignities upon her defenseless head, the wrath of that heroic husband will make you regret, in the bitterness of your cowardly terror, that you were ever born. Instead of a few scattered militia, the land will be full of veteran soldiers, before whose honest faces you will not have courage to raise your eyes from the earth. If permitted to live in the State at all, you will be infamous. You will be hustled from the polls, insulted in the streets, a jury of your countrymen will not believe you on oath, and honest men everywhere will shun you as a pestilence; for he who lacks courage and patriotism can have no other good quality or redeeming virtue." [1]

In a last desperate measure to arouse the public conscience of North Carolina, Vance arranged a series of public meetings in the early months of 1865, but in the face of an approaching victorious foe he feared that they would hardly have their proper effect. He himself, however, addressed the people at two or three points despite his pressing duties; and he promised to order out the home guard in every county to arrest skulkers. Accordingly, he ordered out about March 2 that class of the home guard not subject to field duty to arrest deserters. [2]

---

[1] *Ibid.*, Ser. I, LI, pt. II, 707. See also *Daily Richmond Examiner* of May 15, 1863, for another proclamation of Governor Pettus after the battle at Port Gibson. Equally vitriolic was one of Vance's earliest pleas on the subject, that of January 26, 1863 (*O. W. R.* Ser. I, XVIII, 861–862).

[2] *O. W. R.*, Ser. I, XLVII, pt. II, 1312. Vance's courage and faith were remarkable. On January 18, 1865, he could write to Governor Magrath of South Carolina: "There are enough soldiers absent from their commands without leave to render the armies of the Confederacy irresistible and triumphant if they were all returned. How can this be done?" (*ibid.*, Ser. I, LIII, 392).

In several of the States there is evidence just on the eve of the collapse of the rebellion of the use of State reserves under one name or another for the hunting of deserters. In Georgia, for instance, Governor Brown ordered out what he termed the "reserve militia," men over fifty years of age, while in Mississippi, State reserves, old men armed with shot-guns, were so employed about Osyka and Camp Moore.[1]

A very interesting, if natural, step was a conference of governors. Two such gatherings are recorded: one east of the Mississippi, the other west. The chief executives of Virginia, North and South Carolina, Georgia, Alabama, and Mississippi convened on October 17, 1864, at Augusta, Georgia, for consultation and interchange of counsel, whereupon they agreed to recommend to their respective legislatures the passage of stringent laws for the arrest and return of all stragglers and deserters from Confederate armies or State troops to their proper commands. It was further recommended that it be made the duty of all civil as well as military officers to arrest and deliver to the proper authorities such delinquents.[2]

On August 17, 1863, at the call of General E. Kirby Smith, on whose shoulders devolved the responsibility for the entire conduct of military affairs in the Trans-Mississippi Department, which had been virtually cut off from the rest of the Confederacy by the fall of Vicksburg, a conference of the governors, the judges, and representatives of the States of his command convened at Marshall, Texas. Realizing that the department must depend entirely on its own resources, realizing the despondency which would result from the double disaster of Vicksburg and Gettysburg, he hoped by this measure to restore confidence and to win the coöperation of the civil power. Some twelve men responded, among whom were to be counted the chief executives of all the States of the department, except the governor of Arkansas, who presumably was debarred from coming since the State was otherwise well represented.

It is significant that desertion was not specifically mentioned, though it is impossible to doubt that it was intended by the commanding general to be embraced in one or both of the following subjects submitted by him for the consideration of the conference: "the best means of bringing into use the whole population for the protection of their homes," and "the best means for checking the spirit of dis-

[1] O. W. R., Ser. I, XLVIII, pt. II, 168; XLIX, pt. I, 939.
[2] Ibid., Ser. I, XLII, pt. III, 1150.

loyalty." It is equally significant that though a committee debated those two questions, it had no constructive suggestions to offer, but asked to be discharged from the further consideration of the questions, recommending that they receive deliberation by the entire conference. That body, in turn, could devise nothing better than the time-honored and hackneyed plan of a committee of public safety composed of the governors of the department with corresponding committees in each county and parish.[1]

State legislatures could, of course, aid or thwart the suppression of the ill. On the whole, such assistance would not seem to have reached the maximum possible. Arkansas, Mississippi, and Alabama were the first to take special action. As early as March, 1862, the first named made the offense of discouraging people from enlisting a misdemeanor, entailing imprisonment for from three to five years; and in the following November any effort of a civilian to promote desertion was declared a felony.[2] At a called session of the assembly of Mississippi of the same year it was made the duty of all military officers of the State to arrest all soldiers belonging to the Confederate army absent without leave and to forward them to camps of instruction; it was likewise made the duty of all civil officers in each county to arrest deserters on the requisition of the commanding officer.[3] A special session of the assembly held in December in Alabama required each of her sheriffs to arrest deserters or absentees who might be passing through his county, authorizing him to call on the citizens for a posse comitatus, or on a military commander for a sufficient body of troops to accomplish his purpose. Clerks of court, probate judges, justices of the peace, and constables were required to furnish the sheriff with information and aid.[4]

When the evil was arousing general concern in 1863, a number of the legislatures placed on their statute-books laws designed to check it. Alabama made it the duty of all citizens to give any information in their possession which might lead to the return of deserters; they were to arrest and confine in State and county jails any stranger in the county who could not produce proper warrant for his presence; it was made the duty of all civil as well as military officers to cause the arrest of deserters with the assistance of the full military force of the county; citizens were held guilty of felony,

---

[1] *Ibid.*, Ser. I, XXII, pt. II, 1003–1010.
[2] *Acts of the Assembly of Arkansas*, 1862, pp. 14, 44.
[3] *Laws of the Assembly of Mississippi*, 1862, chap. I, sec. 5.
[4] *Acts of the Assembly of Alabama*, 1862, chap. XVI, secs. 2, 5, 6, 7.

subject to fine and imprisonment, who gave food or shelter to a deserter or who aided him to escape; the governor was authorized to order out the militia in any part of the State; and a generous appropriation, considering the finances of the State, was made for the execution of the law.[1] Laws, roughly similar, though with variations in detail, were passed by South Carolina, by Texas, by Georgia, and by Virginia. Texas prescribed hard labor for a period up to five years for aiding desertion.[2]

Complaint was made of the indifferent spirit of a majority of the legislators of North Carolina, but it must be admitted that an act of July, 1863, went as far as those of the other States by penalizing the abetting of desertion with a fine of $500 and imprisonment for four months. But the act of May 28, 1864, which laid penalties on a person for attempting to prevent the execution of a writ of habeas corpus or for transporting a civilian outside the State by force directly hampered the effort to seize skulkers.[3] The resolution of thanks to Major Bingham for capturing deserters and bushwhackers in Watauga and adjacent counties should not pass unnoted.[4] Charges of disloyalty were hotly resented by the legislators. They passed a resolution denouncing the charge and denying any desire to conflict with the Confederate government as "grossly untrue, illiberal and slanderous."[5]

Lee's plan, to deprive deserters of their political rights and of such civil rights as title to property as one means of reaching the problem, was never translated into law by any State.

The provisions made by the various States for the care of soldiers' wives and children was regarded as an effort to combat desertion and this task, everything considered, was courageously under-

[1] *Acts of the Assembly of Alabama,* called session, August, 1863, No. 3. The sum appropriated was $100,000.

[2] *Acts of the General Assembly of South Carolina,* December, 1863, No. 4666. *General Laws of Tenth Legislature of Texas,* December 16, 1863, chap. XLVI. *Acts of the Assembly of Georgia,* 1863, No. 61. *Laws of Virginia,* Called Session, 1863, chap. 29; Session of 1863–1864, chap. 12.

[3] *Public Laws of North Carolina,* Adjourned Session, 1864, chap. II, 26. The State also insisted on its claims for expenses incurred in the arrest o deserters and conscripts by State forces (*ibid.,* 1864–1865, p. 78). The first named act was inadvertently omitted from the published laws of that session and is found published later. Louisiana lacked specific laws and special officers on this subject which was hardly surprising in view of Federal occupation of a considerable portion of that State.

[4] *Ibid.,* Adjourned Session of 1865, p. 65.

[5] *Daily Richmond Examiner,* May 15, 1863.

taken. Arkansas spent $62,000 to help soldiers' families in 1862; Mississippi appropriated $500,000 in the session of that year; Tennessee set aside $450,000 for that purpose in February, 1862; Texas increased her appropriation of $600,000 in 1862 for that purpose to $1,000,000 for the years 1864–1865, in addition to donating 600,000 yards of cloth and the excess of material manufactured at the State penitentiary; and the Louisiana Assembly, sitting at Shreveport in May, 1863, set aside $300,000 for citizens expelled by the United States from New Orleans.[1] Most surprising of all, in view of the divided sentiment in the State, was the sum of $3,000,000 appropriated by North Carolina for the families of indigent soldiers killed in Confederate service.[2] This action was undoubtedly in response to the gubernatorial recommendation that the State should assume the support of the families of soldiers, instead of imposing it on the counties.[3]

Georgia in 1862 appropriated $2,000,000 to relieve the families of soldiers who had enlisted into the Confederate service from that State. In the early part of 1863 when much suffering began to be manifest in that State from lack of food, even more liberal arrangements were made for these dependents of the fighting men. In Muscagee County, to take one instance, the grand jury made an assessment of $60,000 for the benefit of the poor. And the State appropriation to the county amounted to $33,000 for the relief of indigent families of soldiers, whether the absent father were living or dead. There was also a relief association at Columbus with a capital of $100,000, which furnished provisions to these families at less than market prices.[4]

Though there is no record of legislative action to supply relief in Alabama, there was an effort, apparently by private benevolence, to meet the need, as at the beginning of 1862, some eighteen hundred persons were supplied with food at a free market which had been opened in Mobile.[5]

[1] *Acts of the Assembly of Arkansas,* November-December, 1862, p. 16. *Laws of the Assembly of Mississippi,* 1862, chap. II. *Laws of the 34th Assembly of Tennessee,* chap. 52. *General Laws of Ninth Legislature of Texas,* Extra Session, chap. XVIII. *General Laws of Tenth Legislature,* chap. 34. *Acts of Louisiana,* Special, May Session, 1863, No. 24.

[2] *Public Laws of North Carolina,* 1864, chap. 33.

[3] *American Annual Cyclopedia,* 1864, p. 590.

[4] *Ibid.,* 1862, p. 495; 1863, p. 447. The relief association was probably conducted by private philanthropy.

[5] *Ibid.,* 1862, p. 9.

In Virginia a bare reference to "County agents for supplying soldiers' families" is sufficient evidence of some attempt at local aid,[1] while the statistical record in Florida in 1863 of 3,398 soldiers' families or 11,673 persons needing help argues some slight concern by that commonwealth concerning her obligations in this respect.[2]

The insistence of the various parts of the Confederacy on State rights must be constantly kept in mind. While no attempt can be made in this study to go into that big question, it is present and explains the lack of more aggressive support of the central power in curbing the ill of desertion. It may be seen in the reluctance with which President Davis was granted authority to suspend the writ of habeas corpus which has been discussed earlier. The insincerity of support by the various States is perhaps sufficiently manifest when the reader recalls that the Georgia legislature declared the Congressional act of February 15, 1864, suspending the habeas corpus unconstitutional, while Mississippi and North Carolina voiced their opposition to the act by resolution. In North Carolina the writ was never suspended during the entire period of the war.

There prevailed among the States and people great jealousy of their liberties. They believed strongly and deeply in the doctrine of State rights; they held that the central government possessed no powers except those specifically granted, and whenever there seemed to be a conflict of authority, they gave the benefit of the doubt to the State or to the individual. Pretty generally throughout the Confederacy there was a minority which complained of the acts of the powers at Richmond. And under the leadership of Vice-President Stephens, of Toombs, and of Governors Vance and Brown, this opposition became articulate in the legislatures. Insisting upon the theoretical rights of the States, they sowed dissension among the people until all spirit of coöperation between the States and the Confederate government was destroyed. The situation can be put fairly in the conclusion of a recent writer on this question: "Instead of pooling its resources of men and equipment in the hands of the Confederate government, each state insisted upon the right to maintain 'troops of war,' and, at times, withdrew thousands of men and sorely-needed arms from the general service and employed them for local defense, thereby weakening the Confederate government without gaining the equivalent . . . The states rights leaders put

[1] *American Annual Cyclopedia*, 1864, p. 808.
[2] *Ibid.*, 1863, p. 413.

all sorts of impediments in the way of Confederate impressment of supplies, and finally contributed largely to the complete breakdown of the impressment system." [1]

Nowhere perhaps is the picture of the State standing squarely on its rights more trenchantly put than in an address by Governor Milton to the legislature of Florida. "Shall the planters of Florida crook the 'pregnant hinges of the knee' to the military authorities for the humble privilege of saving, by the fruits of their own industry, the families of the soldiers and their unfortunate fellow-citizens from starvation . . .

"I have unlimited confidence in the wisdom and integrity of the Confederate Government when justly administered; but at the same time can only be sensible of its appropriate influence in the maintenance of the sovereignty of the States. Better that Florida should be a waste of flowers, enriched with the blood of her brave citizens, than to be inhabited by them as slaves or willing to be slaves." [2]

This feeling found frequent expression in the newspapers, early and late in the war. The following excerpt from the *Richmond Daily Whig* of September 17, 1862, may be regarded as typical: "We do mean that liberty as we understand it, liberty guaranteed by organic forms and regulated by law; the liberty of the citizen and the sovereignty and rights of the States, can be preserved in this country only by a strict adherence to the Constitution, and by a rigid observance of its limitations. The abolition of the Constitution, for any purpose whatever, can lead to but one of two results—either the disintegration of the Confederacy, or the substitution for our present system of a centralized despotism." [3]

---

[1] Owsley, State Rights of the Confederacy (University of Chicago Press), pp. 3-4.

[2] *O. W. R.*, Ser. IV, II, 975–976.

[3] Note also the *Daily Richmond Examiner* of June 6, 1863, in its comment on an order of General D. B. Hill, "Overbearing as are some of our military rulers, it is yet almost incredible that such insolent excess of authority, as is indicated by this order, could be committed within the limits of this Confederacy."

CHAPTER VIII

Results of Desertion in Losing the Cause

The results of defections from the Confederate army were both widespread and profound. Two ways in which the absentees benefited the cause may be conceded. No furloughs were granted, naturally, to men whose homes lay within the Federal lines; the men in gray took French leave whenever opportunity offered, but still often rendered service in some form as partisan rangers or as independent scouts. A very small number of the Stonewall Brigade,[1] living in the mountainous country of northern Virginia adjacent to the Baltimore and Ohio Railroad, would in parties of eight to ten make raids on that road. They would tear up the track, burn a bridge, or capture a train with valuable stores or funds,[2] with the result that the Federal army had to keep 10,000 to 12,000 troops of cavalry, infantry, and artillery along the road from Cumberland, Maryland, to Martinsburg, Virginia, to preserve communication. A by no means negligible body of Union soldiery was thus subtracted from the forces on the battle-field. Hence, although irregular and condemned by the Confederate government, the activity of these deserter raiders did render some service to the cause. As they were operating in a mountainous country and as they were mobile, the Federal forces very seldom succeeded in capturing any of the small band.

Furthermore, those men, who, though deserters from the regular army, still attached themselves to Mosby's Rangers, performed a certain police duty. The region in which this body ranged, disputed

[1] Casler (*Four Years in the Stonewall Brigade,* p. 292) gives the number as fifty, though common sense would indicate that he has greatly exaggerated the size of the Union forces and minimized the number of partisan rangers.

[2] The most valuable capture made by raiders which the writer has encountered was the seizure of a train near Harper's Ferry on October 14, 1864, on which a Federal paymaster was traveling with $60,000. ($80,000 is stated in another account.) This was probably more of a success to the South than it was disaster for the North, but the Union authorities at once ordered a mounted escort for the paymasters (*O. W. R.,* Ser. I, XLIII, pt. II, 368, 370, 377, 382).

territory between the lines, was left entirely unprotected during the war by civil and military authorities of the Confederacy alike. If it had not been for Mosby's soldiers, the defenseless residents would have been at the mercy of the roving bands of deserters, turned bushwhackers, who had been left in the wake of both armies as they moved back and forth over the country from Washington to Richmond. The mountains were filled with horse thieves and desperadoes who were ready to prey upon the miserable inhabitants, regardless of which cause the latter supported. In this chaotic situation, Mosby's men functioned roughly as a police force, in which Mosby played the rôle of military judge; he kept the lawless in check and settled disputes without the tedious process of litigation, but also without favor.[1]

Another raider, Morgan, operating in Kentucky, and many deserters from the Texas regiments joining partisan corps in the northern part of that state, where Indians were driving whites from their homes,[2] performed a similar service of keeping Union troops fruitlessly occupied in various parts of the Confederacy in petty warfare and in guarding the Indian frontier.

It is on record that despite the fact that men were sufficiently out of sympathy with the Confederacy to leave the service in the field to return to their homes in the border region, their homes remained the haunts of bushwhackers, for old acquaintanceships are not easily broken. Many bits of information relative to the Union movements were thus transmitted to the rebels through "loyal disaffected" across the Tennessee River or across the Mississippi.[3]

The debatable land of Virginia, naturally sterile and sparsely settled, became more thickly settled in 1864 than since colonial days by deserters, who, caring little for either side, grew rich by selling the booty salvaged from the Union camps to Richmond, thus rendering by their greed some slight service to the Southern cause.

The balance of debits on the other side of the ledger far outweighed those few items on the credit side. The first result can be seen in

[1] Williamson, *Mosby's Rangers*, p. 105. Lee states that many deserters from his army had joined Mosby (*O. W. R.*, Ser. I, XXIX, pt. II, 652). As evidence that Mosby caused concern to the Union forces, might be cited the dispatch of an officer on October 19, 1864: "In consideration of the almost nightly depredations by parties of Mosby's men, I would suggest that a small infantry force may be sent to Fall's Church, to remain until the return of Colonel Jansevoort's party" (*ibid.*, Ser. I, XLIII, pt. II, 415.)

[2] On the authority of General Steele. *Ibid.*, Ser. I, XXII, pt. II, 806.

[3] *Ibid.*, Ser. I, XXXII, pt. II, 132–134.

1862 when the heavy desertion made it impossible for the South to reap the fruits of her victories in the field and to invade the territory of the enemy. Senator Hill's bitter claim that the Battle of Missionary Ridge was lost because of absenteeism was doubtless not overstated and was not an isolated instance, for Lee himself admitted that desertion was the main cause of his retiring from Maryland in the fall of 1862.[1]

In the next place, the defections weakened and sapped the strength of the Confederacy by the steady diminution of forces to oppose to the foe faster than additions could be made by conscription. The presence or absence of a hundred thousand men from duty was a factor of stupendous importance. It should be recalled that practically each man carried off his arms, equipment, and, if mounted, his horse, with frequently additional ammunition borrowed from his comrades—all subtracted from the resources of the State.[2]

Not enough that the deserters withdrew themselves from the forces in the field, they also caused the withdrawal temporarily from service of the regular troops sent to capture and return them, and this often occurred when the latter were urgently needed for a battle. Furthermore, good soldiers sent after bad not only often failed to secure the recreants, but became worthless themselves and deserted. Lee was only too conscious of this loss, as his statement to the inspector-general sufficiently proves: "These detachments weaken the army, and I have only resorted to them when in despair of otherwise mitigating the evil."[3] General Ransom complained that the Fifty-sixth North Carolina Infantry had been detached for two months[4] to arrest deserters as well as 150 other men.

Those Confederates who delivered themselves up to the Union

[1] *O. W. R.*, Ser. I, XIX, pt. II, 622–623. See also Henderson, *Stonewall Jackson and the American Civil War*, II, 441; Rhodes, *History of the United States*, V, 432.

[2] Some of it was, it must be added, doubtless recovered, for soldiers occasionally scattered it along the line of travel, and Lee suggested that enrolling officers be directed to make diligent search for it. (*O. W. R.*, Ser. I XXIX, pt. II, 647). Occasionally, if a sick or discouraged soldier deserted the line, he abandoned his firearms at the first opportunity, concerned only to relieve himself of all impedimenta (*ibid.*, Ser. I, X, pt. I, 785). And often he sold them to citizens for ready cash.

[3] *Ibid.*, Ser. I, XXXIII, 1063. Lee also criticized General Chalmers for having so many men engaged in this service (*ibid.*, Ser. I, XXXI, pt. III 828–829). Governor Milton of Florida complained of the same thing (*ibid.* Ser. I, LIII, 347).

[4] *Ibid.*, Ser. I, LI, pt. II, 780.

armies strengthened those forces proportionately. While deserters were assured that they would not be forced into service against their former comrades, they were, as has been stated, accepted for service against the Indians in the Department of the Northwest. The regiment of 1,000 such "volunteers" released an equal number of regular Union troops for service in the South. Furthermore, the ready sale of the arms, horses, mules, and accouterment, which they had brought with them, at high prices, meant not only the subtraction of so much in the way of supplies from the South, but widened the differences in material equipment by the addition of so much to the North.[1]

There was still another way in which the absence of the recruits from the armies operated to the distinct disadvantage of the Southern cause. According to Governor Vance, hundreds of thousands of bushels of grain were spoiling at the various depots of the South in 1863 because of the lack of transportation; and the inability to transport supplies was partly due, at least, to the lack of soldiers to protect the transport trains.[2]

The information conveyed by deserters to the Northern commanders of a general and specific nature of the exact location of the troops, of the numbers opposing them, of contemplated military maneuvres, of shifts and changes in the Confederate army, was inevitably a result of considerable consequence. But probably the most valuable information was that of discouragement abroad through the South, of the want of food, of the lack of resources, and of the lack of courage. Indeed, the very fact of the desertion itself to the lines of the enemy in such overwhelming numbers put added courage and spirit into the Northern army with the feeling of certainty that the foe was almost at the last gasp. The North knew of the desertion and trafficked on the knowledge.

On the other hand, the desertion indubitably and inevitably contributed to break down the morale in the South. The citizenry was thoroughly terrorized and dispirited by the organized bands of outlaws who threatened their lives and property if they dared to aid the constituted authorities in arresting the marauders. They lost all faith in a government unable even to preserve law and order or to protect its citizens, in a government which was constantly deceiv-

[1] The records show demands on the ordnance department for money to pay for the arms brought in by deserters so that it is clear that advantage was taken of the Union offer to buy equipment (*ibid.*, Ser. I, XLVI, pt. III, 38).

[2] *American Annual Cyclopedia,* 1863, p. 623.

ing them with vain hopes of victory; possibly the government of the old Union looked attractive by contrast. They saw their country lapsing in certain sections into anarchy and barbarism. It discouraged all belief in ultimate victory until the foundations of the Confederacy were utterly undermined by discouragement and despair. This terrorization of the civilian population wrought other strange political results, affecting elections and public sentiment. In Alabama, for instance, it was believed that hosts of deserters appeared at the polls where they were not guarded by military force with the result that men pledged to encourage desertion but scarcely known to be candidates, were elected to the State legislature and to positions of public trust.

On the other hand, it is possible that the presence of a large number of rebel stragglers and deserters in West Virginia deterred men whose sympathies were with the United States from going to the polls in the November election of 1864, as some citizens of that section feared would be the case. Had the election been close, this might have proved a factor of consequence.[1]

Utter demoralization of the moral character of both deserter and civilian was the inevitable result in those parts of North Carolina, Georgia, Florida, and Mississippi, which were given over to the marauding bands. Men could not give themselves over for periods of twelve months, eighteen months, or even two years, to lawless living outside the bounds of organized society, to pillage, arson, robbery, and murder without death to their better instincts for abiding within the law. Consorting with desperadoes soon reduced all to the same level of outcasts from society, whether crowded in the slums of a city or congregated as free companions in the Alabama hills. Men became unwilling to work for a living when it was to be had for the taking. Robbery, in turn, discouraged the law-abiding citizen if he were to be defrauded of the honest fruits of his toil. It may not be far-fetched to see a logical preparation for the lawless Ku Klux Klan of Reconstruction in the lawless bands of the Civil War deserters.[2] For a period of a few months after Lee's surrender, before the Federal government had taken firm charge, the very bonds holding society together seemed to be dissolving.

The wanton destruction of which the deserter bands were guilty

[1] O. W. R., Ser. I, XLIII, pt. II, 547.

[2] The complete breakdown, most apparent in the southwest after Lee's surrender, may be seen in Colonel Richardson's General Orders No. 13 of May 19, 1865: "The major portion of this command having deserted camp and

exhausted more quickly the strength of the Southern States and their resources, where such depredation was practised. It as definitely abstracted supplies from the wealth of the Confederacy and did as serious damage to the cause as if the deeds of destruction had been the acts of the foe and was far more demoralizing and depressing.

Furthermore, the presence of deserters and disloyal men laid additional burdens on the various State governments by creating two serious, if obvious, problems: first, the protection of the loyal element of the population, which was attempted where possible; and, secondly, the support in camps or asylums or homes of women and children, abandoned and despoiled by the deserters and conscripts.

One natural result, that of dissension within the States of the South between loyal and disloyal citizens which would naturally have left a rankling bitterness and have placed the ex-Confederates into two camps after the war, failed to become a reality only because the North by its blundering reconstruction policy threw them all into the same camp. The initial meetings just after the war were awkward, but disloyalty was forgotten when the deserters, formerly Republicans, began to fall back into the ranks of the Democrats to oppose reconstruction.[1]

In conclusion, it is apparent that there was an appalling, incredible amount of desertion from the Confederate armies; that it existed in all ranks, among officers as well as enlisted men, though naturally in lesser degree among the former; that it was to be found among the troops from every command, that deserters lurked in every State of the Confederacy; that it appeared in all classes, but especially in the lower and middle classes; that the efforts to curb it only inflamed it the more, for there existed a determination not to fight for the Confederacy which could not be crushed because of the tremendous numbers involved, because of the existence in the South of many remote, inaccessible places of refuge and because of the sympathy of the civilian population with the renegades.

gone to their homes, all the Government animals and most of the wagons having been forcibly taken possession of and carried away, the Quartermaster's and commissary departments of' this command and the post at Mansfield having been pillaged by the troops" . . . he authorized the disbanding of the troops (*ibid.,* Ser. I, XLVIII, pt. II, 747. See also p. 929). An assistant adjutant declared on May 17, 1865, "All is confusion and demoralization here; nothing like order or discipline remains" (*ibid.,* p. 1310.) For a raid by deserters and disbanded soldiers on May 9, on United States army stores at Thomasville, Ga., see *ibid.,* Ser. I, XLIX, pt. II, 683–684.

[1] Dodge, "Cave Dwellers of the Confederacy," *Atlantic Monthly,* October, 891, LXVIII, 521.

The government and military authorities were unduly lenient, but faced, to all appearances, an impossible situation; to stamp out desertion when it first reared its head was impossible because the Confederacy was a house divided against itself—Congress in opposition to the executive, and the States in opposition to the central government. The only thing which could have checked it was military victories and they were not to be had.

It does not materially affect the conclusion to admit, as President Davis did, that a great error was made in the beginning in allowing troops to be used for the defense of their own homes, as that policy offered constant temptation to the men to absent themselves from duty. The best generals agreed that the discipline and efficiency of the army were far greater when the troops were operating at a distance from their homes. But even if that error had not been committed, nothing could have staved off ultimate abandonment of the cause in the face of superior numbers and inexhaustible resources on the part of the foe.

Recognition should be frankly made of the fact that the attitude of 1861–1865 toward the question is not that of to-day. Desertion soon lost its stigma, if, indeed, it ever really had any, with most of the Civil War soldiers. The writer is forced to agree with many of the Confederate leaders who insisted that many offenders had little conception of the gravity of their offense in military law, though the existence of a large number in the army who execrated the "crime" should not be overlooked. The soldier volunteer did not feel morally obliged to fulfill a contract, the terms of which he found different from what he had understood in entering upon his enlistment; the conscript did not feel obliged to fight a war for which he had not personally voted; as free-born Americans they refused to be slaves of a government rebelling against slavery to the North. The effort to bring in the deserters and to stamp out desertion brought ill-will to the Confederacy and became in its turn a source of fresh desertion.

All in all, desertion certainly contributed definitely to the Confederate defeats after 1862 and was a prime factor in precipitating the catastrophe of 1865. It could not be claimed that the presence of all the deserters in the ranks would have altered the ultimate result; but their presence might have postponed the inevitable end a few years longer—a fact which would have, of course, been a misfortune. The miracle is not that the Confederacy fell, but that it did not collapse in 1863.

PART II

DESERTION IN THE NORTHERN ARMY

CHAPTER IX

ROOTS OF THE DISEASE

A close parallelism runs through the underlying causes which produced the evil of desertion in the armies which opposed each other in the Civil War, as might be expected where the combatants on both sides were, after all, one people. At base, the main strain was British and the environment which had fixed the character and temperament of the privates on both sides was fundamentally the same. Some men on both sides came from the frontier; all had but recently, in a country which was scarcely three quarters of a century old, emerged from the pioneer stage.

The causes may be grouped under perhaps nine heads. There was, first of all, that body of citizens who were out of sympathy with the thought of coercion of the South by military force. Sentiment ranged here all the way from honest Quaker objection to war anywhere and any time to genuine Southern sympathy on the part of men who wished ardently to fight but on the Confederate side. Evidence is not lacking of men who deliberately enlisted in the Union forces in order to be carried South on to Confederate soil in order more easily to cross the lines to join the Confederates. One conspicuous example is a man who joined an artillery troop in Baltimore because he had heard that it was going into Virginia, where he planned to desert. When he found, however, that the company was to be stationed at the north end of the Chain Bridge over the Potomac he decided to desert across the eastern branch of that river and delivered himself to General Holmes, by whom he was permitted to join a volunteer company just being raised.[1] The frank admission by a western paper of the existence of such a motive is illuminating: "The loyalty of the great mass of soldiers in the army is beyond suspicion . . . That here and there one has enlisted for an unworthy purpose—that he may desert or otherwise aid the cause of the enemies of the country—has

[1] *O. W. R.*, Ser. II, II, 1428–1429. For another such instance see Goss, *Recollections of a Private,* p. 328.

been made but too evident. But such are rare exceptions to the general rule." [1]

Defection for this cause was undoubtedly greatest in the border states, in Missouri, in particular, judging from the evidence. General Ewing in 1864 requested authority to order most of the militia on duty in his district out of service, as nearly half of them had deserted.[2] About the same time a provost marshal warned an officer that most of the men drafted into the Union army from Calloway and Boone Counties, Missouri, would desert to join the bushwhackers.[3] The evidence of General Forrest is conclusive when he reports that of 130 men conscripted by the Federals in Mississippi, over 100 escaped to his command.[4]

The hardships of war were just as inevitable in the Union camps, though less severe during the latter half of the war, as in the Southern camps, and nothing could make filth, the hard marches, exposure to all sorts of weather, to say nothing of the dangers of battle, a welcome experience. Without drawing fine-spun distinctions as to the degree of difference in hardships between the two combatants, it will perhaps be profitable to study the physical discomforts of the Northern soldier in his unfamiliar environment. Above all the point should be made that there was acute suffering on this account, but that this condition steadily improved as the North grew better able to avail itself of its great resources, while it steadily grew worse in the South; so that as a primary cause of desertion lack of food and clothing operated in inverse proportion in the two sections.

The clamor for clothing, particularly for shoes, was incessant at first. General Schofield reported many of his men as barefoot in July, 1861; General Patterson declared that his men were barefoot and indecently clad and had just cause of complaint.[5] Generals sometimes felt that their commands were discriminated against and sent wails such as the following when their men were traveling with frozen feet. "If you can, for God's sake, send me all the shoes to spare and at once." [6] Lack of shoes was a general cry through 1861

[1] *Daily Illinois State Journal,* February 4, 1863.
[2] *O. W. R.,* Ser. I, XLI, pt. IV, 310–311.
[3] *Ibid.,* pt. III, 35.
[4] *Ibid.,* Ser. I, XXXI, pt. III, 789.
[5] *Ibid.,* Ser. I, III,· 408; II, 165, 170.
[6] *Ibid.,* Ser. I, XVI, pt. II, 227. It is rather distressing to find horses being shod when men had to go barefoot. Meade wrote in October, 1862, "I can't get a shoe for man or beast. I had to send money today to Frederick to buy shoes, to have my horses shod, which article the Government is

and 1862 and undoubtedly operated as a cause in the failure of the three-months' men to-reënlist.[1] As late as October, 1862, General Meade was unable to secure shoes, blankets, or overcoats for his men and received marching orders although he had declared that he could not move without those necessities.[2] Even in December, 1863, the quartermaster's department was not yet able to meet the demands for clothing, as the report of a medical director from Tennessee attests: "Having just returned from a personal inspection of the men in this command, I have the honor to report that I find them exceedingly destitute of clothing. The entire outfit of many soldiers consists of a blouse, worn as a shirt, a pair of pants, well worn, a pair of shoes, and in some instances not even those, an oil or woolen blanket, and a hat or cap." Some complaints of barefoot men occur as late as December, 1864.[3]

This same inadequacy of supplies extended to blankets, tents, ambulance and baggage trains, and, during the early years, to knapsacks. In August of the first year of the war one regiment had no blankets, save private property, and only the clothing in which they had enlisted. Rosecrans's troops were without tents or shelter for thirty-eight days in 1862; with their clothing worn out, their shoes gone, and without pay for four months, he held it small wonder that they stole and marauded.[4] Exposure to a violent storm without tents filled the hospitals, and hospital tents there were none.

Before the commissary department was organized so as to function properly—and ponderous bodies get under way slowly—the troops, in Missouri at least, at no time had full rations of bread, most of the time no coffee or sugar, while on some occasions they went without a morsel of food for twenty-four hours and longer.

---

bound to furnish me with, and yet they won't send them" (*Life and Letters*, Charles Scribner's Sons, N. Y., I, 320). Gen. Emory in 1864 charged partiality (*O. W. R.*, Ser. I, XLIII, part II, 329). See also *ibid.*, Ser. I, III, 46; IV, 325; VIII, 57–58.

[1] *Ibid.*, Ser. I, III, 408; II, 165.

[2] Meade, *op. cit.*, I, 321. Occasionally the lack may have been due to the carelessness of officers in making requisitions.

[3] *O. W. R.*, Ser. I, vol. XXXI, pt. III, 409. See also DeTrobriand, *op. cit.*, I, 277–278.

[4] *O. W. R.*, Ser. I, III, 43; XII, pt. III, 81. It did not relieve the distress nor improve the temper of the recruits that the government was the victim of fraud. The soldiers received blankets of light, open fabrics instead of the heavy, woolen blankets which the government had ordered and paid for. Uniforms were in rags after a short period of service while a pair of shoes often lasted less than a month (DeTrobriand, *op. cit.*, I, 139–140).

This occurred sometimes, it must be confessed, because in the confusion of the early battles, they threw away their haversacks, or they would eat up the rations at once instead of making them last for the proper period. Privations during General Frémont's campaign in West Virginia, when fresh beef with a little salt was the only food to issue, brought one body of troops almost to a state of open mutiny; while forced marches day and night through an already devastated country reduced another command to the verge of starvation so that the very horses staggered in the ranks from weakness and exhaustion.[1]

There was, while the Confederates were busily purchasing arms and ammunition abroad, a great deficiency of arms in the Union army. The arms placed in the hands of the men at first were mostly the old flintlock, the "Tower" musket, and others of still more inferior quality; Belgian and Austrian muskets of old and indifferent pattern were being carried by many of the men in Frémont's division a year and more after the outbreak of war, while half of an Indian regiment was almost unarmed. There was sad lack of ammunition and cartridges to fit the arms for which they were distributed. This lack of arms may partially explain some of the early Union reverses, for, as an officer justly reported in 1862, his men could scarcely cope with a well-armed foe. For his entire company he had but twenty-eight pistols, which had been long before condemned as unfit for service because they were spurious, made of cast-iron, and half the time refused to cock or to revolve.[2]

The hardships incident to bitter fighting and prolonged campaigns had to fall upon the Union men in equal measure with their foes. Exposure to the bitter cold of winter or to the drenching rains of spring, the grinding fatigue of the march, and consequent illnesses would wear down the morale of any body of men. The soldiers of the Army of the Potomac experienced forced marching in mud knee-deep, forded streams through water to their waists with the rain falling in torrents; at the close of the day they struck camp where

[1] *O. W. R.*, Ser. I, III, 58, 64; II, 316; XLII, pt. III, 1037; XII, pt. I, 11, 25, 642. But in general the food was adequate after the first year. It may be interesting to note the typical ration for comparison with that for the Confederate soldier: ¾ pound of pork or 1¼ pounds of fresh or salt beef; 1 pound of hard bread or 22 ounces of flour, ample coffee, rice, sugar, beans, salt, vinegar, molasses; potatoes, onions, dried apples, vegetables when practicable (Noyes, *Bivouac and Battlefield,* p. 60).

[2] *O. W. R.*, Ser. I, VII, 442; XII, pt. I, 8; X, pt. I, 79; XIII, 666.

there was no place to sit except in slush a foot deep and where men were continually slipping on the hard icy bottom under the slush so that they were wet through.[1] The change from rain and slush was sometimes no gain if it was to pitch camp and attempt to sleep on ground thickly covered with rocks and stones.[2] Sometimes the torture took the form of a lack of water, as when for three successive days a body of troops in the Cumberland Mountains was limited to the water of stagnant pools or had to clamber to holes eighty or a hundred feet down among the cliffs.[3]

It would be difficult to exaggerate the discomfort which the Army of the Potomac suffered from Virginia mud. Though the soldiers waxed facetious over it at times with such remarks as "it was verily heavy marching," and "If Virginia was once in the Union, she is now in the mud," and alluded playfully to the "Mud March of Burnside," because his mules, hitched to the pontoons, floundered to their bellies in the sticky paste, we cannot doubt that they also waxed vehement against it at times. They also were probably not able to smile at the humor of the Confederates when the latter stuck up a large placard on the opposite side of a stream but plainly visible to the Northerners, *Burnside, Stuck in the Mud.* "The foot sank very insidiously into the mud, and reluctantly came out again," wrote one private, "it had to be coaxed, and while you were persuading your reluctant left, the willing right was sinking into unknown depths; it came out of the mud like the noise of a suction-pump when the water is exhausted." And no one could blame them if when they awoke to find the mud oozing around their rubber blankets, they cursed it roundly.[4]

This same mud when the hot sun of summer had baked it dry was almost as great a trial. Suffocatingly on hot summer days the dust rose in clouds, completely enveloping the marching army; it filled the nostrils and throats of the men and covered their clothing

[1] *Soldiers' Letters,* p. 146.

[2] *O. W. R.,* Ser. I, XVII, pt. I, 574.

[3] *O. W. R.,* Ser. I, XVI, pt. I, 991, 995. Buell reported one occasion when his men had had to do without water for thirty-six hours previous to and during a battle (*ibid.,* pt. II, 612).

[4] Goss, *Recollections of a Private,* pp. 23–26, 139. Ellis, *Camp-fires of General Lee,* 228–229. Sometimes the men were so soaked with rain and snow that as they turned over at night, they could hear the swish of the water (*Personal Narratives of the Battles of the Rebellion of Rhode Island Soldiers* [R. I. Cavalry], Ser. I, No. 3, p. 6).

as if with ashes, while sometimes from the cracked earth of the fields rose fever miasmas and plagues of flies.[1] The diseases which Sherman contemptuously termed "infantile," [2] measles, mumps, diarrhea, exacted their toll from new regiments.

The picture drawn by General Crook could hardly be exceeded by the Southern army, but it should be noted that it was not typical of the entire Northern army nor of his army for the entire period of the war: "For twenty days I have been constantly marching, and part of this time in a drenching rain, and have only drawn three days' rations in that time. A great many of my men are nearly naked. A great many of my horses are barefooted and worn out." [3]

The effect of hardships, when combined with defeat, was about to destroy the Army of the Potomac by 1863. The continued fighting at a disadvantage without success, in addition to frequent night marches, had exhausted and disheartened them. These hardships were recognized by Schurz as a fundamental cause of the growing desertion.[4]

It could hardly be surprising that the soldier of the infant Confederate republic had to wait for his pay and then received it in worthless scrip, but it is something of a shock to the modern reader, who thinks of the United States dollar as the world's standard of exchange, to learn that the Union soldier of the Civil War waited weary months for his pay and that Secretary Stanton was then hard put to it to find the funds. From Missouri, Virginia, and Kentucky rose murmurs in July, 1861, of complaints that the three-months volunteers had not received a cent of pay and could scarcely be expected to reënlist.[5] By June of the following year some men had

[1] Goss, *op. cit.,* p. 61. DeTrobriand, *op. cit.,* p. 288.

[2] *O. W. R.,* Ser. I, XXIV, pt. III, 373.

[3] *Ibid.,* Ser. I, XXX, pt. IV, 464. The following excerpt may be set down to "grouching" but affords an interesting comparative statement: "It [a soldier's life] is a horrible life to lead, worse than being in prison so far as comfort is concerned, and there are few here who would not be willing to have some wound to get out of it, if the conversation of the men be believed. I have talked with men who have been in every station of life; men who have been in the navy, and sailed around the world; those who have been in the English and other European armies, and they say, without exception, that this is the hardest scrape that they ever got into".—*Soldiers' Letters,* p. 146.

[4] Rhodes, *History of the Civil War,* p. 323. Schurz, *Speeches,* I, 221.

[5] *O. W. R.,* Ser. III, 395, 416–417, 512–513; II, 169.

received no pay since they had been in the service—nine months—with two more months' pay to fall due in a few days.[1]

The following statement of an assistant quartermaster, made in January, 1862, is probably colored by a natural pessimism but is significant: "No funds; no nothing, and don't seem as though we ever would get anything. Everybody, high and low, in this district is discouraged, and I assure you I had rather be in the bottom of the Mississippi than work night and day as I do without being sustained by Government . . . Government owes everybody and everything, from small petty amounts to large. Liabilities more plenty than Confederate scrip and worth less. Regiment after regiment arriving daily. Nothing to supply them with, and no funds to buy or men to work. No transportation for ourselves or any one else.

"To tell you the truth we are on our last legs, and I have made my last appeal in behalf of Government unless it's to a higher power, for it will kill any man and every man at the head of departments here the way we are now working." [2]

Yet there was some basis for his plaint, as in 1863 we again find companies which had been eight months without pay, a complaint which recurs in 1864 and even in 1865. Some of this delay was probably attributable to the red tape of a big system and to delays in the arrival of the paymasters, but Halleck's frank statement to Grant in February, 1865, goes to the root of the matter. "In reply to your telegram in regard to the payment of the troops before Richmond," he wrote, "I would remark that these troops have been paid generally to a later period than those in the West and South. Some are unpaid for seven or eight months. The fault is not in the Pay Department, but a want of money in the Treasury . . .

"If we pay the troops to the exclusion of the other creditors of the Government, supplies must stop, and our armies will be left without food, clothing, or ammunition . . . What we want is some more great victories to give more confidence in our currency and to convince financial men that the war is near its close. In money matters these are the darkest days we have yet had during the war but I hope that relief is not very distant." [3]

---

[1] *Ibid.,* Ser. I, XV, 503. Rosecrans made complaint for his troops in November, 1862 (*ibid.,* Ser. I, XX, pt. II, 91).

[2] *Ibid.,* Ser. I, VIII, 512.

[3] *Ibid.,* Ser. I, XLVI, pt. II, 561–562.

Natural solicitude for their families entered into the restiveness and discontent of the soldiers, as they received accounts of the suffering of their wives and children, dependent on the scanty pay which was withheld from them. It tended to impair confidence in the government, produced envy of those who stayed comfortably at home, and created a hatred of the service, with a determination to get out of it on any terms.[1] Rosecrans felt that many of his poor men had been led by this cause temporarily to desert.[2]

A fourth cause which underlay desertion was an utter absence of a realization of the obligation incurred by enlistment and failure to impress that obligation on the mind of the soldier by firm discipline. The reader must stop to understand, first of all, that the army had been raised from a population unused to war or to military service for fifty years, except for the brief and insignificant Mexican War. The men had not the slightest conception of the burden and necessity of military law and discipline, however greatly aflame they were with patriotic ardor. They had always followed freely their own wishes, restrained only by the civil law of a free people. And so it is no attempt at palliation to say that many absented themselves in the beginning of the war without thought of wrong-doing, without thought of abandoning the flag. It is sufficient proof of this fact to point out that numbers of the early deserters subsequently joined other commands without inducements and proved faithful soldiers.[3]

A strong sense of independence and of their rights as free-born American citizens and of their importance as substantial men of their communities led early to a mutiny, which McClellan crushed with prompt severity,[4] and to insistence on the part of the Fourth Pennsylvania Volunteers on their discharge at the end of their term of enlistment so that as the army moved forward into battle, they moved to the rear to the sound of the enemy's canon.[5]

---

[1] One general termed the accounts of suffering of their families told him by the soldiers "truly heart-rending" (*O. W. R.,* Ser. I, XXV, pt. II, 82; XXII, pt. II, 253; XLVI, pt. II, 547–548; XIII, 666).

[2] *Ibid.,* Ser. I, XX, pt. II, 91. It is to be noted that several generals, DeTrobriand and Curtis, feared that the large payments being made to the troops would be followed by increased desertion (*ibid.,* Ser. I, XXII, pt. II, 78; DeTrobriand, *op. cit.,* pp. 117–118).

[3] *O. W. R.,* Ser. III, V, 678. See also Meade's early impression of the men, *Life and Letters,* I, 223.

[4] *McClellan's Own Story,* pp. 86–87.

[5] Report of McDowell, *O. W. R.,* Ser. I, II, 325. In the face of such selfishness it is heartening to read of a number of Massachusetts regiments

The absence of an adequate supply of West Point trained officers was a grave problem to the government. The pay of officers was fixed on a liberal scale and so civilians in important social position, as well as those of no standing, aspired to the rank of officers, though utterly untrained. The system of electing the officers by the men was here, as in the Confederate army, fruitful of evil. The men voted without knowledge as to the requirements or qualifications of the person chosen. A dissatisfied, intelligent minority was often the result, while desertion, before and after sufficient trial to test the fitness of the officers, often followed. The deserters regarded their action more as a refusal to ratify a contract than as a crime. The result may be viewed through Meade's eyes: "The men are good material, and with good officers might readily be moulded into soldiers; but the officers, as a rule, with but very few exceptions, are ignorant, inefficient and worthless. They have no control or command over the men, and if they had, they do not know what to do with them."[1] Certainly, the lack of efficient field and company officers seems obvious.

Discipline, which it would have been difficult under any conditions to enforce on an army composed of civilians, became doubly difficult because of an initial laxness which brought sad consequences. Such carelessness as is indicated by the following excerpt is what might be expected in the first months of the war, but is startling when dated August, 1862: "The sleeping of sentinels on their posts appears to have been of no uncommon occurrence, and yet no punishment proportionate to this offense appears to have been inflicted; and from the statement of one of the officers it seems that there was an almost total want of discipline in the command."[2] The fact that it was usual for pickets on the same post to take turns sleeping, that no pickets, mounted or on foot, were posted during the day, and that they were not visited during the night did not tend to discourage desertion.[3]

consenting to serve beyond their term in the Gettysburg emergency (*ibid.*, Ser. I, XXVII, pt. III, 413).

[1] *Life and Letters* Charles Scribner's Sons, (New York), I, 231. McClellan early (July, 1861) reported the discontent of some of his men with their officers and their determination to leave the service (*O. W. R.*, I, II, 752). See also *ibid.*, Ser. I, IX, 604, for the same fact reported from Confederate records.

[2] *Ibid.*, Ser. I, XVI, pt. I, 846–847.

[3] *Ibid.*, 849–850. It was also this second year of the war that one commander was invariably told by a negligent sentinel that he did not know any better, had never been reproved by his officers (*ibid.*, Ser. I, X, pt. II, 270). McClel-

General Gorman thought the material splendid, but the political demagogues among the line officers enough to "damn the best army on God's footstool."[1] But most illuminating is the complaint of General Milroy penned January 16, 1865, concerning the Fifth Tennessee Cavalry: "I have tried every means known to me to bring about order and efficiency in the regiment, but have not been rewarded with success, even unto this day. In fact, the regiment is as far from being an efficient organization as it was in June. The field officers seem to have no conception of their obligations and duties; have no control over their subordinates or men. Officers and men absent themselves without authority whenever they take the notion to visit their homes. The regiment is about 800 strong, and the largest number that can be paraded in camp at any time will not exceed 200. Most of the 600 absentees are unaccounted for."[2] Unfortunately, this was not a single, isolated case of poor discipline.

Sick leave was in one way and another gravely abused—more so than in the South. It was alleged in 1862 that men were placed on the sick list and given certificates of inability as a mere matter of favoritism, in order to enable them to visit their homes or to avoid disagreeable service in the field. On several occasions Halleck ordered medical boards to reëxamine men sent from the field to hospitals in St. Louis, only to have a large portion, perhaps three fourths, reported fit for duty.[3] Many absentees lived openly at their homes, after having exceeded a reasonable period for recovery from wounds or sickness. A lax sentiment in regard to a furlough existed so that soldiers finally regarded it as equivalent to a discharge from the service and resumed their ordinary occupations of peace time.

The government itself was in a measure responsible for this state of things from its neglect to punish abuses of furlough and other privileges and from its clemency toward deserters. The want of adequate means for the arrest of deserters in the early part of the war led to consequent impunity and increase of desertion.

The same disposition to stipulate the place where their service should be rendered, which was such a problem in the Southern army, manifested itself in the Northern ranks. One entire Pennsylvania

lan found that officers and men left camp of their own sweet will (*McClellan's Own Story*, p. 68).

[1] *O. W. R.*, Ser. I, XXII, pt. I, 212.

[2] *Ibid.*, Ser. I, XLV, pt. II, 600. From West Virginia came a similar complaint in September, 1864 (*ibid.*, Ser. I, XLIII, pt. II, 91).

[3] *Ibid.*, Ser. I, VIII, 647.

regiment refused to go to West Virginia; when virtually coerced on to the train, one hundred of them left the cars at different points. The general's solution was to advise the discharge of the regiment, "as the Government had no use for such troops!" [1] Another body expressed its objection to being transferred to the western field, as they were fearful of the climate, by deserting at every opportunity. Individuals refused to go to places personally obnoxious, as when a soldier deserted rather than go to the desolate coral reefs of the Dry Tortugas when his company was ordered there. [2] A group of forty men who had enlisted for service in New Mexico forsook their colors when ordered to Missouri; and numerous instances occur of refusal by militia to cross the State line under the terms of their enlistment. [3] Halleck's admission is significant of the weakness of the government when he said, in October, 1863, "If we had attempted to send them [drafted men] south, most of them would have deserted." [4]

War weariness and discouragement was another potent cause of desertion, which is made vivid by the Comte de Paris: "The old soldiers who had made the campaign of the peninsula could not ponder without bitterness over the fact that, after having seen the spires of Richmond six months before, they were further than ever from attaining the object of their efforts. The newcomers had learned to know the war in its most tragic aspect, and the enthusiasm which had called them to arms had considerably cooled off." [5] Nowhere is the weakened morale more clearly shown than in a soldier's letter: "But, Mrs. . . . my faith is getting weak, and I fear we are gone; the internal enemies are too many and great. Many of our own generals are no more than traitors; the soldiers are becoming discouraged, and we will be compelled, after a while, to yield or to compromise in some dishonorable way, I fear." [6] A few months later a general declared that it was impossible to keep up the morale of the troops and that he was in constant fear that the troops would abandon all organization to go home or turn bushwhacker. [7] Probably worst of all, was the intense bitterness which was manifesting itself among the soldiers because they felt that they were being used chiefly

[1] *Ibid.*, Ser. I, XXVII, pt. III, 707.
[2] Prentice, "Dry Tortugas," *McClure's Magazine,* April, 1902, XVIII, p. 565.
[3] *O. W. R.,* Ser. I, XIII, 455.
[4] *Ibid.*, Ser. I, XXVIII, pt. II, 103.
[5] Comte de Paris, *History of the Civil War in America,* II, 600.
[6] *Soldiers' Letters,* p. 233. Written by Lloyd Knight.
[7] *O. W. R.,* Ser. I, XXXIV, pt. II, 439.

for the benefit of cotton speculators, officers, and outsiders. Such a deadly poison would soon reduce the army to a mere skeleton.[1]

Probably the most serious cause producing desertion was the calibre of the recruits, noticeably inferior after 1862. Reënforcements were constantly being sent to the armies but they were for the most part mercenaries, immoral and cowardly. Substitutes were allowed after August, 1862, when the draft was to be applied to secure quotas, where necessary, and it is significant that they were pretty generally felt to be worthless material.[2]

While there are instances of many foreigners in the ranks, as among the officers, who served the cause with fidelity and honor, weight must be given to the calm opinion of the provost marshal general, deliberately stated after the war had closed. He held that it was a crime of the foreigners, rather than of men of native birth, and pointed to the fact that the great mass of the bounty-jumpers were Europeans and that the manufacturing States, dotted with towns and cities which were crowded with foreigners, ranked high in the column of desertion. The ratio per thousand of desertions to credits throughout the Union States was 62.51; in the State of New York it rose to 89.06 and in the small States near the metropolis it was still higher, while in the West, where large cities were relatively few, the average ratio sank to 45.51.[3] His view is corroborated by army officers of both sides. Meade alluded to the "worthless foreigners, who are daily deserting to the enemy;" Breckinridge spoke of the men, "chiefly foreigners" who had come over into his lines.[4] Among these foreigners the "kidnapped emigrant" who was put

[1] O. W. R., Ser. I, XXII, pt. II, 106. What made the soldiers most angry was to read in the papers that the army was abundantly provided for and living in comfort with nothing to be desired (DeTrobriand, op. cit., II, 8).

[2] Gen. Orders. No. 99. August 9, 1862 (O. W. R., Ser. III, II, 334–335). An officer at Ft. Richmond, N. Y., found most of a group of 154 deserters to have been substitutes (ibid., Ser. III, XLIII, pt. II, 628). See also the opinion of General Meade who found four in delirium tremens the day they joined (Life and Letters, II, 143).

[3] O. W. R., Ser. III, V, 668–669. In New Jersey the ratio rose to 107, in Connecticut to 117.23, and in New Hampshire to 112.22. But the general ratio of New England was but 74.24. They explained the relatively high percentage of desertion in Kansas, 117.54, by the fact that most of the men were in the service but torn by their obligations to their families and by the fact that it was a frontier community. California's high rate, 101.80, he attributed to the fact that a portion of her contingent had been levied in the East and to the cosmopolitan character of her population.

[4] Meade, Life and Letters, II, 251. O. W. R., Ser. IV, III, 863. Ibid., Ser. I, XLII, pt. III, 917.

through the enlistment is probably a picturesque but rare exception.[1] A few specific instances of deserters of British and French birth occur.[2]

The United States does not seem to have met with much success in enlisting Mexicans from New Mexico and the Southwest in its ranks and the few who marched under the Stars and Stripes proved just as in the Confederate ranks utterly undependable. They were of little value for service in Texas or New Mexico, where they were vulnerable to the appeals of their families, who were constantly asking them to return home, and to the inducement of higher pay in specie offered them on the other side of the Rio Grande where, it will be recalled, the French intervention was in progress.[3]

The large and numerous bounties given to volunteers proved undoubtedly an inducement to desert for the purpose of reënlisting, or to enlist when the recruit knew that he had no intention of remaining in the field. Bounties both encouraged and facilitated desertion, and the war, so far as enlistments were concerned, had become a trade. Men were induced to shoulder the musket by bounties from the National government, from the States, the towns, and even from the city wards. The trade gave rise to two classes of professionals: bounty-jumpers, the men who made a practice of repeated enlistments and desertions in order to pocket the liberal bounties; and the substitute-brokers, each of whom tried to outbid the other in his efforts to secure recruits.

[1] *Battles and Leaders of the Civil War,* IV, 91.

[2] Meade, *Life and Letters,* II, 235. *O. W. R.,* Ser. III, I, 835. (Suggests the likelihood of British deserters.) The most interesting case is one told by Prentice, "Dry Tortugas," *McClure's Magazine,* April, 1902, XVIII, 567–568. A British subject enlisted in an Ohio regiment; he twice deserted and reënlisted in another regiment, each time under a different name. After the third desertion, he secured employment as a clerk at General Thomas's own headquarters. But finally he was court-martialed and sentenced to ten years at the Dry Tortugas. He was of such prominence in England that Prime Minister Palmerston tried to locate him.

[3] *O. W. R.,* Ser. I, XXXIV, pt. III, 102. The men here referred to would seem to have become American citizens. Major Wesche gives a report which shows the attitude of the Mexicans. "Accompanied by Adjutant Gonzales I visited the houses of some of the influential Mexicans, and tried my best to make them take up arms in defense of their Government, their homes, and fireside. Vain endeavor! No one responded to the call. Don Pedro Baca went even so far as to say that the United States Government was a curse to this Territory, and if the Texans (Confederates) would take and keep possession of New Mexico the change could only be for the better."—*Ibid.,* Ser. I, IX, 605. See also for desertion, *ibid.,* p. 527.

The bounties were, it must be conceded, munificent. In the beginning of the war, in addition to the pay of $13 a month, a bounty of $100 was offered, payable upon honorable discharge at the close of the war. By July, 1862, payment of one fourth of the bounty in advance at the time of mustering and a premium of $2 or $3 was authorized by act of Congress under insistent urging of civilians and officers. After May 1, 1864, the pay rose to $16 a month and the bounty became $300 to new recruits, with an additional $100 to veterans.[1]

Each State offered an additional bounty, some of which were very substantial, ranging from $12 a month extra pay in the form of a relief fund in Massachusetts, to $17 paid once in New Hampshire.[2] Local bounties from cities and counties swelled the total by large sums. The Board of Trade of Chicago, for instance, raised a bounty fund of $30,000; a fund for the purpose existed in Philadelphia; and there is evidence of local bounties paid in Albany. The bounty of New York County was $300 in cash.[3] Thus a single soldier could cost the country, from first to last, from $500 to $800. Bounties of $5 to $7 from private individuals were the most vicious of all, offered by those whose commissions depended upon their success in obtaining recruits, as it placed a poor officer with scanty funds at a distinct disadvantage with the rich one.[4] The enormous profits of the system produced the class of "substitute brokers,"

---

[1] *O. W. R.*, Ser. I, III, 118. Rhodes, *History of the United States*, IV, 430–431. *American Annual Cyclopedia*, 1865, p. 31. For the pressure for advance payment of bounties see telegrams exchanged between Seward and Stanton, *O. W. R.*, Ser. III, II, 182, 187.

[2] The bounties and extra pay offered by some of the States is shown in the following table:

Maine	$ 10 (*O. W. R.*, Ser. III, II, 266.)
Massachusetts	$ 12 per month relief funds (*ibid.*, Ser. III, I, 655.)
New Hampshire	$ 17 (soon discontinued) (*ibid.*, p. 653.)
New Jersey	$ 6 a month (*ibid.*, Ser. III, II, 202.)
Connecticut	$300 (*ibid.*, Ser. I, XXVI, pt. I, 881.)
New York	$ 75 (Rhodes, *History of the United States*, IV, 430.)
Vermont	$ 7 a month (*O. W. R.*, Ser. III, II, 102.)
Wisconsin	$ 5 a month (limited) (*ibid.*, Ser. III, II, 111.)

[3] *Ibid.*, Ser. III, II, 253, 269, 413. Rhodes, *History of the Civil War*, p. 430.
[4] General Butler protested vehemently against the practice of private bounties. Governor Andrew turned the table on him neatly by stating that the only case which had come to his knowledge was that of a man who in order to secure a commission from Butler himself was offering $5 per man to secure his quota of men (*O. W. R.*, Ser. III, I, 824, 826).

plying the trade of collecting recruits, who were interested only in their brokerage and not in the physical or moral quality of the soldiers furnished.

The vast size of the country, the feverish zeal of each town and city district to fill its quota, rendered it hard to detect the miserable bounty-jumpers. This method of filling up the ranks was shown up at its worst in the large Eastern cities where it raked in a number of criminals, bullies, pickpockets, and vagrants. A great many of them enlisted under fictitious names, such as Abe Lincoln, Johnny Boker, Jim Crow, which names they did not always themselves remember. During a roll-call it was not unusual to see them look into their hats, we are told, to recall the assumed name which they had written there.[1] A recruit's social standing was fixed, in the enrollment camps or forts, by the number of acts of villainy he had to his credit and the number of times he had "lepped the bounty." One hard-faced, crafty pickpocket, who had plied his trade profitably in a half dozen cities, more or less, shamelessly boasted of his agility, and was regarded as a leader and his words of experience stored for future reference. Such arrant cowards were they, when it came to the time for actually being forwarded South, that they cut open the mattresses to crawl into and hide in the straw, from which they were prodded by the guards with bayonets. One despicable wretch actually burrowed into a large garbage box. So eager were they to pursue any possible avenue of escape that in one camp they made up a pot of $1700 and offered it to a young lad of sixteen for his pass. So well was the character of these "soldiers" recognized in the North that the very guttersnipes of New York jeered at them as they were marched to the wharves.[2] It is this class of men whose desertion led the rebels on one occasion jokingly to send word that, since most of the regiment was on their side, it might be well for the Union side to send over the regimental colors.[3] The same scorn led the better class of Union soldiers to call these men "seven dollar a pound fellows." [4]

"The jumper" would enlist, pocket the bounty paid, desert at his first opportunity, change his name, reënlist in another State under

[1] Goss, *Recollections of a Private,* p. 328.
[2] Wilkeson, *Recollections of a Private Soldier,* pp. 2–3, 7. For a vivid, if distressing, account of these bounty-men, see *ibid.,* pp. 1–12.
[3] Goss., *op. cit.,* p. 328.
[4] Adams, "Pensions—Worse and More of Them," *The World's Work,* January, 1912, XXIII, p. 332.

a different name, collect perhaps a more generous bounty, and so play the game until he was caught or until he had deserted so often as to fear detection, when he would desert finally to the enemy. The provost marshal general stated that out of a detachment of 625 recruits sent to reënforce a New Hampshire regiment, 137 deserted on the way to the front, leaving a net total of 370 men![1] In general, those States which paid the largest bounties produced the largest proportion of deserters. Grant showed up the inherent viciousness of the system admirably when he wrote Secretary Seward that for every eight bounties paid, he did not receive one good soldier for the service.[2]

Last, but by no means least, in the catalogue of causes, comes the cowardly or traitorous encouragement of desertion by civilians, from which the Union, as the Confederacy, suffered. The draft riots were a distinct abetting of the soldier in refusal to enter upon his military duty; to desert the field or camp was the next logical step. The existence of disloyal organizations through the North is notorious. There was abundant evidence also that disaffected persons were systematically employed in promoting desertion by enticing men from their regiments or by persuading them to overstay their furloughs until they were afraid to return.[3]

[1] Rhodes, *History of the Civil War,* pp. 301–302. Schurz, *Reminiscences,* III, 49–50. *American Annual Cyclopedia,* 1864, p. 37.

[2] *O. W. R.,* Ser. II, VI, 614. General Thomas said the same thing (*ibid.,* Ser. III, II, 864). The boldness of the bounty-brokers almost surpasses belief, for Sheridan expressed fear that they would solicit soldiers already in camp at Baltimore (*ibid.,* Ser. I, XLVI, pt. II, 72).

[3] *American Annual Cyclopedia,* 1863, p. 24. This encouragement was noted by the press. See *Daily Illinois State Journal,* February 4, 1863. General Logan charged that newspapers with treasonable articles, falsifying the public sentiment, were circulated in the camps and set them down as machinations of politicians, bidding for votes (*O. W. R.,* Ser. I, XXIV, pt. III, 47).

CHAPTER X

Progress of Desertion in the Union Armies

As in the armies drawn from the land south of Mason and Dixon's line, so in those drawn from the territory north of that line desertion began to manifest itself almost at once. Two men found life at Fort Pickens in Florida sufficiently unpleasant already in May, 1861, to lead them to desert without awaiting the dangers of siege or battle. And so the report of a major of artillery bears the terse statement, "I have lost two by death and two by desertion." [1] But it seems clear that during the first year of the war, say from April, 1861, to January, 1862, despite resignation and desertion of commissioned officers to join the Confederates, the enlisted men of the regular army were but little affected by desertion. But that same evil, according to a report of the provost marshal general, manifested itself fairly frequently among the militia and volunteer troops at that time. [2]

By the fall of 1862 desertion had become a problem. By July of the very first year of the war, there had been great complaint of the way Washington was filled with officers and with men improperly absent; citizens as well as military commanders were aware that soldiers were loitering on in their own homes illegitimately, [3] but General McClellan did not seem alert to the gravity of the evil, for he wrote Lincoln in a strain rather remarkable for the man in command of the Army of the Potomac: "I think that the exciting of the public press to persistent attack upon officers and soldiers absent from the army, the employment of deputy marshals to arrest

---

[1] O. W. R., Ser. I, I, 407. The writer is not unaware that some of these early desertions may mean only that some Southerners were making choice of the government to which they wished to acknowledge allegiance. The number which was reported missing after the first Battle of Bull Run, duly recorded by both sides, is also disregarded as not reliable or significant for this study, as many were stragglers, who ultimately returned to their commands.

[2] Ibid., Ser. III, V, 605, 676; Ser. I, IX, 487.

[3] In August, 1862, Simon Draper, for a time in charge of the Deserter Bureau, reported large numbers of absentees in Maine (ibid., Ser. III, II, 325–326).

and send back deserters, summary dismissal of officers whose names are reported for being absent without leave, and the publication of their names, will exhaust the remedies applicable by the War Department." [1]

Perhaps Lee and the commanders in the South saw with the eyes of the Union scout who wrote from Virginia on November 20, 1862, that desertions from the Union lines were so frequent as to be disgusting to the rebels themselves.[2] It is about this time that President Lincoln recognized and presented the situation in realistic terms. He pointed out to a group of women calling upon him that while McClellan was constantly calling for more and more troops, the deserters and furloughed men outnumbered the new recruits; and that while that general had 180,000 men on the rolls for the Battle of Antietam, he had had only some 90,000 with which to enter the battle, as 20,000 men were in hospitals and the rest "absent," and that within two hours after the battle, some 30,000 had straggled and deserted.[3] Pope in September of that year had reported the straggling as so bad that unless something were done to restore tone to the army, it would "melt away before you know it." [4] To recognize the different corps, he brought the army within the defenses of Washington.[5] No less a figure than Halleck charged that not a few voluntarily surrendered to the enemy, in order to be paroled as prisoners of war. Even the vigilance of escorts and guards was materially affected by the alluring thought that captivity meant liberty and relaxation.[6] Many, according to Meade and McClellan, dispersed and left during the fight of Antietam. Every defeat was marked by a long line of stragglers and deserters, who, if the outcome had been different, would probably have remained to press on the advantage.[7] If the number improperly absent in September seemed serious, the number absent without leave in December after Burnside's disastrous campaign was worse. The demoralization of the army was complete.

[1] *O. W. R.*, Ser. I, XI, pt. III, 322.

[2] *Ibid.*, Ser. I, XXI, 824.

[3] Livermore, *My Story of the War*, pp. 557, 558. About 70,000 were absent on leave granted by company officers, who had no power to grant absences. With one of his homely figures, Lincoln compared the task of filling up the army to undertaking to shovel fleas.

[4] *O. W. R.*, Ser. I, XII, pt. III, 797; XII, pt. II, 8.

[5] Schurz (*Reminiscences*, II, 401) speaks of the number of desertions at this time as "alarming."

[6] *Ibid.* Buell, *Battles and Leaders in the Civil War*, III, 32.

[7] *O. W. R.*, Ser. I, XIX, pt. II, 66. *Soldiers' Letters*, p. 63.

The situation was little better in the West at this time. Military reverses had been followed by retreats, in the confusion of which large numbers of deserters and stragglers were left behind. In the late summer General Bragg was writing exultantly of the prisoners and deserters which he was receiving daily from Buell's army, from which fact he inferred that the latter's troops were greatly disorganized.[1] The early delusion of a brief, brilliant campaign had given rise to disappointment, as there were no signs of yielding on the part of the Confederacy. Large numbers got away from the Tennessee front on all sorts of pretexts—with or without authority. Buell in June, 1862, admitted that 14,000 officers and men were absent from the various divisions of his army, some without any authority, others with the permission of officers who had no power to give it.[2] This state of things continued through February, 1863; according to the report of the provost marshal of the St. Louis district it was a growing evil and assuming fearful proportions.[3]

When Hooker took command of the Army of the Potomac on January 26, 1863, the situation seemed almost hopeless; desertions were occurring at the rate of several hundred a day; his carefully compiled returns showed about 25 per cent of the army absent.[4]

The number of missing and of deserters—it is impossible here, because of the method of keeping the records, to discriminate between those taken prisoner by the enemy and those deliberately taking advantage of the confusion to slip away—in the eastern army was more than double the number of those in the volunteer forces in the West. It was estimated in March of 1862 that to replace the losses from these two causes alone, the missing and the deserters, 34,000 men would have to be recruited annually as long as the war lasted.[5] Hooker immediately went to work to improve the situation with regard to desertion, as well as to bring up the morale of the army. He issued stricter rules concerning leaves of absence, whereby they were restricted to fifteen days, and arrested deserters with such energy that by February he reported desertions in his army almost at an end.[6]

---

[1] O. W. R., Ser. I, XVII, pt. II, 677; XVI, pt. II, 775. General Pemberton also reported that many Union men deserted to him, February, 1863.

[2] Buell, Battles and Leaders in the Civil War, III, 32.

[3] O. W. R., Ser. I, XXII, pt. II, 77.

[4] Ibid., Ser. I, XXV, pt. II, 78.

[5] American Annual Cyclopedia, 1862, p. 21.

[6] O. W. R., Ser. I, XXV, pt. II, 10, 52, 78. Rhodes, History of the Civil War, p. 210.

The seriousness of the evil and the extent to which the country was startled by the statistics published led to the appointment of officers to arrest and return the deserters under the provost marshal general, who created a comprehensive system for this work. So effective were these provisions that by the close of the year 1863 the general-in-chief was able to report a considerable decrease in desertion and straggling, although the evil was by no means cured.[1]

While the records show many cases of desertions through 1864, it appeared to the men studying the problem at the time that they were not so numerous as in the preceding year, due to a stricter discipline and to an effort to make the offense appear more odious. Senator Wilson, speaking on the floor of the Senate in March, admitted that common report put the number absent from the armies at 80,000 but affirmed his belief that it was not more than 40,000, as he charged the records with being faulty.[2] During the latter part of the year, when executions were taking place almost daily in the Army of the Potomac, a diminution of the evil was perceptible on that part of the fighting front. Still the number was sufficiently large to cause the government considerable concern and embarrassment. The desertion of drafted men and of substitutes, chiefly the miserable bounty-jumpers, simply could not be stopped.[3] A fresh impetus was certainly given to desertion by a proclamation from General Lee, offering to send Union deserters North, which had been undoubtedly inspired by General Grant's similar offer to Confederate deserters. Even during the early months of 1865, when it was so apparent that the ship of the Confederacy was doomed that the men were deserting it as rats a sinking ship, the Union forces still lost a great many men from this cause.[4] The fact that the army was brought up to its original standard in size may indicate merely that enlistments had been so stimulated as to offset the loss by desertion.

[1] *American Annual Cyclopedia*, 1863, p. 25.

[2] *Congressional Globe*, 38th Cong., 1st sess., 1249. But see Appendix, Table No. III.

[3] *American Annual Cyclopedia*, 1864, p. 37. *O. W. R.*, Ser. III, V, 757–758. There were a great many from the Army of the James in December, 1864 (*ibid.*, Ser. I, XLII, pt. III, 1049). General Stevenson reported to Stanton October 28, 1864: "There are numerous desertions of the substitutes arriving at this post. A party deserted yesterday. I sent today a scout into Loudoun and captured two of them; they belong to the Fortieth New Jersey, a part of the same company that deserted at the Philadelphia depot a few days ago." And he added that many such fellows were arriving every day.—*Ibid.*, Ser. I, XLII, pt. II, 484. See also *The Sherman Letters*, pp. 177, 226.

[4] *O. W. R.*, Ser. I, XLVI, 56.

As has already been intimated, absenteeism on the part of the officers grew to very distressing proportions. It appears to have occurred far more during the early years of the war, 1861 and 1862, than later, and arose, apparently, more from ignorance of the obligations of *noblesse oblige* than from baseness of character. However, it was as late as October, 1863, that General Schofield reported from St. Louis that officers absented themselves from their appropriate duties without due authority, upon frivolous pretexts, or without any pretext at all, because of drunkenness, or merely from disregard of duty. He felt quite hopeless about courts-martial as a remedy, for if such a trial were held for each case of delinquency, a large proportion of the reliable officers would be constantly on such duty. Hence the remedy would only aggravate the evil.[1]

The complaints from the military men were more bitter concerning the volunteer officers in the beginning than concerning the privates, for more was expected of them. Meade's opinion has already been recorded.[2] McClellan wrote with regard to his army in July, 1862, that it was a melancholy fact that, with exceptions, the officers of volunteers were greatly inferior to the men they commanded, though he added that perhaps he should shift his tense as the worst had been sifted out.[3] The laxness took the form of frequent absence from their commands while in camp, from their columns while on the march, and the overstaying of sick-leave though fit for duty.[4] Serious indeed was the situation, if correctly represented by the *New York Tribune* early in 1863, when more than 350 commissioned officers were absent from one grand division of the army, as it calculated, on that basis, 1,200 absent from the entire Army of the Potomac.[5] It was openly charged on the floor of the Senate on January 7, 1863, that many officers had been absent for several months without leave and that there were then 411 absent without leave. The most flagrant case seemed to be that of an officer who, though on the rolls, had

---

[1] *Ibid.*, Ser. I, XXII, pt. II, 597.

[2] See above, page 135. Of course, in noting desertion of officers during 1861, due allowance must be made for the possibility of desertion representing merely a change of allegiance. In that class probably belongs the case of a petty officer, connected with the navy, a native of Virginia, reported to be a relative of Secretary of the Navy Welles (*ibid.*, Ser. I, VI, 184).

[3] *Ibid.*, Ser. I, XI, pt. III, 323.

[4] A colonel reported peremptorily ordering some officers back to their posts from Philadelphia (*ibid.*, Ser. I, XII, pt. I, 563). One captain easily escaped by getting into an ambulance as if ill, and instead of going to camp, having himself taken to Nashville.

[5] *New York Tribune*, January 6, 1863.

absented himself from his command without authority from March, 1862, to January, 1863.[1]

All of the cases of dereliction from duty cannot be attributed to mere ignorance of military usage when we read such statements as the following from Rosecrans: "Desertion by officers of white liver, feeble constitution, and Butternut connections are not utterly unknown to this command, nor are the attempts to draw away others of unfrequent occurrence." [2] Again, even later, we read of a group of 300 unorganized New York recruits whose commissioned officers deserted them after coaxing them into the service. The presence of three officers of the Second New York in New York City shortly after the Battle of Bull Run, though this regiment did not cross the stream, pointed to their determination to run no further risks of battle.[3]

Officers, so dead to the proper sense of obligation to their commissions and to their swords, were, as on the Southern side, to be found usually among the non-commissioned and among the lower commissioned men. The searcher finds now and then the name of a lieutenant or of a captain or even of a lieutenant-colonel, charged with having deserted, sometimes to the enemy, but the number of such items is surprisingly and gratifyingly few.[4] But one can scarcely believe that Halleck was referring only to men of the lowest rank when he declared at the close of 1862 that hundreds of officers were almost continually absent from their commands, and one circular distinctly charges guilt by *superior* officers.[5] However, one is led to the inevitable conclusion that the large number of absences without leave reported for officers, 100 to 200 per month, were but temporary

---

[1] *Congressional Globe,* 37th Cong., 3d sess., pt. I, 215.

[2] Regardless of the above, one finds it hard to credit the rumor that officers encouraged men of the 109th Illinois to stack their arms, and give a cheer for Jeff. Davis! (*Daily Illinois State Journal,* February 3, 1863). And yet corroboration is found in the *Official War Records* in the fact that twenty-one officers, including a colonel, a major, and a captain, were discharged for this cause from their regiment shortly after this date (Ser. I, XVII, pt. II, 590–591, 586).

[3] *Ibid.,* Ser. I, XLII, pt. III, 184; II, 351 (note).

[4] *Ibid.,* Ser. II, II, 327; Ser. I, XXV, pt. II, 605–606. A captain and lieutenant of a yawl went over to the enemy (*ibid.,* Ser. I, XXXIV, pt. IV, 504). The writer, it should perhaps be stated, found but one instance of a lieutenant-colonel who deserted in the face of the enemy to be taken captive (*ibid.,* Ser. I, XVII, pt. II, 586.

[5] *Ibid.,* Ser. I, XIX, pt. II, 225; XIX, pt. I, 6.

infractions of strict military law and did not imply any intention of desertion.[1]

The evil contaminated all classes who were in any way connected with the army: engineers, pilots from the river boats on the Mississippi, and teamsters.[2] One of the most amusing tales which has come down is that of a surgeon's assistant in a skirmish at the Pamunkey River in 1862. When the balls began to whistle, this man, who carried the box of medical stores strapped to his back like a knapsack, dropped on his knees behind a large tree. During the seven days' retreat which followed, he disappeared from view and was not seen again until about a month later when the regiment was mustered out of the service. It proved that he had been hanging about hospitals and convalescent camps since his precipitate departure.[3] There has even been revealed one woman deserter, Sarah E. E. Seelye, who after serving for nearly two years as "Franklin Thompson," deserted and resumed her proper sex rather than face exposure. A bill in 1884 to remove the charge of desertion and award Mrs. Seelye a pension made the story public property.[4]

The record of the negro troops is a respectable one in regard to desertion. The report of a New York captain as to their courage under fire reads well: "I do not remember a single instance, in my labors in the trenches, where the black man has skulked away from his duty, and I know that instances of that kind have occurred among the whites . . ." But in cold statistics they do not show up so well, for the loss by desertion among the colored troops was sixty-seven per thousand, slightly above the general ratio of 62.51 for all volunteers. In exact figures the final report of the provost

[1] One is confirmed in this view by the very small number of officers counted as deserting by Fry: Five in the regular army, 187 in the white volunteer, 24 in the colored—216 in all, which statistics cover, of course, the period only after the establishment of this bureau. This shows clearly that the desertion of officers occurred in the early period of the war (*House Ex. Doc.*, 39th Cong., 1st sess., No. 1, IV, pt. I, 79). See also Phisterer, *Statistical Record*, p. 67.

[2] See the story told by General Lew Wallace of how he stationed a train of cars behind a hill to carry off the wounded from a battlefield, but of how the engineer, frightened by the flying shells, ran off the complete train (*An Autobiography*, II, 773–774). For desertion of a pilot see *O. W. R.*, Ser. I, XXIV, pt. I, 389; XX, pt. I, 656.

[3] Told in *Soldiers' Letters*, pp. 88–89.

[4] Ida Tarbell, "The American Woman," *American Magazine*, April, 1910, LXIX, 807–809. Mrs. Seelye had adopted her masquerade two years before the war broke out, believing she would find the struggle for a livelihood easier as a man than as a woman.

marshal general gives 12,464 desertions from the colored troops, twenty-four of whom only were officers, presumably white men. This record shows 12,440 negro deserters as compared with 186,389 white deserters from the enlisted men.[1] Complaints came to the ears of officers of depredations by armed negroes, presumably deserters.

Dull as statistics usually are, unreliable as they often are, still with all factors duly allowed for and calculated, the number of deserters from the Union forces forms an interesting chapter, especially for comparison with the number of Confederate deserters. No one could follow the monthly and trimonthly returns for the armies with which the *Official War Records* abound without realizing that there must have been a painful number absent without leave, though, as stated earlier, the abstracts merely compare the number actually present with the number recorded present and absent on the muster-rolls and so afford no definite figures on the number of deserters as distinct from those taken prisoner. Some attempt at presenting figures for each year will be made, and then the grand totals, which may prove illuminating, will be given.

From a table furnished by McClellan it is possible to note that on December 1, 1861, only 11,470 were absent from the Army of the Potomac, but the record does not state how many of these had leaves of absence.[2] The exact amount of desertion in the Army of the Potomac comes out glaringly for the first time in 1862 in a communication from President Lincoln to McClellan dated July 13: "I am told that over 160,000 men have gone into your army on the Peninsula. When I was with you the other day we made out 86,500 remaining, leaving 73,500 to be accounted for. I believe 23,500 will cover all the killed, wounded, and missing in all your battles and skirmishes, leaving 50,000 who have left otherwise. Not more than 5000 of these have died, leaving 45,000 of your army still alive and not with it. I believe half or two-thirds of them are fit for duty today. Have you any more perfect knowledge of this than I

---

[1] *O. W. R.*, Ser. I, XXVIII, pt. I, 329; Ser. III, V, 670. Among *Soldiers' Letters* may be found an interesting, though probably not typical, case of a negro deserter, who at first fearing to return because of the warning of a white soldier, finally made his way back to camp after six weeks, preferring to be shot by his Northern brothers to being shot by a rebel 'scription (*op. cit.,* 236). See also Phisterer, *Statistical Record,* p. 67.

[2] *O. W. R.*, Ser. I, V, 13.

ave? . . . How can they be got to you, and how can they be prevented from getting away in such numbers for the future?"[1] This statement then clearly indicates 45,000 deserters in 1862 from the eastern army. But by December, Simon Draper, specially commissioned for the task of dealing with desertion, found upward of 100,000 absent without leave and hence subject to be treated as deserters.[2] When Hooker assumed charge of the army in the East, his returns computed 2,923 commissioned officers and 82,188 non-commissioned officers and privates absent from the Army of the Potomac.

In February, 1863, Halleck computed more than one third of the officers and men in service absent. Official returns in January, 1863, estimated absent from duty from all the armies of the United States 8,987 officers and 280,073 non-commissioned officers and privates; though no attempt was made to estimate the exact proportion of those who were sick or on furlough, it is certain that a large portion were deserters and stragglers.[3]

A study of the monthly table prepared in the office of the provost marshal general of the deserters reported to the bureau by regimental commanders reveals a fairly steady increase, with a few fluctuations, from May, 1863, when the bureau may be regarded as beginning really to function, up until October, 1864, when it reached its apogee in 10,692 men reported improperly missing and therefore technically deserters. Even during 1865 the figures average higher than during 1863.[4]

The average monthly desertion as estimated by Colonel Dodge, an assistant in general charge of the Deserters' Branch of the provost's office, may prove interesting:

[1] *Ibid.*, Ser. I, XI, pt. III, 319. McClellan a few days later, July 28, admitted 38,795 absent, some 3,800 without leave (*ibid.*, 329). In September he charged that 8,000 from one corps of his army were probably at work at home. See *ibid.*, Ser. I, XIX, pt. II, 365. DeTrobriand points out in his comment on the condition of the army at this time the significant fact that the loss from death during the retreat had been but 15,249 (*Quatre ans de campagnes à l'armée du Potomac*, I, 278).

[2] He estimated that a very large proportion, from 10 per cent to 25 per cent in the various States, of the new levies had deserted (*O. W. R.*, Ser. III, II, 939).

[3] *American Annual Cyclopedia*, 1863, p. 24. Rosecrans gives 40,000 absentees for the western army alone in February, 1863, though again the number absent with leave is not given (*O. W. R.*, Ser. I, XXIII, pt. II, 75).

[4] See Appendix, Table No. III, drawn from *House Ex. Doc.*, 39th Cong., 1st sess., No. 1, IV, pt. I, 232–235.

1863	4,647
1864	7,333
1865	4,368

The general average, to put it in round numbers, may be said to hav ranged for the three years around 5,500 a month.

In view of the impression expressed during 1864 that there wa some diminution of the evil, the searcher is startled to find the recor indicating a decided increase. Hence we are forced to scrutinize th table closely and to explain it possibly by two facts: undoubtedly, th military officers were reporting the desertions more carefully and cor sistently, despite the complaints of the provosts of their delinquenc in this respect; and the bureau pointed out the fact that the cour of 1864 included all drafted men, who deserted en route to the fiel and some who deserted even before reaching the general rendezvou a fact whereby it would account wholly for the high average of 1864 But it is the judgment of the writer that the table establishes ir dubitably the fact that the problem of desertion was far from solve by the close of the war.

A scrutiny of the record of Union desertion by States [2] reveals th largest actual numbers from New York with 44,913, from Penr sylvania with 24,050, from Ohio with 18,354, from New Jersey wit the startling figure of 8,468, and from little Rhode Island with 1,38 to its credit. While due consideration must be given to the fact tha each of these States, except New Jersey and Rhode Island, had a initially large population and hence sent a large body of soldiery t the field, the fact remains that they contributed an undue propor tion to the "roll of honor." The figures for several of the border State prove interesting; notably, Maryland, which produced 5,328 deser ers; Tennessee, which furnished 3,690; Kentucky, which yielde 7,227; and Arkansas, which contributed 2,245. Likewise, Indian Wisconsin, and Iowa, where there was considerable disaffection, ran relatively high in proportion to their population.

Usually the recorded statements of specific instances of desertio whether from Union or Confederate reports, show the slipping-awa of individuals or of small groups, varying from five to sixteen c

---

[1] It is no purpose of the author to include in this study any consideratio of desertion of drafted men who failed to report at rendezvous, which wa technically desertion, as data would be too unreliable to be of value.

[2] See Appendix, Table No. IV.

twenty.[1] But the constant defections, one or two at a time even, mounted up in a comparatively short time to large numbers. At Pittsburgh, for instance, complaint was made that more than 300 from two Pennsylvania regiments had absented themselves since their muster; from an Illinois regiment, stationed at Cairo, Illinois, more than 700 men had deserted; 347 men succeeded in making their escape from another Illinois regiment which was placed at Memphis.[2]

There were also to be found cases of considerable bodies departing together. One conspicuous case savored of open mutiny; a group of between 300 and 400 drafted men departed from the forts investing Washington on the 29th of August, 1864. They continued in a body with arms until they had secured citizen clothes, when they scattered in every direction.[3] A body of 100 cavalrymen in Mississippi escaped one night in the fall of 1862, taking advantage of the fact that no guards had been posted.[4] A colonel on another occasion returned from a reconnaissance with forty men to find that the rest of his command of several hundred had decamped.[5] At times it was even worse than these figures indicate, for one general states in the fall of 1862 that, so great was the disorganization, desertions were taking place by the thousand among the men and by the hundred among the subaltern officers. A Confederate officer reported at the opening of 1863 that he had gathered from some prisoners of war that 2,000 men had already deserted from the Union army opposed to him, while others were seeking an opportunity to surrender in order to be paroled.[6] As late as July, 1864, an entire company of Arkansas State troops, sent to defend a point in that State, went over in a body to the Confederates.[7]

The grand total of desertions for the period of the war was reported by J. B. Fry, Provost Marshal General, to Secretary Stanton on March 17, 1866, as 268,530. As many of the men included in those returns were repeaters from various causes—sickness, injuries, accidents, unavoidable overstaying of furloughs—and as others were

---

[1] For Union records see *O. W. R.*, Ser. I, XV, 681; XLII, pt. III, 720, 767, 780, 921; XLVI, pt. III, 72. For evidence from the Confederate side see *ibid.*, Ser. I, XV, 1039, and Gilmore, *Four Years in the Saddle*, p. 50.

[2] *O. W. R.*, Ser. III, II, 864; Ser. I, XXIII, pt. II, 65; XVII, pt. II, 590.

[3] *Ibid.*, Ser. I, XLIII, pt. III, 861.

[4] *Ibid.*, Ser. I, XVIII, pt. I, 143, 144, 145.

[5] *Ibid.*, Ser. I, XXXIV, pt. III, 629.

[6] De Trobriand, *op. cit.*, I, 278. *O. W. R.*, Ser. I, LII, pt. II, 414.

[7] *Ibid.*, Ser. I, XLI, pt. II, 1020.

unintentionally absent and later returned to duty, he estimated that 25 per cent were not deserters in fact, and so deducted that proportion. That would make the total of actual desertions 201,397.[1] Since that date, however, new muster-rolls, returns, and other official papers have been deposited with the government, affording evidence of death, discharge, and desertion, together with amendments of personal records, which were not available for the provost marshal general; many charges of desertion have been removed by the War Department on the ground of manifest error and under the acts of July 5, 1884, May 17, 1886, and March 2, 1889, and by amendatory acts. Livermore, who has made a careful study of the numbers involved on both sides of the war, estimates the number of deserters at only 125,000, a number greatly below that of the provost marshal general, and obviously a mere guess, unsupported by any figures to show the reasons for his variance from his authority.[2]

The War Department estimates the number of actual deserters at large at the close of the war, making due allowance for those incorrectly reported, as 117,247, a figure which has been consistently accepted by the department since 1882.[3] If to this figure we add the 80,000 which it may safely be calculated were returned to the army during the war, we arrive at 197,247, not far from Fry's estimate. The writer has, therefore, been brought to the conclusion that his allowance of twenty-five per cent for error was nearer correct than the officials realized at the time of publication of the *Official War Records,* and that we shall probably not go far astray if we place the total number of desertions, not deducting for repetitions, at 200,000 in round numbers.[4]

---

[1] *O. W. R.,* Ser. I, XLI, pt. II, p. 677. The writer is here using the revised figures of the provost marshal general of March 17, 1866, which differ slightly from his figures of September 11, 1865, and from those of an assistant, who gives 278,644 (*ibid.,* p. 758). Fry does not always give the same figures himself, as note a discrepancy in his tables (*House Ex. Doc.,* 39th Cong., 1st sess., IV, pt. I, 78–81, 232–235).

[2] Livermore, *Numbers and Losses in the Civil War,* p. 48.

[3] The writer is indebted for the above estimate of the number of deserters at large at the close of the war to the present adjutant-general of the army, who states that such research as his office has had occasion to make in recent years would not justify a deviation from this estimate made some years ago.

[4] The writer wishes to be understood as not attempting any exact accuracy in these estimates. As is perfectly obvious, no investigation of the muster-rolls has been made, such as Livermore made for his study of the numbers and losses, since the primary purpose of this study is not a statistical inquiry into the numbers involved, but a general study to throw more light on this neglected phase of our Civil War history.

The ratio of desertions to enlistments stood high: 244.25 per thousand of enlistments in the regular army, while in the volunteer army it rose to but 62.51 per thousand.[1] This leads to a very interesting inference as to the moral fiber of the men in the regular service compared with those who responded to the call of their States, and shows a reversal of the tendency of the first year of the war when the desertions were higher in the volunteer army than in the regular army. A rather interesting comparison of the proportion which deserted is afforded by a statement in 1862 by Rosecrans, who thought that the government was paying 100 men in order to get the services of seventy-five or eighty, and by a statement by Grant in late 1864, who thought that out of five reported as having enlisted, he got perhaps one effective soldier![2] It was an extreme case, however, which General Terry reported in 1864 when, starting with 1,800 men, he arrived with 700.[3]

Figures are obviously difficult to give with any hope of accuracy, especially in view of the repeaters, the number of whom was undoubtedly very large, though we are without any means of determining just how large. This interesting character often coincides with the famous or infamous bounty-jumper. The reports show that the same men had deserted five and six times, and "intended to keep it up;" others confessed that it was a regular business with them. The most extreme case, as already stated, is that of a man who finally landed in the Albany penitentiary for four years, after having confessed to jumping the bounty thirty-two times![4] The supply of deserters seemed inexhaustible, for the same men were arrested, sent to the rendezvous, forwarded to the front, put into

As illustrative of how hard it is to give figures which may be regarded as authoritative, the following story is told, showing how a certain captain had no desertions—recorded: Although a certain captain had been in service for several months, the same number and the same men as had been mustered in were mustered out, when he had in reality lost more than a dozen men in action and as many more by desertion. If his sergeant reported Juan Chacon or Jose de Dios Montoyn y Armijo as having deserted during the night, he would pounce upon the first Mexican peon he chanced to meet and would say in Spanish, "Here, Juan Chacon, get into your place. I have a great mind to shoot you for desertion." If the victim protested, the captain would say, "Close your mouth, you brute. Here, sergeant, give this man a uniform and a horse as I'll excuse him this time" (*Battles and Leaders,* II, 106, note).

[1] *O. W. R.*, Ser. III, V, 670.
[2] *Ibid.*, Ser. I, XII, pt. III, 12; XLII, pt. II, 783. Rosecrans complained of those absent for illness as well as of deserters; Grant stressed desertion.
[3] *Ibid.*, Ser. I, XLII, pt. II, 507.
[4] *Ibid.*, Ser. I, XLII, pt. III, 1038. Rhodes, *History of the Civil War*, p. 301.

the ranks without the pretense of a trial, only to desert again and repeat the whole mockery. The irritation of the officer who called them the "most desperate villains unhung" [1] is understandable. The naïve case of a soldier court-martialed at Columbus Barracks, Ohio, will bear repetition. When asked to plead to the charge of desertion, he innocently replied, "Which one? I have deserted thirteen times." [2]

[1] *O. W. R.,* Ser. III, IV, 1231.
[2] Greenleaf, "Recognition of Deserters," *Journal of the Military Service Institution,* X, 561.

CHAPTER XI

Devices for Escape from the Union Army and Measures of Prevention

The Union soldier was as ingenious in devising methods for effecting his escape from a service which had become irksome to him as his Southern confrère, but certainly in the early stages he had less need of wile.

One of the earliest means scarcely deserves designation as a method; it was merely to refrain from returning from a sick leave or from a furlough. Evidently the abuse of the sick leave was a worry to Halleck while he was serving as a commander in the field, for in July, 1862, he directed that sick leaves cease, as they were destroying the army, for of the thousands sent off sick, scarcely any returned.[1] At about the same time McClellan was bringing the matter to the attention of Governor Morgan of New York, seeking that executive's help to secure the return of many thousands in the North who were fit to rejoin their regiments.[2] The former complained also to General Thomas that the convalescent soldiers habitually returned to their homes when allowed to leave the hospitals as convalescent. He accompanied his charge with the startling statement that it was the experience of every commander that not more than a tenth of the soldiers left behind sick ever returned to their companies. He cited as evidence the fact that a regiment stationed as depot guard with his army had sent some 500 sick to hospitals in the rear and had received back some fifteen or twenty.[3] It must be confessed that his statement is fairly well borne out by the figures of the medical director of the Army of the Potomac concerning hospitals located near Washington for about two months of the year 1862. Of the total number of patients, nearly 52,000, only about 7,000 were returned to duty, or somewhat more than an eighth; as compared with 7,000 convalescent men who returned to their posts, 597

[1] *O. W. R.*, Ser. I, XIII, 477.
[2] *Ibid.*, Ser. III, II, 225–226.
[3] *Ibid.*, Ser. I, XIX, pt. II, 365.

deserted on the way.[1] Even when the physicians learned to retain near the front the men who would soon be able to return to duty, the latter would slip off in the night to escape service. Self-inflicted wounds are not a discovery of the modern factory workman, for this same medical director reports that about 5,000 sick and slightly wounded men, "many of the latter self-mutilated," did not go to the field hospitals according to orders but straggled to Fredericksburg at different times, relying upon the agents of the Sanitary Commission and other relief organizations for food, keeping as much as possible out of the way of the medical officers.[2] Well men made care of the sick a pretext for leaving the battle-field in the confusion incident to carrying away the wounded after a battle.[3] In taking care of the sick, the able-bodied managed to get on board hospital boats, as there was always confusion and haste in shipping and caring for the wounded after an engagement. There was, naturally, no time for nice examination of permits to pass here or there.[4]

The confusion of battle also favored desertion, especially if during an engagement a regiment became scattered.[5] Slipping to the rear and then from the field was a common trick.

Purposeful capture by the enemy in order to be paroled to their homes belongs in the class with self-mutilation as a means of evasion. The bitter denunciation of it by Rosecrans as more base and cowardly than desertion, which had a "semblance of courage when contrasted with voluntary capture," and the threat to arrest all soldiers captured and paroled while straggling was, however, mere bluster.[6]

Escape while on the march or en route to the front or to a camp, easy at first, became increasingly difficult. Straggling was, as usual, the stepping-stone to desertion and was promptly recognized by the officers for what it was. How great the straggling was in August, 1861, is sufficiently indicated by General Schurz when he declared that his regiments entering Culpepper on August 8, 1861, looked little

---

[1] O. W. R., Ser. I, XIX, pt. I, 111.

[2] Ibid., Ser. I, XXXVI, pt. I, 235, 233. See also Noyes, The Bivouac and the Battlefield, p. 59.

[3] Officers learned to forbid men to leave the field of battle to carry off the wounded (O. W. R., Ser. I, IX, 71).

[4] Ibid., Ser. I, XI, pt. III, 322.

[5] One bit of such testimony comes from the side of the enemy. A Confederate major writes: "Some of the enemy were scattered around the town and when they heard firing, made good their escape" (ibid., Ser. I, XXI, 692).

[6] Ibid., Ser. I, XX, pt. II, 49.

larger than color-guards, though they later resumed almost full strength.[1] It is not at all unusual to read of thousands of stragglers after a battle, or of the whole country being overrun by renegades. In 1862 some 20,000 stragglers from Pope's army were reported scattered between Centreville and Alexandria in northern Virginia; the country near Chattanooga was said to be filled with 5,000 stragglers.[2] The cavalrymen were particularly troublesome and a general nuisance to the citizens because of their greater freedom as they lounged about the villages and drinking places, since depredation went hand in hand with straggling.[3]

Remedial measures began to be taken in the spring of 1862 by general orders to brigade commanders, by orders from the War Department, and by efforts to collect the men. But, unfortunately, straggling did not disappear with the progress of the war; indeed, one commander reported it in 1864 as increasing in Louisiana and threatening serious consequences to the army. Even in Virginia after the Battle of Cold Harbor in June, 1864, 4,000 missing were coolly regarded merely as missing stragglers who would come in; and 850 stragglers were collected and brought in to be put to work in the trenches.[4]

There was, however, considerable deliberate desertion from the ranks while being moved from one point to another. This tendency was greatly increased if troops were ordered to march to a point of unusual danger or to a section of the country which they did not wish to visit. Laxness in discipline on the part of company officers greatly facilitated such escape, naturally. One officer was irritated into writing that he found too many company officers who were totally unconcerned as to whether their men marched in ranks or went along the road "like a flock of geese." [5] The opportunities were not far to seek: bridges, where ranks were perforce broken, and transference from distribution camps, due to the lack of the required number of officers and guards.[6] A striking example can

---

[1] Schurz, *Reminiscences,* II, 354.

[2] *O. W. R.,* Ser. I, XXX, pt. III, 805; XII, pt. III, 773, 798. See also *ibid.,* Ser. I, XII, pt. III, 791; XLI, pt. IV, 472; XIX, pt. I, 319, 335.

[3] *Ibid.,* Ser. I, VII, 8–9.

[4] *Ibid.,* Ser. I, XIX, pt. II, 319; XXXIV, pt. IV, 187–188; XLII, pt. III, 877.

[5] *Ibid.,* Ser. I, XVII, pt. I, 183. A large number of the First Kentucky cavalry refused to go into the mountains, while many who started, deserted en route (*ibid.,* Ser. I, VII, 32).

[6] *Ibid.,* Ser. III, III, 693; Ser. I, XXXIV, pt. I, 103.

be cited where a group of 800 men sent to Harper's Ferry in charge of *one* officer, lost 132 men en route and were turned over to an insufficient guard. One officer complained bitterly that the "object of officers in charge of camps of distribution seems to be to get rid of men in as large numbers as possible. They arrive here generally in the night and without sufficient officers to take care of them. All who wish to get away." [1] It was indeed heyday for bounty-jumpers. Usually there was some leakage on railroads and steamers.

Cavalry men could effect their escape more easily than men of the infantry. On one occasion a company, pitching camp just at dark, unsaddled the horses and scattered to cut corn, without posting a guard. About 100 men escaped, including one company which had not yet unsaddled their horses. [2]

Once in camp, or at the front, the most favorable opportunity for taking French leave was from the picket line, preferably, of course, at night, though occasionally early in the morning. The phrase occurs sufficiently often to have been disturbing to the government: "Two men [one man, or ten men, as the case might be] deserted from the picket-line last night to the enemy." The favorite time with the Northern picket for slipping over to the enemy's line was during the first tour of the picket-duty, in order to afford him the maximum time possible for effecting his escape. [3]

Charles Francis Adams tells of how two new recruits were posted at an important point on the extreme front of the Union line. Their failure to return was generously interpreted as capture by the enemy until their horses were found several days later tied to a tree near their posts, one already dead of starvation, the other too weakened to recover, whereupon the disappearance of the recruits was ascribed to the proper cause. [4] Frequently the escape was rendered possible by the connivance of the pickets posted on each side of the criminal. If the plan was not escape to the enemy, once through their own lines they often boldly borrowed horses from plantations in the

[1] *O. W. R.*, Ser. I, XLIII, pt. II, 189.

[2] *Ibid.*, Ser. I, XVII, pt. I, 143–144.

[3] *Ibid.*, Ser. I, XLII, pt. II, 28; pt. III, 733, 1056. *Battles and Leaders of the Civil War*, IV, 93. Ellis tells an amusing tale of how a Union soldier swam the Rapidan to talk with the boys in gray (*Camp-fires of General Lee*, 335–336). For other instances of fraternization see von Borcke, *Memoirs of the Confederate War for Independence*, p. 75; Wise, *End of an Era* pp. 348–349; Goss, *Recollections of a Private*, p. 329.

[4] *O. W. R.*, Ser. I, II, 115. *A Cycle of Adams Letters*, I, 247–248.

vicinity, in order to reach some section of the North where they would be safe.¹

Some statistics concerning a detachment of 625 recruits sent to reinforce a New Hampshire regiment in the Army of the Potomac, shed some light on the relative ease of escape by various methods; 137 deserted on the passage, eight-two to the enemy from the picket line, and but thirty-six to the rear.²

Escape was also effected under veil of some disguise or other. Hiding in a sutler's wagon, pretending to be a teamster, and posing as a telegraph repairer, were devices which sometimes worked.³ Citizen clothes were, naturally, at a premium. Friends and relatives abetted the would-be deserters by sending packages containing such clothing, to the army under the name of provisions. The matter was brought conspicuously to the attention of an officer of the One Hundred and Thirty-second Pennsylvania Volunteers by an anonymous note from a Pennsylvania town, warning him that citizen clothes were being mailed to soldiers. He immediately had the mails searched and detected two packages of clothing, one accompanied by a letter of advice from a relative, revealing clearly the object for which the clothing was intended. Failing such accommodating relatives, the soldiers often exchanged their uniforms for civilian clothing, probably of inferior quality, or bought them in the vicinity of the camp, before or after escape, from inhabitants, who, driven by want or by the threats of the deserters, became accomplices of their flight.⁴ One disguise, revealed by its failure, may have often proved successful. A soldier, deserting from an Ohio Regiment in Tennessee in female attire, was detected by the conductor on the Covington and Lexington Railroad after he reached Kentucky.⁵ Escape by means of forged passes and false paroles, secured from citizens, falls into the category of escape under false pretenses.

¹ *O. W. R.*, Ser. I, XXXIV, pt. II, 118.
² *American Annual Cyclopedia*, 1864, p. 37.
³ Hooker had an order issued on February 18, 1863, which declared: "No sutler's wagons, teamsters, nor passage of any kind through our lines in that direction will be allowed, and all persons representing themselves to be telegraph repairers must be furnished with the most undoubted authority upon the subject."—*Ibid.*, Ser. I, XXV, pt. II, 86.
⁴ Comte de Paris, *History of the Civil War in America*, II, 600; III, 3. *O. W. R.*, Ser. I, XXXIV, pt. II, 233; XXV, pt. II, 73; XLIX, pt. II, 293. One officer was of the opinion that many had been assisted in their escape by the government mails.
⁵ *Louisville Daily Democrat*, January 14, 1863.

Once outside the Federal lines, the adherents of the Confederacy, actuated by various motives, aided the escape. The importance of this aid was recognized by the rebel authorities who directed citizens to afford every facility to the Northern renegades. Sometimes the chief use of boats and dugouts was to carry deserters across rivers.[1] A ready market for the Federal uniform was found among Confederate soldiers, willing to exchange the tattered gray even for the blue to hide their nakedness.

Zeal on the part of the soldiers to devise ways of escape promptly led to zeal on the part of the authorities to prevent possibility of escape. On June 12, 1862, an order issued directly from the War Office declaring that a furlough from a captain or colonel, granted on any pretext whatever, would not relieve a soldier from the charge of desertion. All the methods to anticipate and circumvent the wiles of the soldier, with which the reader is already familiar from the tricks of the Confederate soldier, occurred in the Northern army.[2] Hooker established a system of regular furloughs in 1863, securing to the most meritorious an opportunity for revisiting their families for a few days at a season when military operations were impossible. This greatly ameliorated the situation. Great strictness with regard to passes for leaving camp, or even for going from the front to the rear of the army, was exercised by commanders;[3] medical officers were enjoined to practise severity in passing upon cases of sickness and to provide prompt care for the disabled; roll-calls were heard with burdensome frequency, as often as every hour until tattoo in one command as early as March, 1862.[4] Even when on the march at least three roll-calls a day were prescribed. Company and regimental commanders were required to march opposite the rear of their respective commands; the commanders of rear guards were ordered to arrest all stragglers and to report them for punishment, using their bayonets freely, and, if necessary, their guns; provost marshals, who were provided, together with a suitable guard, for every corps,

---

[1] O. W. R., Ser. I, XLII, pt. III, 526, 1038; XXXV, pt. II, 273. Occasionally a family living near the Union camp became suspect and was closely watched.

[2] Ibid., Ser. III, II, 146.

[3] Ibid., Ser. I, XIX, pt. II, 509. In one division only two passes were allowed to a company (ibid., p. 477). See also ibid., Ser. I, XLIII, pt. II, 35.

[4] Ibid., Ser. I, XVI, pt. II, 26; XVII, pt. II, 321. In March, 1862, one general ordered roll-call every hour until tattoo "to insure that all remain with their regimental and company lines" (ibid., Ser. I, XI, pt. III, 51–52). In the Army of the Cumberland in November, 1862, roll-calls were held at reveille, dinner, retreat, and tattoo (ibid., Ser. I, XX, pt. II, 108).

division, and brigade after December, 1862, followed up and flanked the march of the column with cavalry to drive up loiterers; courier stations were instructed to pick up stragglers to be sent to the nearest post; during action provost marshals were often placed to the rear of their respective corps, out of range but within sight of the field, in order to force the return of stragglers and skulkers to their regiments; halts were to be made on open ground; and camp guards were to be established before the troops stacked arms. Every soldier having permission to leave the ranks while on the march, was required in one command to leave his musket, haversack, and knapsack to be carried by the soldiers of his company until his return.[1] By 1864 vedettes and pickets were being instructed to shoot any man crossing the outer line of vedettes at night, if they could not apprehend him, and no men were allowed to pass the picket-line in the daytime unless by permission of an officer of the picket who was responsible for his return.[2] Responsibility for their pickets was squarely placed on the superior officers, who were often arrested for neglect of duty.[3]

A further effort to check desertion by preventing it took the form of special inducements to the soldiers to catch the men attempting it by offering the former furloughs with expenses defrayed and recommendations for promotions. "Do this as a solemn duty to your country and our cause," one commander urged, "and you shall be rewarded by a furlough and a recommendation for promotion."[4]

As the draft was applied, the government learned to have the provost marshals collect and guard the victims of the draft and the bounty men at the several places of rendezvous, like veritable prisoners and the criminals they often were, so as to prevent their untimely departure. Escapes, which were so easy at first as to make bounty-jumping a most lucrative business venture, became one of the hazardous trades at the close. And yet, so determined were they never to face the enemy's guns, that some of them would make the attempt after they had seen their comrades actually shot as they broke from the ranks while being marched from the station to the

---

[1] *Ibid.,* Ser. I, XLII, pt. II, 516; XXI, 985; XLI, pt. IV, 455; XXXVI, pt. III, 135; XLIII, pt. II, 150; XIX, pt. II, 226–227.

[2] *Ibid.,* Ser. I, XLII, pt. III, 568–569, 580, 1049–1050; XL, pt. II, 594.

[3] *Ibid.,* Ser. I, XLII, pt. III, 569, 625.

[4] *Ibid.,* p. 623. Another offer held forth a furlough of twenty days with money to defray expenses to the soldier's home (*ibid.,* p. 692); another, a month's furlough and $30.00 (*ibid.,* pp. 1049–1050).

wharf at some terminal.[1] Officials learned to send detachments on railroads and steamship lines under charge of an officer, and to prefer the water as a means of transportation south for recruits from Boston, New York, Philadelphia, or even Baltimore.[2] They also learned to station dependable troops with companies which were unreliable, in order to counteract the poison at work.[3] The Adams Express Company was notified of restrictions placed on packages for soldiers: clothing and liquors were prohibited, though no objection was raised to "underclothing, mittens, or other little articles." [4]

The leakage due to convalescents, discharged from hospitals, who never reported at camp was stopped by sending them forward under reliable officers to superintend their muster and embarkation when they were reported by the surgeons fit for duty. They were transferred to hospitals in the North, if it seemed advisable, in parties but not allowed to go individually, while great care was used to keep them constantly under military control and with men of their own companies.

The measures to provide for the support of the families of enlisted men, very noticeable in New England, was a step of prevention.

---

[1] For interesting and dramatic stories of how these men were guarded see Wilkeson, *Recollections of a Private Soldier*, pp. 12–13.

[2] *O. W. R.*, Ser. III, II, 739–740; Ser. I, XIX, pt. II, 509.

[3] *Ibid.*, Ser. I, XXV, pt. II, 149–150.

[4] *Ibid.*, p. 73.

CHAPTER XII

Union Remedies for Desertion

In an Anglo-Saxon state the logical starting point in the discussion of the cure for an ill in the body politic seems to be the law. And so we shall notice first the Military Code which was in effect at the outbreak of the war, the same which had been passed when the republic was an infant in 1806. Despite the common popular impression that the penalty of desertion is death, Article 20 of the Military Code provided that "all officers and soldiers who have received pay, or have been duly enlisted in the service of the United States, and shall be convicted of having deserted the same, shall suffer death, or such other punishment as, by sentence of a court-martial, shall be inflicted." [1] The law was explicit that no sentence of death for this offense should be executed until approved by the president. This provision was altered in the session of 1862–1863 by amendment of the militia law of July, 1862, by repealing the provision which required the approval of the president to execute the sentence of a court-martial against any person convicted as a spy or deserter, so that thereafter only the approval of the commanding general was required. In addition, the offenders forfeited all pay and allowances due at the time of desertion. But many delays and a vast increase of the problem had been necessary before Congress was brought in March, 1863, to so amend the law. [2] And it must be recalled that there always existed the presidential power of pardon after a trial had condemned a deserter.

The law on the subject of reward for apprehension of deserters must also be noted. Prior to April, 1861, the Army Regulations authorized payment of $30 for the arrest and delivery of a deserter to an officer of the army at the most convenient post or recruiting station. It was made the duty of every officer to arrest deserters,

[1] *Articles of War*, sec. 57. Passed by 9th Cong., 1st sess., April 10, 1806. It is interesting that the penalty for plundering was death, without exception.
[2] *Statutes of the United States*, 1862–1863, chap. 75, sec. 21, 26.

but the duty did not appertain specifically to any class of officers.[1] This clause was modified in September, 1861, so as to substitute $5 for $30 as the amount to be paid in such cases.[2] This reward was interpreted to include the remuneration for all expenses incurred for apprehending, securing, and delivering the delinquent.[3] The reward, as a provost pointed out, was entirely inadequate, with the result that a sufficient number of the right kind of men could not be found to enlist in the business of deserter hunting.[4]

There remains only to notice the penalties imposed by the law for aiding desertion. The early military law of 1806 treated the offense by a soldier or officer exactly as if he were himself deserting. But a civilian who enticed a soldier from his duty was subject to a fine of $300 or imprisonment for one year.[5] When the matter proved during the war a menacing evil, Congress raised the penalty for harboring or aiding deserters to $500 *and* imprisonment for a period ranging from six months to two years.[6] In the very closing months of the war steps were taken to make even more stringent the laws and rules on the subject. On February 8, 1865, the adjutant-general issued a revision of Section 158 of the Army Regulations to the effect that deserters must make good the time lost by desertion, unless discharged by competent authority.[7] The last act on the subject during the war, that of March 3, 1865, provided in addition to the other penalties, that all deserters failing to return within sixty days should lose their rights of citizenship and be disqualified from ever holding office. This law made the original party, if he had furnished a substitute, immediately liable for service for the unexpired period if that substitute deserted with the knowledge or aid of the original. This act furthermore provided in Section 18 that any officer who knowingly mustered into the service a deserter should be dishonorably discharged.[8]

The proportions which desertions reached in the Union army may be directly due, as Provost Marshal General Fry charged, to

[1] *Army Regulations,* par. 152 (edition of 1861). *O. W. R.,* Ser. III, V, 676.

[2] *Ibid.,* Ser. III, I, 488.

[3] *Ibid.,* Ser. III, II, 924. *Revised Army Regulations,* 1861, sec. 156.

[4] *O. W. R.,* Ser. III, V, 834. For another opinion see *ibid.,* Ser. III, V, 858.

[5] *Military Laws* of 1806, pp. 116, 179.

[6] Act No. 54, sec. 24, of Congress, approved March 3, 1863.

[7] *O. W. R.,* Ser. III, IV, 1155–1156. *Revised Army Regulations,* Art. XLIII, sec. 158.

[8] *Statutes of the United States,* chap. 79, session of 1864–1865, sec. 20, 21. *O. W. R.,* Ser. III, IV, 1225.

the leniency with which it was treated in the beginning.[1] The authorities at Washington evidently felt it impolitic to pursue too drastic a policy when they were first made aware of the dimensions of the evil.

Effective steps to deal with desertion among officers came much more promptly than among enlisted men. As early as June 7, 1862, General Orders No. 61, emanating from the War Office, restricted the granting of leaves of absence to the Secretary of War, according to General War Regulations, except under medical certificate when life would be endangered by continued presence in camp, under which contingency a commander of an army, department, or district could grant a leave of twenty days; it also ordered all officers, except those paroled, to their posts within fifteen days.[2] By November of that year the evil was being abated by summary dismissal of officers for this offense "without honor and without pay."[3] More than any one preceding him, General Hooker, who was placed in command of the Army of the Potomac in January, 1863, brought the officers to a sense of their duty and of the respect due their chiefs by a few sharp examples.[4] General Pope's ironical offer of five cents for the apprehension of absentee officers in August, 1862, had been intended undoubtedly to have a wholesome effect on the crowds swarming about the hotel bars in Washington, Baltimore, and New York.[5] The commander-in-chief, in order definitely to check the bad example of dereliction of duty by officers, instructed courts-martial in all parts of the country in 1863, in accordance with the Conscription Act which had been passed in March of that year, that they had power to sentence absentee officers to be reduced to the ranks to serve three years or for the period of the war.[6]

There had been set up in 1862 two examining boards, one at Annapolis and one at Cincinnati, to inquire into cases of absence from duty by officers with the effect by 1864 of diminishing the

---

[1] He states in his final report, "There can be no cause so just or so beloved that war in its behalf will not be attended by desertion among its defenders. The extent of the evil is governed by circumstances, but it is always directly affected by the relative leniency or severity with which the crime is treated." —*Ibid.*, Ser. III, V, 676.

[2] *Ibid.*, Ser. III, II, 112.

[3] *Ibid.*, Ser. I, XIX, pt. 1, 6; Ser. III, II, 935.

[4] Comte de Paris, *History of the Civil War in America*, III, 4.

[5] *Chicago Tribune*, July 28, 1862.

[6] Statement of General Halleck. See also *American Annual Cyclopedia*, 1863, p. 25; *Daily Illinois State Journal*, January 8, 1863.

number of cases of absence without leave from an average of 150 to about thirty-three a month.[1]

On June 12, 1862, the government took its first tentative step toward recognizing desertion among privates. An order from the adjutant general's office directed each military commander to publish three times in some newspaper a notice requiring all soldiers who were physically able to report to their regiments without delay on penalty of being considered deserters.[2] The final date permissible varied, naturally, with the commands: Rosecrans set July 10; Sherman, August 11. It did not conceal the outstanding fact of clemency and laxness that General Buell tried to camouflage his offer of pardon as a command to all men absent without direct authority from his headquarters to rejoin their regiments by July 10, 1862, or to account satisfactorily for themselves on pain of being reported as deserters.[3] This action was followed shortly by an order from the War Department under the direction of the president that all leaves of absence and furloughs, unless granted by the War Department, be revoked to end on August 11, 1862; and that all officers, on pain of dismissal or court-martial sentence, and all privates rejoin their regiments for a general muster to be held on August 18.[4] Officers were peremptorily ordered to their commands on September 15, 1862, by order emanating from Washington.

The War Department made a brave show of preserving a firm attitude, for when Secretary Stanton was besought to hold out the olive branch to some deserters in Canada, he replied on September 8, 1862, that it had been a rule rarely departed from to make no terms with deserters, though clemency was often extended to them if they surrendered unconditionally. "The crime is too serious in its consequences to be made light of even for the sake of securing the return to the ranks of a few effective men." [5]

The hope of restoring to the service much of its proper material

[1] *American Annual Cyclopedia,* 1864, p. 37.
[2] *O. W. R.,* Ser. III, II, 146. Gen. Orders No. 65.
[3] *Battles and Leaders of the Civil War,* III, 32.
[4] Gen. Orders No. 92. *O. W. R.,* Ser. III, II, 286–287. In order to comply with the spirit of the general muster, Sherman felt obliged to announce that all soldiers reported as deserters on the muster-rolls of his army on June 30, 1862, were declared pardoned and those only who were absent on August 18 would be held deserters (*ibid.,* Ser. I, XVII, pt. II, 166).
[5] *Ibid.,* Ser. III, II, 527. And in August, 1864, he withheld approval of a pardon by General Couch in connection with the desertion from the draft in Pennsylvania (*ibid.,* Ser. I, XLIII, pt. I, 840).

and of discouraging desertion inspired, doubtless, the insertion of a special clause in the Conscription Act upon which the president based his proclamation of March 10, 1863, which declared that all soldiers improperly absent who would report at certain designated rendezvous by the first day of April, would be restored to their respective regiments without punishment, except forfeiture of pay and allowances for the period of their absence, but that all failing to comply with the order would be punished as deserters. He also called upon all patriotic citizens to aid in restoring soldiers to their proper posts and to aid in the punishment of offenders, thus helping the government and all faithful soldiers.[1]

The clemency was probably more conspicuous and pernicious in the neglect to inflict punishment upon individual deserters when they were returned to their companies. It was represented by the provost in the St. Louis district as a common practice to return deserters to the service of the flag which they had dishonored with scarcely an admonition, let alone a trial as required by the regulations.[2] When the number of deserters so casually restored reached hundreds, and the number of stragglers, semi-deserters, reached thousands, the effect on the morale of the army may be easily understood. The use of stragglers as cooks and nurses in the depot hospitals by the surgeons could scarcely be designated as anything except winking at the evil.[3] Officers were not held responsible for the ill as military usage prescribed. A certain lieutenant-colonel, after being placed under arrest for the absence of thirty men from his regiment for two days, was restored to duty without the formality of a trial.[4] Prominent citizens abetted the crime, when they secured, as did Governor Morton of Indiana, a furlough of ten days for a brigade which had stampeded from Camp Chase and had returned to their homes in Indiana.[5]

A second instance of general governmental clemency was afforded in February, 1864, by President Lincoln's order that sentences of deserters, who had been condemned to death by court-martial, be

---

[1] *Statutes of the United States,* 1863, chap. LXXV, sec. 26. It is noticeable that this course was urged by Governor Todd of Ohio (*O. W. R.,* Ser. III, III, 59). Deserters were not exempt from making up the time lost.

[2] *Ibid.,* Ser. I, XXII, pt. II, 77. Complained of also by the provost marshal of Illinois (*ibid.,* Ser. III, V, 833–834).

[3] *Ibid.,* Ser. I, XXXVI, pt. I, 258.

[4] *Ibid.,* Ser. I, XXX, pt. III, 76 (note).

[5] *Ibid.,* Ser. I, XXIII, pt. II, 390.

mitigated to imprisonment for the duration of the War at Dry Tortugas, Florida. The commanding generals were further empowered in special cases to return to duty deserters whose restoration would, in their judgment, benefit the service. The penalty was later amended to include, in addition to imprisonment for the period of the war, discharge from the service of the United States together with forfeiture of pay and allowances.[1]

In addition to these acts of general clemency, the tender-hearted president pardoned numbers of those deserting from hospitals or failing to return from furloughs, several thousand of whom had taken refuge in British provinces, upon their expressing contrition and a desire to return to duty.[2] Limited pardons, effective only within the boundaries of their commands, were granted by individual generals in a few cases. General Foster, for instance, granted one for the Department of the South in 1864, and such a martinet as Governor Andrew Johnson sponsored and secured from General Thomas a pardon for the Fourth Cavalry of the Army of the Cumberland.[3]

Yet once more, just as the Confederates in their hoplessness of stopping desertion by severity turned to another general amnesty, so the United States authorities felt obliged to try a second general pardon, though it is conspicuous that initiative for both the proclamations of President Lincoln, that of 1865 and that of 1863, seemed to come from Congress. The clemency differs further in the two sections in that the Union proclamations maintained a better degree of dignity, as they were coupled with threats of greater severity, which there was some pretense of enforcing. On March 11, 1865, Lincoln issued his second warning and promise in order to discharge the duty laid upon him by Congress. All persons who had deserted the service or who had left the United States to avoid such service, were ordered to report within sixty days, by May 10, 1865, on pain of forfeiting their rights of citizenship, including the right to hold office, but all who should return to their companies and duty and who served for a period equal to their original term of enlistment, would be pardoned. The proclamation was extensively published, while constant attention was called to its provisions by editorials and comments.[4] It is indicative of the disposition abroad in the

---

[1] Gen. Orders, No. 76. *O. W. R.*, Ser. III, IV, 137, 418. It related only to desertion and not to other crimes.

[2] *American Annual Cyclopedia*, 1864, p. 37.

[3] *O. W. R.*, Ser. III, IV, 621; Ser. I, XXXIX, pt. II, 325.

[4] *Ibid.*, Ser. I, XLVI, pt. II, 926–927; Ser. III, V, 755.

country for clemency that Governor Andrew of Massachusetts urged upon Lincoln extension of the pardon to those who had been convicted and were already undergoing punishment or were then awaiting trial for desertion as a necessary act of justice and a wise measure to secure valuable men to the service.[1]

The early methods to check and control desertion practised by the Union authorities and military men were the obvious ones, dictated by a body of overworked, harassed officials who felt that they were too pressed by all the other problems of winning a war to accord thought to this minor question. It was much like guarding the entrance to a hall while refusing to look steadily at the exit.

The devices of guards and patrols are so similar to those resorted to by the Confederacy that this phase of the subject can be dismissed with a word. Guards were placed, naturally, at the railroad stations, at ferries, and at bridges, especially over the Potomac, and in winter at points on the rivers where the ice would bear a man's weight; patrols were sent out frequently through cities where soldiers were likely to be found and to public houses with orders to arrest all soldiers found without passes. River banks between pickets and roads in the vicinity of Washington were closely patroled and all travelers examined.[2] Rafts, flats, boats of every kind, except at authorized crossings, were destroyed.

Scouting parties, mounted and unmounted, were sent out to scour the woods and hills of the country in the vicinity of the camps, or where an army had recently passed, for stragglers and deserters. It was recognized that they should be detected at military posts in the South before they reached and were lost on the public lines of travel. Small parties were dispatched to the Northern States to search for and return deserters who were brazenly or furtively staying at their own homes, while general warfare was conducted against the deserter bands in the border country, regardless of which side they had abandoned.[3]

---

[1] *Ibid.*, Ser. III, IV, 1249–1251.

[2] *Ibid.*, Ser. I, XVI, pt. II, 115; XLVI, pt. II, 143, 292. General Hooker was alert to the small boats carrying deserters across the Potomac above and below Aquia Creek (*ibid.*, Ser. I, XXV, pt. II, 36). One patrol was suggested in 1864 for Maryland all the way from Port Tobacco to the Patuxent River to catch the men landing below, should attempt be made to make their way up the peninsula (*ibid.*, Ser. I, XLIII, pt. II, 43, 63).

[3] *Ibid.*, Ser. I, XXIII, pt. II, 111; XVIII, 552, XLI, pt. I, 242. Parties varied from three to 200 and more (*ibid.*, Ser. I, XXII, pt. II, 249; XXXI pt. III, 248).

The United States was especially stupid in its handling of pecuniary rewards offered as an inducement to apprehend deserters. In view of the fact that desertions became frequent even during 1861 it would seem that the proper step would have been an increase of the reward from $30, instead of its reduction to $5, as was done on September 7, 1861, this paltry sum also to cover expenses of apprehension and delivery. This economy proved in the end expensive, as it was prohibitory to action. On July 16, 1863, the reward was increased by an order from the adjutant-general's office to $10, which sum was finally in the following September restored to $30 for the remainder of the war. This sum included all expenses.[1] Special inducements were held out to the soldiers by various commanders to aid in detecting and apprehending their cowardly fellows, such as the boon of a thirty-day furlough or a money reward—$30 was frequent—or both.[2]

Civilian aid was early invoked, though perhaps to little purpose. Government agents, especially Federal officials, were expected as early as July, 1862, to assist in curbing desertion to the extent of their ability; boards of enrollment, marshals, mayors, and chiefs of police of towns, sheriffs, constables, postmasters and justices of the peace were authorized to act as special provost marshals to arrest officers or privates absent without cause and to conduct them to the nearest post.[3] At the same time an appeal was sent out to the governors for their vigorous coöperation in searching out the absentees, the adjutant general contenting himself with merely suggesting a system of committees of the reliable and influential citizens of the State to aid in the work.[4] General Foster, located in enemy country in South Carolina, demanded that plantation owners or superintendents and all other civilians arrest and deliver to the nearest military post all deserters on their lands or reveal their presence. Detectives even occasionally lent a hand.[5]

In April, 1862, the first organized attempt to arrest and punish the deserters from the volunteer forces was made by laying the duty of collecting stragglers and deserters on the military commanders of cities, no effort yet being directed toward country districts.

---

[1] *O. W. R.*, Ser., III, V, 676, 752, 753.
[2] *Ibid.*, Ser. I, XLII, pt. III, 1086.
[3] *Ibid.*, Ser. III, II, 286–287; IV, 999.
[4] *Ibid.*, Ser. III, II, 247–248.
[5] *Ibid.*, Ser. III, IV, 621. *The Detroit Free Press,* May 4, 1863.

Very little improvement resulted, because of the limited authority and means of these officials.

The first definite step toward facing squarely the growing evil of desertion was taken by Secretary Stanton on September 24, 1862, when he created the office of provost marshal general to improve the discipline of both the regular and volunteer armies. The appointment of Simon Draper to have supervision and control of the work, to be assisted by one or more special provost marshals in each State, followed on October 1. It was, among other tasks, made the duty of the special provost marshals to arrest all deserters and spies and to send them to the nearest military commander. To perform their duties, they were to call upon any available military force at hand, or to employ the assistance of citizens, constables, sheriffs, or police officers.[1] Although Draper formulated a rather elaborate plan, and though he made some arrests,[2] the abuse was not removed. February 9, 1863, General Buckingham, requested by Stanton to report on the bureau, attributed its failure to the insufficiency of special provost marshals and the uncertainty of the compensation of those officers.[3]

The enrollment act of March 3, 1863, laid the foundation of a system for really attacking the evil. It was made the duty of the provost marshal general in Washington to ascertain and communicate to a provost marshal in each Congressional district such facts concerning the desertion of the men from that area as would be likely to facilitate their arrest. The law required the provost marshals to locate, arrest, and return deserters,[4] and authorized the former to call upon military commanders for aid. The Provost Marshal General's Bureau also had imposed on it the task of enrolling the national forces for draft and the enlistment of volunteers.

Commanders of regiments, battalions, and independent companies,

---

[1] See Gen. Orders, No. 140. *O. W. R.,* Ser. III, II, 937. It should be understood that on July 31, Secretary Stanton had made Simon Draper a commissioner of the War Department with an office in Washington to execute Order No. 92 for the return of absentees (*ibid.,* p. 294). He immediately visited New Hampshire, Massachusetts, and various other eastern States to make arrangements with the governors, military officers, and some special provost marshals appointed by Stanton for the arrest of deserters (*American Annual Cyclopedia,* 1862, p. 21, *O. W. R.,* Ser. III, II, 936).

[2] *Ibid.,* pp. 936–940.

[3] *Ibid.,* Ser. III, III, 37–38.

[4] *Ibid.,* Ser. III, V, 676. All the essentials of the organization were approved by Stanton. Draper became a provost in New York.

surgeons in charge of hospitals, and all officers in control of detached parties were required by an order of the 24th of March, 1863, to report on the last day of every month on a blank to the provost marshal general the names of all deserters from their commands who had not already been reported. This descriptive list set forth the place of residence, amount of bounty, date of desertion, birth, occupation, supposed whereabouts, date of last pay, and all data calculated to help in securing the arrest. The commanders were also to furnish supporting military force.[1]

There followed very shortly, on March 17, 1863, the appointment as head of the Provost Marshal General's Bureau of Colonel James B. Fry, who stayed in this post through the remainder of the period 1863, who remained in this post through the remainder of the period of the war. He immediately took hold of the work aggressively, working out an elaborate system for the bureau, which he organized into seven branches, with the third of which only, that of *Deserters, Arrest, Descriptive Lists, etc.,* we are concerned, extending its network of provosts, deputies, and agents into the towns and counties of all the loyal States.[2]

The reports of deserters began to come into the office early in April; copies were sent to the provost marshal of the proper district. But great difficulty was experienced, as was to have been expected, with busy generals, in securing the reports—indeed the records were never complete and accurate. The force of clerks, which was necessarily large, twenty to thirty, for copying the numerous descriptive lists, was drawn largely from incapacitated soldiers detailed from the Veteran Reserve Corps.[3]

The method of work by a provost in a typical section might be presented. The devotion to duty of these men became, at times, almost as obnoxious as the red tape of the similar officials at Richmond. This zeal, added to the attractiveness of the bounty when it was raised to $30, naturally led to some improper arrests and to very detailed regulations. Every deserter, however arrested, must be delivered to the provost marshal of the district, who then examined

---

[1] *O. W. R.,* Ser. III, III, 84–85; Ser. I, II, 586. (Held over from Gen. Orders, No. 140 of September 24, 1862.)

[2] Sections 6, 7, 24, 26 of the act. For the regulations governing the bureau see *ibid.,* Ser. III, IV, 651–656.

[3] *Ibid.,* Ser. III, V, 751–752. A report from Illinois gives some hint of the enormous amount of clerical work involved: 13,977 lists were received; 20 copies of each were made for the provost marshals and assistants of the State (*ibid.,* pp. 809–810). The work in some sections was less efficient (see *ibid.,* Ser. III, IV, 993).

him, placed him in irons, and turned him over immediately to the commandant of the post with duplicate descriptive rolls, one of which was receipted by the latter and returned to be forwarded with the monthly report to the provost marshal general.[1] Safeguards had to be erected for the men who claimed to have been discharged or who had never enlisted nor been drafted, and for the government against false claims of rewards; and soldiers were cautioned to preserve about their persons their passes in order to avoid improper arrests.[2]

Considerable conflict of authority arose early in 1863 because of the issue by State courts of writs of habeas corpus, which fact led provost marshals in many instances to give up the deserters to the civil authorities, during which proceeding the deserters often escaped. This difficulty was adjusted by vesting the provost with the right to resist State interference by force after he had made due answer to the writ.[3] The provosts were held responsible for the arrest of all deserters in their districts, and for their safe custody until delivered over to the army. Hence it is little surprising to read of dozens of pairs of handcuffs and a strong guard-house as a part of the equipment of the provost's office.[4] Frequently they were sent to Camp Distribution, Alexandria, Virginia, to await escort to the front.

One of the most interesting arrests noted by the writer was one made in New York on March 10, 1865, and told in the following

---

[1] *Ibid.*, Ser. III, V, 858. Occasionally the provosts encountered real difficulties as when one had to deal with an organized band of deserters and draft-dodgers in Pennsylvania (*ibid.*, Ser. III, IV, 607, 620–621). Discussed in Chapter XIV.

[2] Naturally the expense incurred was great and so the government had to be careful that the men actually turned over were deserters, while on the other hand the reward, if bona fide, needed to be paid with as little delay as possible in order not to discourage the apprehension of deserters. When the reward was but $5 and expenses, the vouchers had to be carefully scrutinized, which involved the expense and delay of clerical labor to establish the proper amount allowable.

The decision was reached before long that so-called special agents should not be paid the reward of $30 unless they elected to relinquish their monthly pay, and to receive only the reward (*ibid.*, Ser. III, III, 995).

When requisition for transportation was issued to deputies or special agents sent in pursuit of deserters, that fact had to be entered on the stub of the requisition book, in order that the expense incurred might be charged to the deserter, if apprehended (*ibid.*, Ser. III, IV, 482).

[3] *Ibid.*, Ser. III, V, 752. As this suggestion was approved by Stanton, presumably it went into effect.

[4] *Ibid.*, Ser. I, XLII, III, 1087. Men were sometimes returned to the front, handcuffed and "strung on a chain." (*Daily Illinois State Journal*, January 8, 1863; *Soldiers' Letters*, p. 325.)

words: "I made my contemplated raid on the bounty-jumpers yesterday and succeeded in capturing 590 of the most desperate villains unhung. Most of them have enlisted and deserted from three to twenty times each. They are most all in irons and will go to the castle on Governor's Island today. I have been requested to pass them down Broadway in order that the people may have a sight of them. Is there any objection?" The reply of Mr. Fry was brief and pointed: "Do not march the deserters down Broadway, and do not iron them or any other men." [1]

The peak of activity in the bureau seems to have been reached in December, 1864, when twenty-five clerks and copyists were employed in Washington on the descriptive lists, on the deserters-arrested book, and on the letter books. At this time the desertions reported averaged about 6,000 a month while the arrests averaged only about 3,300 a month. Some conception of the amount of business transacted may be conveyed by stating that it required nineteen volumes to record the deserters arrested. [2]

The cost to the government for paying for provost marshals, agents, clerks, and transportation for the apprehension of deserters was very great. The item entered for the fiscal year ending June 30, 1864, was $157,031.21; for the year ending June, 1865, $450,020.16. In November, 1865, the amount reported as disbursed for incidental expenses alone by the Quartermaster General's Department for apprehension of deserters was $12,158.58. But the item in each case probably covers merely the rewards paid out for apprehension, for Draper explicitly estimated relatively early in the war the cost to the government of coping with the ill of desertion at over $10,000,000 up to the close of 1862. [3]

The provost marshal worked out a system of Veteran Reserve Corps to render service in connection with arresting and guarding deserters, in order to relieve the regular troops who would otherwise have been detailed for this duty. So great was the drain of the war on the able-bodied men of the Union that the government early utilized the services of men disabled or unfit for field duty, or elderly, discharged soldiers (over forty-five) about hospitals, camps, and forts in order to release the able-bodied for service at the front.

---

[1] *O. W. R.*, Ser. III, IV, 1231, 1232. Mr. Fry changed his mind on the question.
[2] *Ibid.*, Ser. III, V, 757. See Appendix, Table No. V.
[3] *Ibid.*, Ser. III, IV, 876; V, 252, 489; II, 940.

An embryonic organization into military detachments under the charge of officers was effected, but it remained for Mr. Fry shortly after he took office as the provost marshal general in April, 1863, to organize the partially disabled soldiers into an Invalid Corps to constitute a military police and garrison force. The corps by October, 1864, attained the very respectable size of twenty regiments with an aggregate of 28,738 men. Due to an absurd, if understandable, prejudice against the word *invalid,* which had led the men in the field to throw aspersions on a garrison organization, the name was changed in the spring of 1864 to Veteran Reserve Corps, a change which also permitted the enlistment of discharged soldiers, not incapacitated but no longer subject to the draft.

The services performed by the corps were various, but that which challenges attention for purposes of this study was in connection with the deserters. They arrested deserters from the draft and persons engaged in resisting it; they stood guard at camps of rendezvous to stop desertion at its source; they caught a large number of Federal deserters; they guarded these at various posts separately or with other prisoners; and they escorted soldiers of various classes, very often deserters, to the front. Their relation to desertion is indicated by the fact that one regiment forwarded 1,019 deserters; another arrested 100 deserters; another took 1,355 deserters and 3,062 stragglers to the front; one company guarded the military prison at Alexandria with a monthly average of 400 bounty-jumpers, a total of 2,900, with the admirable record of but three escapes. One of the most interesting regiments was the Fourteenth, which served at Camp Distribution, Virginia, where the daily number of recruits, conscripts, convalescents, and deserters awaiting escort to the front varied from 2,000 to 10,000. The officers of this regiment made sixty-seven trips in charge of convalescents, conscripts, and deserters, escorting in all 14,793 men with a total loss of but 325, a remarkable record considering the fact that thousands of the men were professional bounty-jumpers and desperate characters. The Sixteenth conducted a campaign of several months duration in the mountainous section of Pennsylvania where hundreds of deserters and recusants were arrested and where treasonable organizations of 500 to 600 persons were broken up. Especially noteworthy was its record of 2,810 deserters from regiments in the field and of 3,743 deserters from the draft captured and forwarded with but fifty-three escapes.

But even such an apparently honorable organization was not untouched by the common plague, as Fry records 2,538 losses from this corps from desertion.[1]

The worthwhileness of any effort or system must be tested by its results. Judged by this measuring-rod, the presidential pardons of 1863 and 1865 as a means to win men back to service were a failure. Some, but relatively few, returned to their posts. The proclamation of 1863 was followed by the return of from 12,000 to 15,000 men, but the indignation of their old comrades at their restoration without punishment was so great that it was later proposed not to return deserters to their old regiments.[2] The second promise of pardon, despite extensive publication, did not meet with the anticipated response, as only 1,755 deserters surrendered themselves, leaving 117,000 still at large.[3]

There is, of course, no way of estimating the number who returned voluntarily after periods of longer or shorter absence, though it is a well-known fact that numbers did so return.

There are no records to show just how many deserters were arrested by Draper as provost marshal from September 24, 1862, to April 1, 1863, when Fry took charge. The former himself claimed 3,000 as returned to their regiments in the eastern States; and judged that the number in the western States was probably as large.[4]

Fry thought he detected results almost immediately after the creation of his bureau, for he found that the number who deserted in September and October, 1863, was but one half as great as the number in May and June.[5] The number arrested and returned to the army after April 1, 1863, until the close of the war was 75,909, making an average of about 2,500 a month.[6] The same authority presents

[1] This brief account is based on the report to the provost marshal general (*O. W. R.*, Ser. III, V, 543–567) ; for total desertion see *House Ex. Doc.*, 39th Cong., 1st sess., No. 1, IV, pt. I, 234.

[2] *American Annual Cyclopedia*, 1863, p. 24. *Globe*, 38th Cong., *1st sess.* 1250.

[3] *O. W. R.*, Ser. III, V, 109.

[4] *Ibid.*, Ser. III, II, 939. His estimate for the West receives some corroboration from the fact that an officer reports nearly 2,600 deserters and stragglers arrested in Indiana within "the past few weeks" (*ibid.*, Ser. III, 19–20).

[5] *Ibid.*, p. 1052.

[6] The provost marshal general gives 76,526 (*ibid.*, Ser. III, V, 600), though the report of Dodge, who had this particular branch in charge, gives the figure quoted above. The writer prefers for that reason to accept the more conservative figure. The two officers also differ as to the monthly average, giving respectively 2,412 and 3,000. The loss in percentage was given as 24 per cent for the regular army, but 6 per cent for the volunteers (Fox, *Regimental Losses in the American Civil War*, p. 531). The figures also differ from Table No. V given in the Appendix.

a table which shows that of the deserters reported, 92,095 or nearly two fifths, deserted prior to April 1, 1863, or before the bureau properly began to function. Thus the claim that nearly two thirds as many deserters were arrested and returned to the service as deserted while the bureau was functioning seems justified.[1] If we allow 5,000 as a conservative estimate for those arrested by Draper, we arrive at about 81,000 as the total of recorded deserters, arrested and returned to the army, and when it is recalled that some of the absconders went over to the enemy, and more went to foreign ports, it may be fair to admit that not an enormous number remained at large in their home States, though the promptness with which they materialized in those communities after the close of the war argues a not too distant abiding place during the war.[2] But such results were not discreditable to the bureau. The period of highest monthly returns was September, 1863, when 5,002 men were arrested.[3] Throughout 1864 the number ran between 2,700 and 3,800 and even in 1865 it reached over 2,000.

Of course, not even relative accuracy is attainable, for there is no way to estimate the number who were recovered by the efforts of military officers and others prior to August, 1862, when Draper began his activity. It is interesting that of the deserters regained under Fry's régime, about 42 per cent were arrested by special officers, 33 per cent by citizens, while 25 per cent surrendered voluntarily, including those under the president's proclamation.[4] It is certainly a modest statement to assert that the bureau aided materially in restraining desertion by the prompt arrest of absentees, by their return to their regiments, and by charging the $30 reward for their apprehension against their pay.

For a long time the death penalty seems to have been practically abolished from the Northern army, and the activity of the provost marshals had in consequence little effect. Some of the generals of West Point training were by the winter of 1863 urging the inevitability of severity and the sad effect of long delays to secure presidential confirmation of the death sentence. Rosecrans, for one,

[1] *O. W. R.*, Ser. III, V, 677. One provost for the district of Missouri, Iowa, Minnesota, and Michigan attained the high rate of returning 40 per cent of the deserters reported to him (*ibid.*, p. 809).
[2] *Ibid.*, p. 111.
[3] *Ibid.*, p. 755. *House Ex. Doc.* 39th Cong., 1st sess., IV, No. 1, pt. I, 236. After dropping to about 2,000, it rose again in the fall of 1864 to 3,000.
[4] *O. W. R.*, Ser. III, V, 755.

begged the power of promptly executing sentence of death for this crime and power of sending details to arrest absentees. He was sternly reminded by Halleck of the law which required approval by the president and assured also of the former's disapproval of the sending of details into another department for deserters as unwise.[1] But Rosecrans pressed for the extreme rigor of the law from his courts-martial since "no adequate punishment had been heretofore inflicted" for the offense. As noted earlier, it became necessary to lodge the power of approving the death penalty with the commanding generals.

During the early years of the war the punishments were notoriously mild. A group of officers, including a lieutenant-colonel, for deserting their commands in the face of the enemy and for encouraging their men to desert, suffered no graver penalty than dismissal with loss of pay.[2] Loss of pay and bounties, to which were added the expenses of apprehension, as well as making up the time lost could hardly be expected to be efficacious as a deterrent.[3]

By the beginning of the year 1863 the officers were taking sharper measures against stragglers. One general asked if he might have them drummed out of the service, as court-martialing was too slow. Other generals were by 1864 ordering field officers to hold courts-martial in each regiment of their command with power of summary punishment to be inflicted in the presence of the command to which the culprit belonged. Such punishments as tying up, placarding, forcing men to ride a wooden horse, tying them behind a wagon during the march, in addition to the loss of six months' pay, were recommended by one general as within the province of such a court and sanctioned by usage.[4] Sometimes deserters were placed at hard labor

---

[1] In view of the rigor of later steps, it is curious to read Halleck's statement: "In regard to authorizing you to send officers and armed men into other departments than your own, to look up and arrest deserters, it is believed that such a measure would weaken rather than increase the numbers of your army, besides the risks of conflict between the civil authorities and indiscreet officers sent on that service. The results of sending such parties from the Army of the Potomac, to arrest deserters, have proved that the plan is not a good one."—O. W. R., Ser. I, XXIII, pt. II, 75.

[2] Ibid., Ser. I, XVII, pt. II, 586.

[3] Ibid., Ser. III, II, 924–925. Even after the war had ceased, deserters who had returned under the president's last pardon, were to be mustered out with forfeiture of pay and allowances (ibid., Ser. III, V, 4).

[4] Ibid., Ser. I, XXXVI, pt. II, 912; XLV, pt. II, 25. See Noyes, Bivouac and Battlefield (p. 52) for other punishments. Shaving one half of the head was also prescribed as a remedy for straggling (O. W. R., Ser. I, XX, pt. II, 89).

on the fortifications or in the trenches.[1] Despite the fact that flogging in the army had been abolished since August, 1861, the officers of the guard at a New York fort inflicted severe corporal punishment without awaiting formalities.[2]

The government had no compunctions about shooting or hanging deserters entering the service of the enemy if they fell again into Northern hands; or shooting those who persisted in the attempt at escape when caught in the act, or who resisted arrest.[3] But it was loath to come to the issue of the firing-squad at daybreak for attempted desertion. The question of making an example was seriously debated at a cabinet meeting on February 3, 1863, and a case, thought a strong one, was unanimously assented to as a necessity to check the rapidly increasing evil.[4] It was by prompt approval and execution of the death sentence in the presence of the troops that General Hooker, temporarily at least, repressed desertion.[5] And now examples began to be made in Meade's and in Sheridan's armies, as the only method to deter others from following a bad example.[6] Meade recounts a most significant remark made by a number of his men after witnessing the execution of five deserters, "Why did they not begin this practise long ago?" Not a murmur was heard against the propriety, as they knew that their own security would so be enhanced.[7] A gallows and shooting-ground were provided in each corps and scarcely a Friday passed during the winter of 1863–1864 that some wretched deserter did not suffer the death penalty in the Army of the Potomac. During the latter part of 1864 the death penalty was

[1] *Ibid.*, Ser. I, XXXIV, pt. IV, 188; XIX, pt. II, 376, 509.

[2] *Ibid.*, Ser. I, XLIII, pt. II, 613. Probably an isolated instance.

[3] *Ibid.*, Ser. II, V, 673; Ser. I, XLII, pt. III, 121. *Louisville Daily Democrat*, May 20, 1862. *O. W. R.* Ser. I, XLI, pt. II, 459. *Boston Daily Evening Transcript*, January 10, 1865.

[4] *Diary of Gideon Welles*, I, 232. Welles did not himself regard it as an aggravated case. The president a little later wrote Meade that he desired to consult him on that subject (*Life and Letters*, II, 164).

[5] Comte de Paris, *op. cit.*, III, 4.

[6] *O. W. R.*, Ser. I, XXIX, pt. II, 102. Sheridan, *Personal Memoirs*, I, 301–302. Sheridan's comment after an execution in the presence of the whole division shows that it had not yet become common in his army at least. "It was the saddest spectacle I ever witnessed, but there could be no evasion, no mitigation of the full letter of the law; its timely enforcement was but justice to the brave spirits who had yet to fight the rebellion to the end." (November 12, 1863.) Meade, however, remitted a sentence to imprisonment at the Dry Tortugas for a bounty-jumper, a Frenchman (Meade, *op. cit.*, p. 235). Schurz secured a pardon for one of his lads (*Reminiscences*, III, 47–49).

[7] *Life and Letters of General Meade*, II, 146.

so unsparingly used that executions were of almost daily occurrence in most of the armies.[1] In May of that year Secretary Stanton sharply ordered that deserters from the Army of the Potomac be at once brought before a drum-head court-martial and executed, if found guilty. He made short shrift of the practice of officers who enticed recruits from another battalion to enlist them in their own— an evil which assumed such menacing proportions in the South.[2]

The melancholy details of an execution in the Union army, as told by De Trobriand, were arranged to have their maximum effect on the soldiers who were obliged to witness it. The procedure, it will be noted, differed in some respects from that followed in the Stonewall Brigade, as told by Casler. The condemned man marched out between the two ranks of the regiment, preceded by the musicians, playing a funeral march. The provost guard, as an escort, carried the coffin. The victim was conducted to the edge of the grave, which had already been dug. After the sentence was read, he was seated, blindfolded, upon a board at the foot of the open coffin, into which he fell backwards when the firing squad had discharged its sad duty.[3]

Officers were held responsible for desertion under charges of neglect of duty. While the method of execution seems to have been generally shooting, hanging seems to have been used occasionally, apparently for desertion to the enemy and hence for an act worthy of a more ignominious death.[4] The severity was, of course, relaxed after the war and deserters who had gone over to the enemy were paroled and allowed to go home; those who had forsaken the Union army without identifying themselves with the Confederacy forfeited pay and allowances for the period of their absence—scarcely less could be done—and all held as deserters were discharged.[5]

---

[1] *Battles and Leaders of the Civil War*, IV, 91–93. *American Annual Cyclopedia*, 1864, p. 37.

[2] *O. W. R.*, Ser. I, XXXVII, 406; XLIII, pt. II, 314, 360.

[3] *Quatre ans de campagnes à l'armée du Potomac*, II, 330.

[4] *O. W. R.*, Ser. I, XLII, pt. III, 921; XLIII pt. II, 721, 727. *Boston Daily Evening Transcript*, January 10, 1865.

[5] *O. W. R.*, Ser. I, XLVIII, pt. II, 862.

CHAPTER XIII

Southern Hospitality to Northern Deserters

The famed hospitality of the South did not fail even during the war. Northerners, of a kind, were welcome, even ardently desired, although their hosts did not have the wherewithal with which to spread an abundant table. And so their makeshifts often assumed the character of speeding the parting guest.

Oddly enough, Federal soldiers do not seem to have been so welcome during the early years, and, instead of being treated as honored guests, they were treated as prisoners of war—and worse. The gain to the South through the loss to the North by large defections was fully appreciated, but the problem was what to do with Northern renegades, for a land, hard put to it to feed its own soldiery and loyal citizens, obviously could not feed guests.

The initial disposition of Union deserters seems to have included the following steps: They were brought at once by the Confederate pickets to the headquarters of the officer in immediate command, who examined them closely and then sent them to the nearest provost marshal.[1] By December, 1862, the practice seemed to be, in the eastern theatre of war at least, to send them to Richmond. But willingness to take the oath of allegiance was by no means sufficient to gain the confidence of the rebel authorities. The deserters were kept in even closer confinement than the prisoners of war, and received the same food; the sole privilege accorded them above their compatriots in misfortune was that they were set to work under strong guards to clean the streets, cover them with lime, whitewash the public buildings, saw wood for the hospitals and the prisons—all this, naturally, without the slightest compensation.[2] These Northern

[1] *O. W. R.*, Ser. I, XV, 825. The writer finds no hints to guide her in conclusions on this subject of the treatment accorded Federal soldiers surrendering to the rebels earlier than August, 1862 (see also *ibid.*, Ser. I, XI, pt. II, 956).

[2] *Ibid.*, Ser. I, XXI, 824. This statement is based on the report of a Union scout in General Sigel's corps, who allowed himself to be taken to Richmond as a prisoner during October and November of 1862. In March, 1863, the cavalry

deserter-prisoners suffered discrimination at the hands of their captors as compared with Confederate prisoners of war. The prisons were rife with "mugging," an argot expression for robbing, and one of the most popular words in the Southern prison lexicon. Although the chief offenders in "mugging" were rebels who had violated the Confederate military law by desertion and theft, and although the Yankees were the chief sufferers, since the Southern captive had little to lose, no effort was made to protect the Northern prisoner against the nefarious practice; but when a dozen Union deserters proved guilty of the same action at the military prison located at Salisbury, North Carolina, they were tied to a whipping post and mercilessly lashed with a leather thong by a muscular sergeant.[1]

The miserable bounty-jumpers were a nuisance wherever they were. The Confederate authorities kept them, when they had presented themselves as deserters, at Castle Lightning for a time, but very soon, estimating their character aright, the officers sent them in among the prisoners of war at Andersonville and Libby, as they considered it the better part of wisdom to trade them off for a genuine rebel soldier, as it was a matter of indifference to the Confederacy how soon the Union government shot them as deserters.[2]

The rigor of treating Yankee deserters as prisoners of war appears to have relaxed during the winter of 1862–1863 when so large a number of them had accumulated in the military prisons that the Secretary of War gave instructions to allow such of them as were willing to take the oath of allegiance to the Confederacy, and then to permit them to seek work where it could be found. Accordingly, a number were employed by a director of the Tredegar Works at Richmond, who forwarded them to labor in Rockbridge County, Virginia, where their presence duly alarmed the Confederate House of Representatives.[3] Somewhat more than a year later, in June, 1864, an

of the Army of Northern Virginia was ordered to send all prisoners and deserters by the most practicable route to Richmond (*O. W. R.*, Ser. I, XXV, pt. II, 857).

[1] Told by a Federal prisoner of war (Browne, *Four Years in Secessia*, pp. 339–340).

[2] McElroy, *Andersonville*, pp. 112, 239.

[3] *O. W. R.*, Ser. II, V. 841. The writer is led to conclude that the oath here referred to is probably rather an oath of neutrality, such as was exacted a few months later, about June, 1863. If not, a change in practice was instituted and an oath of neutrality substituted for an oath of allegiance.

enrolling officer attempted to conscript some Yankee deserters, who, under an oath of neutrality, preferable to an oath of allegiance as it could not be broken by conscription, had secured work near Salisbury, North Carolina, where their conduct had been unexceptionable, against the protest of the captain commanding the post. The War Department, as consistency demanded, discharged the men as protected by their oath of neutrality.[1] But at the same time there were deserters from the Union army who preferred to be treated as prisoners of war.[2]

By the spring of 1864 it is apparent that the general rule prevailed in the western theatre of war, east of the Mississippi at least, of forwarding Federal deserters who were residents of that general section of country to Richmond, with the single exception of those employed by competent authority in the niter and mining operations, whose names would be reported to the Niter and Mining Bureau in Richmond. The great importance of the niter operations and the necessity for guarding against any interference with those operations dictated the policy of utilizing deserter labor on the niter mines in Tennessee and the West.[3]

Beginning with the middle of 1862 a distinct effort was made by the Confederate authorities to encourage desertion from the Union armies. It was at first directed to the inhabitants of Tennessee in the hope of detaching that State from Northern strength to at least neutrality. All citizens of east Tennessee in the United States army were addressed by General E. Kirby Smith in seductive phrases: "You must all now be convinced that you have been grossly deceived by the misrepresentations of those under whom you are serving. I therefore announce to you that a final opportunity is afforded you to return to your homes and your allegiance. I offer you a general amnesty for all past offenses, the only condition being that you take the oath of allegiance to the Government and that you conduct yourselves as becomes good citizens." He offered them a fair price for any arms, ammunition, or equipment which they might bring back with them, but he did not hold out specifically, as was

---

[1] *Ibid.,* Ser. II, VII, 227, 445.

[2] A number of Yankee deserters at Salisbury, North Carolina, requested to be sent to Andersonville as prisoners of war! The request was granted (*ibid.*).

[3] The dispatch cited here is dated March 23, 1864, from Greenville, east Tennessee (*ibid.,* Ser. I, XXXII, pt. III, 670).

suggested to him earlier by Secretary Randolph, exemption from enrollment as conscripts.[1]

By 1864 the desire was keen to gain deserters of all sorts and conditions, not merely from the border States but also from the Northern States. But the question of their disposal was one of great difficulty and continual embarrassment, partly due to the bad character and conduct of the deserters, and partly due to the prejudice of the Confederate citizens against them. Some of them, undoubtedly, were destitute of principle, men of bad habits, some few criminals; all were restless and rebellious at the scant fare, the hard labor, and restraints to which every living soul within the limits of the Confederacy must perforce submit. The plan of allowing them to secure work under an oath of neutrality had not worked well.

The inherent scorn and prejudice of loyal Southerners for men capable of such baseness as desertion was only deepened by their conduct into a bitter hatred. Public opinion compelled men who needed and wished their services to refuse their labor. Feeling was so inflamed in parts of the South, that if a planter hired a deserter, he was mobbed. In the cities their turbulence had produced disorder and crimes. The efforts to employ them for wages in workshops failed, for, when they did remain at work, they were disorderly, or the people of the vicinity remonstrated at the effect which the presence of this element produced upon the slaves. In some mining and manufacturing establishments, slaves who were at work in these factories were withdrawn by their owners, while the residents of the vicinity clamored for the removal or confinement of the deserters. The greater number, among those allowed to take work, deserted their employers and roamed about the country, committing depredations on persons and property. In some instances, the renegades themselves disappeared after a brief period only to be recognized as guides of raiding parties of the foe. In consequence deserters were for the most part held as prisoners of war.[2] Even in the prisons they were regarded as the worst element. And so the government found it desirable to induce Southern loyalists living

[1] General Smith's message is dated August 13, 1862 (*O. W. R.*, Ser. I, XVI, pt. II, 756). Randolph had written him on June 23 a dispatch prompting such a proclamation (*ibid.*, p. 703).

[2] The above is based on the report of a Virginia gentleman who stated that he had been studying the question from November, 1863, to May, 1864 (*ibid.*, Ser. IV, III, 376–377). See also a statement from Seddon (*ibid.*, p. 563).

behind the enemy's lines to aid and speed the deserters on their way to the United States.

The instances of deserters actually serving the Confederate flag seem relatively few. And suspicion and distrust, when they did, were keen. A story told by a Confederate soldier well illustrates the distrust with which they were viewed. A sergeant, who had deserted a New York cavalry regiment, ostensibly because of his lack of sympathy with the Emancipation Proclamation, but really because of some personal wrong, if the Confederate officer's secret suspicion was correct, rose to a lieutenant's stripes in the Confederate service, but only after his fidelity had been thoroughly tested. For long, to satisfy the men of the company that he was not a spy, he was not allowed to carry any arms.[1]

A thousand Irish Catholic soldiers deserted the Union cause after they had been captured in battle, declaring they would rather fight for the South than the North. On that declaration they were equipped and sworn in to serve till the end of the war. But when they were sent up to meet a raid in Mississippi, as soon as they saw the blue uniforms, they raised the white flag and surrendered in a body.[2]

The Confederacy made serious efforts in the prisons to induce the Union prisoners of war to become deserters. A story is told by a Northern prisoner of how an officer addressed the Yankees at Andersonville, insisting that the Federal government had abandoned them, and that the Confederacy was certain to succeed. He held out the lure of release from the confinement of prison, of good food and clothing, of a generous bounty, and at the end of the war of a land warrant for a farm. The great mass of the men turned their backs on the speaker and marched back into the stockade. And a group, self-appointed guardians of the Union, disciplined the cowards who manifested a desire to accept the terms with a flexible pine board. The number of men who yielded to the temptation was very small, perhaps 500 out of the 12,000 prisoners in Andersonville; and some of those held that an oath taken under compulsion was not binding, but was to be utilized merely as an opportunity

---

[1] *Battles and Leaders of the Civil War*, III, 149. Scott says that Mosby was won by his frank and soldierly bearing (*Partisan Life with Colonel Mosby*, pp. 32–33).

[2] *O. W. R.*, Ser. IV, III, 694. Maury, *Recollections of a Virginian*, pp. 191–192.

for escape.[1] Another battalion of so-called Galvanized Yankees was made up of Federal prisoners of war, who were not originally deserters, apparently. They were placed into the lines at Savannah upon taking the oath of allegiance, but troops to their right and left had orders to fire on them at the first overt act of treachery. Shortly before the evacuation several of them were put to death for acts of mutiny and attempted desertion at another point. It is curious and interesting to find the name of Galvanized Yankees applied to them, the same name which had been fastened in the North on Southern deserters serving against the Indians.[2]

A solution of the problem, since the methods of incarceration and paid labor seemed closed, was offered by sending the deserters abroad. A Virginian, who had received some slight encouragement from the vice-consul of France with regard to deserters of French nationality, suggested that the Confederate government send foreign deserters to some port—possibly a Mexican port—from which they could be embarked for points outside the United States, the expense for transportation from the port to be borne by their respective governments on the certification of their consuls. The Secretary of War eagerly snatched at this straw as a solution of the problem and authorized further negotiations with the French consul, and at least 500, nearly all foreigners, were run through the blockade to some foreign port.[3]

It was from the military commanders in the field, who, more than any one else, must have been aware of how the country to the rear of the enemy's lines was filled with Union deserters, that suggestions came which finally fixed the Confederate policy. It was as early as February 5, 1863, that General Pemberton was urging on Richmond that he be allowed to parole the Northern deserters and permit them to go home.[4] It was about a year and a half later that General Beauregard urged his belief that desertion could be increased by an order from the War Department or by an executive proclamation, advising all dissatisfied and drafted persons in the Federal army to

---

[1] McElroy, *Andersonville*, pp. 466–470, 552. Browne, *Four Years in Secessia*, p. 327.

[2] *Battles and Leaders of the Civil War*, IV, 669. After the war the general by whose order the execution took place for attempted desertion and mutiny, was tried by a Federal military commission for murder but acquitted.

[3] *O. W. R.*, Ser. IV, III, 376–378; Ser. I, XLII, pt. III, 608.

[4] This was a renewal of his application, so that he had apparently urged it earlier (*ibid.*, Ser. I, XXIV, pt. III, 616).

come over into the enemy's lines, where they would be furnished with food and sent as soon as practicable at the expense of the Confederate government to those points of the Confederacy nearest to their homes, or to the places where they might choose to go. But if any skilled workman among them preferred to remain, he should be allowed to remain to give his labor in return for fair wages. He added the suggestion that arms, horses, and accouterments should be purchased at liberal prices.[1]

It is interesting that on the very same date, July 19, 1864, Lee made a similar suggestion to encourage the disposition of the enemy to desert, which he felt was great and restrained only by the difficulty which they experienced in getting home. He drafted an order in which the Confederacy promised to receive them and offered them facilities to reach the North by a safe route,[2] which order he thought might be published and circulated among the Union armies. As has been pointed out elsewhere, this proposal of Lee's, which took form as Confederate General Orders No. 65, had been inspired undoubtedly by Grant's General Orders No. 64 of the same purport. President Davis and Secretary Seddon agreed in disapproving the promises suggested by Beauregard, especially the work for skilled workmen and the pledge to subsist and to permit Union deserters to go where they pleased. But while they both saw objections to Lee's plan, Davis felt that the objections to allowing enemy deserters to remain at large in the Confederacy might be overcome by close surveillance and thought that the attempt as an aid to the successful prosecution of the war should probably be made, though he pointed out the difficulty involved in the possibility of slaves deserting from the Northern army and then insisting on being transported to the border, a proposition which he could not entertain.[3]

And so, slightly modified so as to apply to foreigners and thus by implication to exclude escaped slaves, the plan appeared as the famous General Orders No. 65 under date of August 15, 1864:

"It having been represented to the War Department that there are numbers of foreigners entrapped by artifice and fraud into the military and naval service of the United States who would gladly withdraw from further participation in the inhuman warfare waged

---

[1] *Ibid.,* Ser. I, XL, pt. III, 785–786.

[2] *Ibid.,* pp. 781–782. As the draft was almost the same as that issued by Seddon, the purport is not repeated here.

[3] See the endorsements on the two plans (*ibid.,* pp. 782, 786).

against a people who have never given them a pretext for hostility; and that there are many inhabitants of the United States now retained in the service against their will who are averse to aiding in the unjust war now being prosecuted against the Confederate States; and it being also known that these men are prevented from abandoning such compulsory service by the difficulty they experience in escaping therefrom; it is ordered that all such persons, coming within the lines of the Confederate armies, shall be received, protected, and supplied with means of subsistence, until such of them as desire it can be forwarded to the most convenient points on the border, where all facilities will be afforded them to return to their homes." [1]

Lee, detecting, as he thought, about a week later some happy effects, expressed the hope that the order be translated into German [2] and that a considerable number of copies be sent to all the Southern armies for distribution. He felt that it was especially desirable that some enemy deserters be forwarded North so that they might spread among their friends in the Federal army the story of the kind treatment received from the Confederacy. [3] General Bragg suggested that a large number be printed also in French and thought it possible to introduce a goodly number of copies within the enemy's lines. [4]

That Lee was not mistaken in believing that the Confederate offer would stimulate desertions is evidenced by a statement from Grant, in which he admits that bounty and substitute men had been deserting immediately on their arrival at the front to take advantage of the Confederate offer to send them through the lines. The Richmond papers on September 5, 1864, announced that several hundred Federal deserters had already availed themselves of the offer and were waiting to be sent off. It may possibly have affected several thousand soldiers all told. [5]

But there were complaints of the practical working of the system,

[1] O. W. R., Ser. I, XLII, pt. II, 529. This order parallels Northern Gen. Orders, No. 64.

[2] The large number of Germans, naturalized or merely resident citizens, in the Union armies, was well known, of course, to the Confederate leaders. Some desertions from the German regiments spread the idea of widespread disaffection.

[3] O. W. R., Ser. I, XLII, pt. II, 1200.

[4] Ibid., Ser. IV, III, 6.

[5] Ibid., Ser. I, XLIII, pt. II, 29. American Annual Cyclopedia, 1864, p. 37. Daily Richmond Examiner.

as most of the deserters were sent from Richmond to Abingdon or Bristol, Virginia, to be sent through to Kentucky. No discretion as to their disposal was allowed, although in most cases, according to General Breckinridge, they asked to be permitted to remain in the Confederacy as mechanics or laborers. The experience of those who went home must indeed have had a wide effect, but not of the kind which Lee had fondly hoped, for they had to march on foot through a barren frontier of several hundred miles infested with lawless bushwhackers who stripped them of everything, even of the very clothes on their backs, before they reached the Federal lines. At first they got through the latter safely by representing themselves as rebel deserters,[1] but as soon as Northern spies had ascertained the Confederate disposition of this class of deserters, they were promptly arrested for what they were when they reached the Northern line.[2] Almost 150 mechanics, teamsters, and laborers were allowed during November, 1864, to remain at Abingdon by a special government commissioner, who shrewdly exacted an oath of good conduct as friends of the Confederacy but not an oath of neutrality, as he conceived that by long-continued residence they might become liable for future military duty.[3]

Meanwhile secret agents were often at work with the Northern forces stationed as advanced posts in the South. It was thought that some of Mosby's men were serving in certain Union commands in the character of spies to influence the men to desert; certain it is that a considerable number of them did join Mosby for the sake of plunder; civilian agents located in the vicinity of such Union camps spent most of their time in paroling deserters from Northern regiments. Efforts were particularly directed to detaching Mexicans

[1] *O. W. R.*, Ser. IV, III, 863–864. Breckinridge also pointed out the short-sightedness on the part of the Confederates in not retaining the labor of which they were so greatly in need (*ibid.*, pp. 864, 865). Before the deserters were permitted to remain, they were required to secure some definite work from persons known to the provost marshal (*ibid.*, p. 865).

[2] A man in the office of the provost marshal at City Point, Virginia, was sent on September 18 to the enemy's lines as a deserter to learn the ropes. He was soon lodged in Castle Thunder where he had to remain about three weeks until a sufficient number had collected to be forwarded to Abingdon. One hundred and five were sent away the day he arrived (*ibid.*, Ser. I, XLII, pt. III, 608).

[3] The oath required that the deserters demean themselves peaceably as friends of the Confederate and State governments, obey all the laws and give no aid or comfort to the enemy during the continuance of the war. The exact number so paroled was 134 (*ibid.*, Ser. IV, III, 865).

from the Yankee service, while agents were kept busy buying arms from such deserters, both profitable businesses for the South.[1] The Confederates were as anxious to correct the impression that deserters would be put in the Southern army or conscripted for the fortifications as were the Federals to correct the impression that deserters from the enemy's service would have to face their relatives and former friends in the ranks.[2]

Many visionary projects were presented. An enthusiast, acting as a secret agent through the North, persuaded himself that certain Northern conscripts, who were opposed to coercing the South, could be induced to make their way South to join the Confederate service in sufficient numbers to make up a division,[3] especially if the Confederates opened a road to the Ohio. Another urged on President Davis a plan whereby deserters from the foe should be won to fight in the rebel ranks by the promise of a negro and fifty acres of land to each such convert upon honorable discharge after his term of service, and by the further promise of all the negroes which he could capture from the enemy. This was intended as an attempt to outbid Lincoln's rewards—bounties, presumably—and the originator of the scheme was sure that "men from all quarters of the globe" would take up arms in defense of the Confederate cause as the South had the more alluring bait, and he was confident that his idea would reduce Grant's and Sherman's armies by one half.[4]

Southern zeal for promoting Northern desertion was fired, not only by the desire to deplete the ranks of their foe, but also by the knowledge that men so disgusted or disheartened by a service as to abandon it would, undoubtedly, yield considerable military information. That information was probably not of as great value to the Confederacy as the information similarly secured by the United States because the actual number of Confederates who deserted to the enemy was proportionately greater. While the records show an absolute total of desertion greater for the North than for the South, there can be no doubt that most of the Northerners returned to their own homes or, at least, to some section of the North. The constant reiteration by

[1] *O. W. R.*, Ser. I, XXIX, pt. II, 24; XVII, pt. I, 515; LIII, 994.

[2] A sergeant of the thirty-ninth New York told the Confederate officer that the Union soldiers would come over in "swarms" if they thought they could get work (*ibid.*, Ser. I, LI, pt. II, 864; XXIV, pt. III, 176–177).

[3] *Ibid.*, Ser. I, XLIII, pt. II, 935. This was in December, 1864, when the more far-sighted on both sides knew that the South was defeated.

[4] *Ibid.*, Ser. IV, III, 1041–1042.

Union generals of the surrender of Southern deserters indicates a larger proportion of deserters so disposing of themselves after escape than was true on the other side. Where one reads in terms of 100 or 500 Northern deserters at Richmond after the announcement of General Orders No. 65, it is but necessary to remind the reader of the thousands of Southern deserters to whom the oath was administered by United States officials between September, 1864, and January, 1865, at one post alone—Nashville.[1]

The subjects on which the Confederate commanders gleaned information of value may be roughly grouped under four heads: the number of the foe with which they had to deal, military movements under way or projected, the location of troops and ships, and reports of discontent and discouragement, subjects certain to be from their very nature paramount in the mind of the Confederate officer examining a deserter as it would be in the mind of the Union official striving to gather information from the lips of the rebel renegade. General Jackson listened to the estimate of a deserter that there were thirty-four regiments in front of him with a cavalry of four regiments and sixty pieces of artillery, but, weighing it beside his information from other reliable sources, dismissed it as too large.[2] It is noticeable that deserters tended to exaggerate the numbers. For instance, when deserters and prisoners placed Halleck's army on the retreat from Corinth on June 2, 1862, at 125,000 or 130,000 men, General Beauregard calmly based his estimate at about 90,000 effective men, as he had already learned the fact of the presence of only three corps with one reserve corps.[3] While the statements of the deserters are occasionally vague, they generally indulge in surprisingly definite figures. A Yankee deserting from Yorktown in February, 1863, who reported the presence there of some 6,000 troops and the constant landing of fresh troops, was furnishing information of value.[4] Apparently the report of 10,000 troops at New Berne under the command of General Palmer on April 13, 1863, was important data for General Hill, as it was promptly transmitted. Even though the information may have been a bit antiquated by reason of the long interval between desertion from the Federal line and confession to a Confederate provost marshal, the facts that the army was

[1] *Ibid.*, Ser. I, XLV, pt. I, 47, 48.
[2] April 12, 1862. *Ibid.*, Ser. I, XII, pt. III, 846.
[3] *Ibid.*, Ser. I, X, pt. I, 777.
[4] *Ibid.*, Ser. I, XVIII, 892.

composed of forty regiments of infantry of 500 men each, of 2,000 to 3,000 cavalry, of ten batteries of light artillery of six guns each, of ten siege guns, and of one battery of flying artillery were likely to remain facts until the two armies encountered one another.[1] On one occasion Lee owed knowledge that General Butler had been reinforced by a complete army corps to the report of a deserter to Beauregard.[2] Accurate data as to figures could affect an entire campaign, as when General Johnston learned that the draft for 300,000 men in the North had actually yielded only 50,000 men and that many of these had deserted, for he probably reasoned that the enemy would not then send another army to invade Tennessee.[3]

An artillerist from Cairo gave the enemy warning of a movement by the Federals on Columbus, Kentucky, the latter part of the following week in November, 1861; and likewise two deserters confirmed a concerted movement in the direction of Corinth.[4] Lee owed to the same source the information that Burnside, who had already left the peninsula for the Potomac, was preparing to join Pope, while a part of McClellan's army had embarked on transports at Harrison's landing.[5] Just to know the direction of a movement was a factor of the utmost consequence, as when Lee had to decide whether his opponents' army was intended for Tennessee or North Carolina.[6] And it is not hard to imagine that definite information that 50,000 Yankees under General Dix were moving up the peninsula from Yorktown with the fleet ready to move up the river as soon as the fort was destroyed, set some camp all aflutter with excitement and preparation.[7]

Occasionally the record bears on its face evidence of the reliability of the deserter's information and the damage to the Union cause, as when a certain major operating in Arkansas dispatched 100 of his best horses across the Red River, but their best speed could not outdistance the deserter who had given the rebel camp notice of their approach. Again, a deserting officer from the frigate *Minnesota* communicated to a Southern commander news of the sailing of a large

[1] *O. W. R.*, Ser. I, XXVI, pt. II, 380.
[2] *Ibid.*, Ser. I, XL, pt. II, 653.
[3] *Ibid.*, Ser. I, XXXI, pt. III, 878.
[4] *Ibid.*, Ser. I, IV, 550; X, pt. II, 509.
[5] Henderson, *Stonewall Jackson and the American Civil War*, II, 136.
[6] *O. W. R.*, Ser. I, XXV, pt. II, 627.
[7] *Ibid.*, Ser. I, XXVII, pt. III, 1004; see also *ibid.*, Ser. I, IV, 672–673 for an earlier event.

fleet from New York and confirmed it unwittingly by letters found in his possession.[1] General Hébert was obviously disturbed by the report of several Yankee deserters that the commander of the squadron which they had just deserted had sent a steamer to Pensacola for five more gun-boats, as it was his intention to ravage the whole coast of Texas, since the former had no boats with which to resist the foe; and General Bee was equally excited when he was informed by deserters that the Federal navy intended to attack Galveston on the first of September, 1863.[2] Sometimes the statements of several deserters brought in on different days and strangers to each other tallied.

Another striking case was a Union captain who left with the utmost secrecy at night to cut off a guard near a bridge at Franklin, Virginia, only to find all ready for a warm reception: artillery, infantry, and guns. Two men, who had deserted thirty minutes before he left, had carried the information of the attack to the foe.[3]

It is also indisputable that the Confederates owed some knowledge concerning the location of the troops of their enemy to the statements of Northern deserters. The following unquestionably was a choice titbit for General Ewell during McClellan's peninsular campaign: "A deserter from Sickles' brigade, brought in by my pickets yesterday, says that there are but two regiments left on the other side of the Potomac, the balance having gone to Old Point."[4] Equally significant to Secretary Randolph and President Davis, in danger of being bottled up in Richmond in April, 1862, was the report from Hill, which he had gleaned from an enemy deserter, that sixty mortars had been landed and that McClellan was threatening a complete investment of the entire Confederate front and that his works bristled with artillery.[5] It was as disadvantageous to Grant as it was advantageous to Johnston to have a Yankee deserter betray on September 1, 1862, the presence at Lake Providence, forty miles above Vicksburg, of seven iron-clad gun-boats and five transports filled with troops.[6] The mere fact of desertion sometimes altered a maneuvre, as when on October 3, 1862, General Dix felt obliged to send out couriers to recall a force of 2,000 cavalry, artillery, and

[1] *Ibid.*, Ser. I, XXXIV, pt. I, 641; IV, 686.
[2] *Ibid.*, Ser. I, XV, 147; XXVI, pt. II, 180.
[3] *Ibid.*, Ser. I, XVIII, 551.
[4] *Ibid.*, Ser. I, XII, pt. III, 847–848.
[5] *Ibid.*, Ser. I, XI, pt. III, 461.
[6] *Ibid.*, Ser. I, XV, 805.

infantry which had been sent out to attack the Confederates at Franklin, Virginia, to cripple the floating bridge on the Blackwater at that point, because two "scoundrels" from New York had been seen before daylight riding rapidly through the lines to the enemy.[1]

Naturally, many items should be verified before their true value to the Confederacy could be proved, but certainly Grant would have preferred that a deserter had not reported to Lee his presence at Old Point Comfort on August 8, 1864, and his meeting with Butler at Dutch Gap on the eleventh during his campaign of attrition.[2]

When prisoners and deserters agreed in the statement to Lee of August 11, 1864, that the Eighteenth Corps and a portion of the Nineteenth, operating near Lee's headquarters, had withdrawn, that wily general was probably justified in planning demonstrations against Washington.[3] Obviously he would check up his information by other deserters, by scouts, and by scraps reported by his different commanders.

Knowledge of depression of spirits among the Union troops and of a state of pessimism abroad in the North was as eagerly hailed by Confederate leaders as data concerning the extent of Southern discouragement was hailed by Grant and Lincoln, and undoubtedly kept alive fictitious hope for ultimate victory. The numerous allusions to Yankee deserters which occur in Lee's dispatches show how eagerly he watched this secret aid, even when he saw the problem with such clarity as the following note indicates: "The enemy has suffered from straggling as well as ourselves (I believe to a greater extent), but his numbers are so great he can afford it; we cannot." [4]

As in every war, false rumors were easily started, news given in good faith as in bad by deserters. One striking instance was the news that Grant had been killed which received rather wide credence; it proved to have been first given out by a deserter from the Union army and then was reported as extracted from Northern newspapers.[5] While there must have been some basis for the report of

[1] O. W. R., Ser. I, XVIII, 15. He also dispatched a strong force to support the troops.

[2] Ibid., Ser. I, XLIII, pt. I, 997.

[3] Ibid., p. 995.

[4] Ibid., Ser. I, XIX, pt. II, 625. For other instances of anxious noting of Federal desertion see ibid., Ser. I, XXV, pt. III, 624, 703; XXIII, pt. II, 677; XV, 1039.

[5] Ibid., Ser. I, XXXV, pt. II, 196.

dissatisfaction among Federal soldiers over Lincoln's negro proclamation," its efficacy in securing desertions was wildly exaggerated
in the South; men believe what they wish to believe.[1]

---

[1] Occasionally a Union officer even learned of desertions from his own
ranks from enemy deserters (*ibid.,* Ser. I, XL, pt. III, 315).

CHAPTER XIV

SANCTUARIES OF THE UNION DESERTERS

The question where the thousands upon thousands of deserters from the Union armies bestowed themselves discovers a very interesting answer. First of all, a certain, small percentage deserted to the enemy; generally among the vast horde of deserters those thus going over to the enemy were the worst characters of the entire group.

Oddly enough, the records do not yield many instances of Northern men surrendering themselves to the Confederates until late in 1862. But there occur then and in February of the succeeding year defections from the Mounted Rifles to the other side.[1] An incomplete table subjoined below, compiled from reports and statements made by both sides, indicates a goodly measure of defection.[2] There is not lacking proof that a trickling line went from the Northern to the Southern side during 1864 and 1865, but, if we may trust Grant's opinion, and he certainly should have been in a position to know, relatively few of the large number of deserters went over to the enemy at that time.[3] One deterrent may have been the fact that the

---

[1] *O. W. R.*, Ser. I, XVIII, 15, 540, 541, 550. Of course, there are a few earlier records (*ibid.*, Ser. II, II, 327; Ser. I, II, 297–298, August 31, 1861).

[2] Desertions to the Southern forces from the Union army were reported by Confederate officers on each of the dates given below and in many of the reports they were said to be occurring every day:

April 12, 1862	February 5, 1863 (daily)
April 13, 1862	March 10, 1863
May 10, 1862	March 18, 1863
August 12, 1862 (daily)	March 20, 1863
August 24, 1862	April 25, 1863
September 1, 1862	May 4, 1863
September 27, 1862	September 18, 1863
October 10, 1862	September 19, 1863 (daily)
October 15, 1862	November 28, 1863 (*O. W. R.*)

[3] This statement evidently represented his matured opinion, for it was made to Seward on August 19, 1864 (*ibid.*, Ser. II, VII, 614). But for desertion to

danger of deserting from the picket line was greater at this time than earlier, as soldiers were immediately fired on if detected in the act, or executed if recognized upon later capture.

Some of those thus surrendering themselves to their foes were, as has been stated, found taking service with the very men to whom they had recently been opposed. A deserter from the Sixth Kansas regiment became a lieutenant in Stand Watie's Indian Brigade under the Confederate flag.[1] Such semi-lawless service as that with the partisan rangers, Mosby and Mobberly,[2] seemed to appeal to the more reckless of them.[3] They even turned freebooters on their own account, attacking wagon trains in order to carry off the booty. The mere taking of the oath of allegiance, which term seems to have been loosely used to cover anything from an oath of neutrality to service under the Stars and Bars, might mean nothing. General Foster complained rather bitterly in the fall of 1864 that the concern of the citizens of Charleston in relieving the necessities of the Union soldiers had been fraught with disastrous results—to the Union—as nearly 400 had been induced to take the oath of allegiance to the Confederacy and to go to work in the shops of Charleston. The evil was only partly mitigated if the oath were taken by men whose terms of service were expiring.[4]

While some of the Northern deserters made their way back to the Union as soon as permitted by the Confederacy to do so, some few remained scattered throughout the South. Especially were they to be found in the border territory—using this term roughly to designate that region in which most of the fighting took place, whether in the Confederacy or just adjacent to it; whether Missouri, Kentucky, Tennessee, or Texas; whether Arkansas, Louisiana, or Virginia. As the armies swayed back and forth over this territory, there was left in the rear of each a host of deserters of both faiths. In

the enemy see also *ibid.*, Ser. I, XL, pt. II, 653; XXXV, pt. I, 66; XL, pt. III, 315; XLII, pt. III, 720; XLVI, pt. III, 99; XLVI, pt. II, 290.

[1] *Ibid.*, Ser. I, XXXIV, pt. I, 101.

[2] *Ibid.*, Ser. I, XLIII, pt. II, 634. A report to General Stevenson read, "French Bill, of Mobberly's freebooters, was yesterday taken by Keye's men, I understand; if so, he is an important capture, as he is a deserter from Twenty-eighth New York Volunteer Infantry. . . . Colonel Root, of Fifteenth New York Cavalry, now at Pleasant Valley, will furnish you evidence against French Bill; also a clerk in employ of Mr. Bush, who was sutler for the Twenty-eighth Regiment."—*Ibid.*, p. 721.

[3] *Ibid.*, Ser. I, XVIII, 33. See above, page 191.

[4] *Ibid.*, Ser. I, XXXV, pt. I, 25–26.

Missouri, it was a wild, frontier life that they lived, where even the United States mail was attacked in true Western fashion.[1] The region in the vicinity of the Boston Mountains, Arkansas, was infested with small bands of deserters from both armies, all alike rebels against law and order.[2] It was notorious with the commanders of each army that as the authority they represented held possession of Kentucky and Tennessee, recruits flocked to their standard, only to fall away as fortune forsook that banner, when the recruits became fugitives lurking in the mountains. In periods of defeat and consequent discouragement hundreds of Union soldiers from north of the Ohio would wander about Tennessee in search of a Confederate officer by whom to be paroled.[3] Naturally, they were not one whit better than the rebel deserters, and turned, as easily as did the rebel outlaw, bushwhacker, and deserter, to depredations upon the lives and property of Southern citizens until many of the latter had to leave their homes. The great difference between the Northern and Southern renegades seems to have been that the former were not united into large bands. A considerable number of deserters lurked along the Rappahanock, robbing for subsistence, and waiting to slip through the Federal lines or to be picked up and paroled by the Confederate cavalry.[4]

Sometimes, to escape contact with the Confederate officials, they penetrated into the rebel's own deserter country, into the mountains of North Carolina, Virginia, Mississippi, and Alabama, where they outrebeled the rebels in lawlessness, and where a society, hybrid indeed, threatened anarchy instead of civilization: marauders, bummers, strolling vagabonds, negroes, rebel deserters, Union desert-

[1] The episode here referred to occurred in that chaotic period just after the cessation of warfare, but before peace had yet been established, May 4, 1865 (O. W. R., Ser. I, XLVIII, pt. II, 314).

[2] Ibid., Ser. I, XXXIV, pt. IV, 453. The foot-hills of the Ozark Mountains have been for generations known as the Boston Mountains.

[3] Louisville Daily Democrat, January 4, 1863. O. W. R., Ser. I, XX, pt. II, 428.

[4] Ibid., Ser. I, XXXVI, pt. II, 652–653. Some citizens of Johnson County, Tenn., petitioned Breckinridge for help "against the bushwhackers, murderers and deserters, who are depredating upon the lives and property of southern citizens to such an alarming extent that a great many of them had to leave their homes. . . . There is a very large number of deserters from the Federal army lurking in the woods with guns of the best quality, and could, if they were to unite, destroy every southern family in the country in a short time and is threatening to do so if we attempt to arrest them."—Ibid., Ser. I, XXXIX, pt. III, 873.

ers, all bent on committing outrages. Insults, rape, plundering, and murder were the order of the day.[1] It is interesting that deserters from the Union forces made their way to northern Alabama, Coffee and adjoining counties, as early as the spring of 1864 to remain there in hiding until the close of the war. A band of about fifty men, chiefly deserters from the First Florida Cavalry of the United States army escaped capture by either Northern or Southern government by operating over a large stretch of territory extending from Coffee County to contiguous counties in Florida where the soil was too poor to maintain a pursuing force in that locality. They billeted themselves upon the country, taking whatever they needed without any regard to the status of the party from whom it was taken.[2] It should be recalled that parts of these mountains had harbored thieves before the war so that there was only a change in degree and kind of lawlessness.

Sometimes it was an individual deserter who parted from his companions in desertion to go to acquaintances or relatives in the South while his fellows turned their faces North, as he preferred to seek work South to courting risk of detection in his home locality.[3]

The influence of the presence of the Northern deserter in the interior of the South was far-reaching in unexpected ways, as medical officers attributed the spreading of yellow fever in the fall of 1864 to the large number of Yankee prisoners and deserters, especially the latter, who would readily fall a prey to it and yet who could not be easily restricted to given localities.[4]

A foreign country, for those who could reach it and who could support themselves there, was probably the most comfortable portion of the globe for the deserter, and men were not oblivious to its advantages, especially when there was a portion of the British dominion so accessible as Canada. The government anticipated this avenue of escape and endeavored as promptly as the draft went into effect to block it, for on August 8, 1862, it was ordered by direction of the president that no citizen subject to the draft be allowed

[1] *Ibid.*, Ser. I, XLIII, pt. II, 739. A "bummer" was defined as a raider on his own account, who temporarily deserted his place in the ranks while the army was on the march, for an independent foraging expedition (Nichols, *The Story of the Great March,* p. 240).

[2] *O. W. R.*, Ser. I, XLIX, pt. II, 1045.

[3] *Ibid.*, Ser. I, LI, pt. II, 864.

[4] *Ibid.*, Ser. II, VII, 825.

to go to a foreign country. This rule was to be rigidly enforced at all ports on the seaboard and on the frontier.[1] Although departure for Canada may have been accelerated in August, 1862, by threat of the draft,[2] it certainly did not begin then, for within less than a month Commissioner Draper, who was later to head the Bureau of Deserters, urged upon Secretary Stanton that a number of deserters in Canada were eager to bargain for their return to their regiments.[3] The next summer an assistant provost marshal at Elmira, New York, declared that Canada was the asylum of more than half the deserters from the New York volunteer companies. While this declaration could not be regarded as precise, it gives some clue to the importance of Canada as an objective for the deserter.[4] Life in Canada was not so simple as it seemed, for the deserters scattered up and down the land found but little opportunity for work and pay, while the supply of laborers was being constantly augmented by fellow-countrymen seeking this more salubrious climate. Probably no exact figures of the number who had fled over the border will ever be available, and so the best we can do is to accept the rough figures of Senator Wilson who held that there were in March, 1864, from 10,000 to 15,000 deserters in Canada.[5]

These deserters who congregated in Canada let themselves be heard from in the fall of 1864 in a very dramatic fashion. The country became excited and disturbed on the morning of October 20 to learn that a band of about twenty-five men, made up, as it later developed, of Confederate plotters, deserters, and draft dodgers from Vermont regiments, had raided and robbed three banks of $200,000, in St. Albans in Vermont across the border from Canada the preceding afternoon. After seriously wounding two citizens, they seized a number of horses and made their escape, the whole episode consuming less than half an hour, as the boldness of the attack had paralyzed the citizens of the town. On their retreat the marauders attempted unsuccessfully to enter the bank at Sheldon,

---

[1] *O. W. R.*, Ser. II, II, 370. Gen. Orders No. 104.
[2] A telegram to Stanton from Rochester, New York, dated August 8, 1862, says: "Many men are leaving for Canada" (*ibid.*, Ser. III, II, 320).
[3] *Ibid.*, p. 527.
[4] *Ibid.*, Ser. III, III, 425–426.
[5] *Congressional Globe*, 38th Cong., 1st sess., pt. II, 1249. *American Annual Cyclopedia*, 1864 (p. 37), says merely several thousand had gone to the British provinces. The *New York Daily Tribune* says that there were at least 10,000 in Canada, March 7, 1864.

Vermont. And in both places they made abortive attempts to set buildings afire. Once across the frontier, they supposed themselves safe and so became less vigilant; but about half of the band were captured and lodged in Canadian jails, while about $75,000 of the booty was recovered. It was thought the whole scheme had been executed under instruction from active rebel agents and it was feared that other outrages of robbery and incendiarism would be perpetrated on unprotected towns and villages along the border to confuse the impending presidential election. And it was feared that the rebel agents plotted to send across the line a large number of refugees, deserters, and enemies of the Federal government, to colonize them at different points, so that they might vote against the government and war party at the election. Stanton was very zealous that a cordon should be drawn on the Canadian frontier sufficiently strong so that the miscreants should be caught as they attempted to flee again into Canada after having crossed to cast their votes.[1]

Occasionally, though rarely, one finds a band boldly staying within sight of the camp of a Union general, in no fear of him and he quite indifferent to them. The most striking case which has come to the attention of the writer is that of a band of some 400 stragglers who deserted General Sigel in July, 1864, and then returned to the field; when it was suggested to General Lew Wallace to use them at the Battle of Monocacy, he refused, as he was unable to place any confidence in them. They took possession of the wooded hills to the east of his camp where the smoke of their camp-fires was plainly visible, but General Wallace contented himself with forbidding them rations from his supply.[2]

The remainder of the vast army of deserters, other than the 15,000 or 16,000 in Canada, Mexico, and abroad, and the possible 2,000 or 3,000 within the limits of the Confederacy, were scattered about in their own homes or throughout other states of the North.[3] McClellan

---

[1] *O. W. R.*, Ser. I, XLIII, pt. II, 455–457, 463–464, 532. See also Headley, *Confederate Operations in Canada and New York*, pp. 258–263. *American Annual Cyclopedia*, 1864, p. 178.

[2] Lew Wallace, *Autobiography*, II, 725 (Note).

[3] General Wool's comment of July 21, 1862, to Stanton shows very clearly where the men were then: "Measures ought to be adopted to apprehend and send back to their regiments the thousands of deserters scattered throughout the country" (*O. W. R.*, Ser. I, XI, pt. III, 331).

in September, 1862, estimated that there were probably 8,000 at home at work.[1] It is difficult for this generation to understand the boldness with which the soldiers, men and officers, showed their faces in their own homes. It began with the very beginning of the war, for many of the Eleventh New York Zouaves, reported among the casualties of the first Battle of Bull Run, had merely absented themselves after the battle and had returned to New York.[2]

At no time, probably, was absenteeism more brazen than during the height of the Copperhead sympathy in 1863 when Rosecrans charged that there were some 30,000 men belonging to his army in the states of Ohio, Indiana, and Illinois alone—improperly absent.[3] A scene in Indiana almost defies belief. Usually it required an armed detail to arrest the deserters, as the oath of the order, Knights of the Golden Circle, required the adherents to desert with their arms. In one case some seventeen members fortified themselves in a log cabin with an outside paling and a ditch for protection, within which, supplied with food by their neighbors, they bade defiance to law. They surrendered only after eight of their number had been seized by a body of troops.[4]

From Rushville, Illinois, came the report of a large armed mob led by deserters in Fulton County, who boldly threatened and drove away the enrolling officer and opposed to the point of force the arrest of deserters; likewise in Brown County an organized band had established themselves near LaGrange, pledged to resist the draft, the further arrest of deserters, and to destroy the provost's rolls in the event of a draft. Probably the boldest act was the attack by a mob of 400 men at DuQuoin, Illinois, in July, 1863, on a deputy provost marshal and the wresting from him of some deserters whom he was guarding.[5] The employment of force in the arrest of deserters in Franklin County shows how scattered were the renegades and the determination of the citizens to support them.

Even from Iowa came echoes of the disturbance, for an officer wrote Stanton that a collision must be expected when his deputies

---

[1] O. W. R., Ser. I, XIX, pt. II, 365; IX, 671.

[2] Ibid., Ser. I, II, 322.

[3] Ibid., Ser. I, XXIII, pt. II, 60.

[4] Ibid., Ser. III, III, 19–20. See also the accounts given in the Daily Illinois State Journal, February 3 and 4, 1863, which argued against a mistaken clemency. There were also disorders in Sullivan County, Indiana, in June, 1863 (O. W. R., Ser. III, III, 392).

[5] Ibid., pp. 505, 506, 509–510.

made a descent on the deserters harbored in Clark County. He was fully satisfied that the men involved in the violence, numbering several hundred in the county, were thoroughly organized, and that they had been drilled by a man who had until a few months previous been serving as a captain in the rebel army. Here the variety of society called the Sons of '76 existed side by side with the Knights of the Golden Circle, but whatever the name, they were belligerent in their defense of deserters. Several deserters were advised by lawyers to go back to their farms to work.[1]

Even distant Oregon was not untouched by the defection, as the reader finds an instance where it was feared a California deserter would be warned and abetted by Copperheads of Oregon.[2]

So far as there was a *deserter-country* in the North, it was to be found in the mountainous region of western Pennsylvania. No later than the winter of 1863 a member of the secret service reported to Halleck that in his travels through Pennsylvania he had found a great number of deserters all through the State, as well as an immense lot of government property, which had been carried off by those renegades and by absconding settlers. Almost every man in the State, he declared, had a rifle, saddle, or some piece of government property.[3] A few months later when a small party of ten men attempted to arrest a deserter in Monroe County, in the extreme eastern part of the State, they were overpowered by an armed band and compelled to release him.[4]

It was only in the fall of 1864, after the government became sincere in its discouragement of desertion, that parts of Pennsylvania began to assume the character of northern Mississippi. It began to be known that in several counties large bands of deserters and delinquent drafted men were banded together, armed and organized for resistance to the Federal authorities, and encouraged by the political opponents of the administration party. The band in Columbia County numbered about 500, while that in Cambria was thought to be larger. Schuylkill County was one of the bad districts where it was estimated there were scattered between 400 and 500 deserters and drafted men who had not reported. In October it was known that very few of the men drafted from Luzerne,

[1] *Ibid.*, pp. 70, 125.
[2] *Ibid.*, Ser. I, L, pt. II, 1035.
[3] *Ibid.*, Ser. I, XXV, pt. II, 81.
[4] *Ibid.*, Ser. III, III, 357.

Wyoming, and Bradford Counties had reported. Many were openly working, following their peace-time vocations, well-known by the residents of the region; but no arrests were made [1] as the laborers at the mines joined the draft-dodgers in rioting and so terrorized the citizenry. It proved very difficult to catch them, as small detachments of troops in disaffected districts only excited the indignation and contempt of the organized malcontents, and at the very first appearance of troops they fled to the hills. The cavalry stationed at Pottsville was sent out in detachments of six and eight almost every night and proved successful in making some arrests, although the outlaws, secreted near the roadside or among the rocks on the sides of the hill, did not hesitate to fire upon them. What largely resulted was that the deserters were forced, in order to escape arrest, to leave their homes and hide in the mountains and wooded districts. The nearest approach to the situation which prevailed so long in the Alabama mountains and Mississippi swamps was to be found in Clearfield and Cambria Counties where there had congregated from 1,200 to 1,800 absconders from duty. They were frankly engaged in lumbering on Clearfield River and were said to have erected a fort at the head of the river, well beyond the terminus of the railroad, in which to resist the law if driven to extremities. In this section nature fought for them: the roads were impassable for troops for a portion of the year, and a rise of the river would enable them to escape down it on their log rafts in early spring if attacked in their lair by troops. They committed many outrages, even killing a detective while he was attempting to arrest a deserter, and on another occasion threatening to drive out some inhabitants until the approach of troops caused them to flee. [2]

It was early found that the only arm of the service of any value in the mountainous districts, wooded and sparsely settled, was the cavalry where fifty men could perform the service of a thousand infantry. The raids had to be made at night, the detachments moving under cover of darkness and with rapidity enough to pursue the deserters. The usual outrages silenced the loyal residents, so that they were afraid to point out the hiding places, unless amply protected by the presence of the troops. Two distinct cavalry scouts were made on November 7 and 8 from Pottsville, and one on December 13 from Harrisburg toward the north central portion of the

[1] O. W. R., Ser. III, IV, 607; Ser. I, XLIII, pt. II, 481–482.
[2] Ibid., pp., 525–526, 527, 589.

State. The first group accomplished little beyond frightening off the gang, but the second surrounded a house in which was hidden a gang of a score of deserter desperadoes, and was able to kill the leader and capture the entire force. But the provost's hopes of dispersing all the bands were not fulfilled, for even in July and August after the close of the war there were still a goodly number of deserters abroad in Pennsylvania and Illinois whom the provost was unable to arrest.[1]

Another portion of the Union where the presence of deserters produced a certain lawlessness was in the Territory of Wyoming, into which deserters and secessionists thronged the early part of 1864, when the pursuit in their home States began to be keen.[2] The nearness of Maine and New Hampshire to the border probably explains the condition which prevailed there in August, 1865, when provost marshals complained that the close of hostilities and hence of danger of arrest had brought deserters back across the border until their districts were overrun with them. As the only penalty imposed upon the deserters was forfeiture of pay and allowances, and disfranchisement by the central government, which power does not, it must be recalled, fix the qualifications of voters, these returning deserters were insolent and abusive to the crippled soldiers who had endured the perils and losses of the service. They began to appear in various places in New Hampshire the last of May.[3] But all through that summer word went out from many of the States of the presence of deserters reappearing from Canada, and "other parts unknown." In New Jersey men who had fled after being drafted brought dissatisfaction to the loyal portion of the community by their return to lucrative posts; citizens in New York felt apprehensive for the security of their property and good order because of the large number of returned deserters; the governor of Minnesota desired the War Department to hold the returning poltroons in that State to strict accountability for their infamous conduct. From Wisconsin in September came complaints of turbulence in the town of Benton, due to disloyal men and the returned renegades from duty.[4] The disloyal element in Indiana was increased by the return of some draft-dodgers.

[1] Ibid., pp. 589, 793; Ser. III, V, 111.
[2] Ibid., Ser. I, XXXIV, pt. III, 305.
[3] bid., Ser. III, V, 110, 111.
[4] Ibid. The town of Benton, Wisconsin, was complained of as disloyal throughout the war.

There can be no doubt that much of the problem of desertion was due to the aid furnished by civilians. The instances of enticing soldiers to desert which occurred in 1861 were probably due to sympathy with the Confederacy,[1] but the later cases were undoubtedly inspired, in part at least, by weariness with the length of the war. One of the actuating motives of the Knights of the Golden Circle and of the Sons of '76 was to embarrass the government by procuring desertions, which were at their height during 1863. Hence, the government was forced early to take steps to combat this insidious evil. In October, 1861, the arrest of persons inducing soldiers to desert was authorized by the Department of State.[2] And stern measures were taken to combat the activity of the treasonable societies, as is well known, even to the suspension of the habeas corpus, the prohibition of the general sale of arms and ammunition, and censorship of the press.[1] The Enforcement Act of March 3, 1863, took hold of the problem aggressively by penalizing the crime of enticing a soldier to desert, or of harboring, concealing, giving employment to, or carrying him away, or of purchasing his arms by imposing imprisonment for a period of six months to two years and by a fine of $500.[3]

[1] Marcus C. Stanley was a conspicuous case. Charged with breaking up the Empire City Regiment of New York City by the many desertions which he induced, he was arrested September 11, 1861, and released September 21 by order of the State Department (*O. W. R.*, Ser. II, II, 766).

[2] *Ibid.*, p. 118.

[3] *Ibid.*, Ser. I, L, pt. II, 150. General Wright excluded from the mails several newspapers published in California and Oregon because of their violent denunciations of the government.

[4] *United States Statutes at Large*, 1862–1863, chap. LXXV, sec. 24. *O. W. R.*, Ser. III, III, 128.

CHAPTER XV

COMPLEXITIES IN DESERTION

Pretense, dishonesty, and double-dealing in desertion are factors which complicate for both sides [1] a problem already sufficiently involved. When the investigator learns of spies assuming the rôle of deserter as a convenient guise in which to enter the enemy's lines, when he encounters genuine deserters driven to pretending allegiance to the other flag when the vagaries of fate threw them once more within the power of their true country, the maze of deception becomes so tangled that he despairs of unraveling all the snarled threads. And such crossing back and forth through the picket lines, such double-crossing, and such easy throwing off and on of allegiance places at least an interrogation point behind all attempts at exact figures. Probably, however, the actual number of cowards and scoundrels who played such hare and hounds with the flags of the two republics were comparatively few. But some recognition of the existence of such duplicity is necessary so that the reader shall not conceive of this subject as a simple tale.

Evidence is indisputable of spies who pretended to the Confederates that they were disgruntled deserters from the Union army; and the Federal officials had good cause for their concern lest repentant Southern deserters returning to the fold prove in reality dangerous spies. Several striking instances are worth recounting.

A man employed in the office of the provost marshal general of the United States entered the Confederate lines in Virginia about the middle of September, 1864, as a deserter, was taken to Petersburg, and eventually landed in Castle Thunder in Richmond, where he was detained three weeks. From there he was sent to Lynchburg, Virginia, and from that point to southwestern Virginia, whence he was marched under guard to the border of Kentucky to be liberated. By November 11 he had made his way back to his headquarters

---

[1] For the sake of clarity and simplicity the writer is treating here a subject which logically should have treatment in each of the two parts into which this study is organized.

at City Point, Virginia, via Cincinnati and Lexington. To him the Union officials owed their information concerning the Confederate disposition of Northern deserters and the detection of many of them as they attempted to slip through the picket lines from Kentucky.[1]

Another party of eight Union soldiers set out from a camp in Tennessee in December, 1862, to ascertain the situation of the enemy near Lebanon and to pick up whatever information they could acquire. After crossing the Cumberland River and penetrating well within the enemy's lines, they stopped at a house, roused the woman occupant to be informed of the location of the nearest Confederate commander to whom they might make their surrender as deserters to be paroled. As the woman was readily duped, she applauded their purpose and contributed considerable valuable information. Even when the men were captured by a band of twenty Confederates, who surrounded the house where they had stopped for breakfast, they insisted upon their status as deserters with such vehemence that even the Southern leader was convinced of their sincerity. Imposing on his credulity, they watched their opportunity, took to the brush under some trivial pretext for turning aside, and made good their escape.[2]

A very interesting hoax of two Galvanized Yankees failed of complete success. Two Germans, who had surrendered and taken service with the Confederates at Mobile, were preparing to desert back to the Union army, carrying off as booty drawings and plans of the defenses of that important port. But a Southern detective, who had been set to catch them, pretended to enter into their plans, and by accompanying them from Mobile toward the United States lines succeeded in securing possession of the valuable papers.[3]

From the casual way in which one Union general alluded to a "spy, pretending to be a deserter," as brought into his camp and revealing certain information concerning the disposition and strength of the Confederate forces opposed to him,[4] the practice would appear to have been very familiar to the Union generals as one of the tactics of their side in 1862.

Sometimes, as has already been stated,[5] the Southerners, to their

[1] O. W. R., Ser. I, XLII, pt. III, 608–609.
[2] Ibid., Ser. I, XX, pt. II, 157.
[3] Maury, Recollections of a Virginian, p. 193.
[4] O. W. R., Ser. I, X, pt. I, 52.
[5] See above, page 186.

disgust, recognized would-be deserters turning their newly acquired knowledge of Southern geography to good account by leading and directing a movement of Union raiding parties against those to whom they had just professed to be friends and brothers.

Southern officers were alert to the possibility of such imposition, as is evidenced by a letter from General Beauregard to General Cooper: "Deserters from the Federal Army are continually arriving within our lines, and from their statements many are, no doubt, honest in their action and intention, while others are probably impostors and commit the act for the purpose of gaining information, or to perform any other crime that may prove injurious to our cause." [1]

On the other hand, the Confederates resorted to the same device as a ready and plausible disguise for their spies to assume. The Northern officers early became suspicious and attempted to prevent the acquisition of any information by such persons. [2] In 1862 Stanton was warned by General Boyle from Kentucky that deserters, taking the oath and being paroled, were agencies in the hands of the Confederacy—no more or less than spies. [3] By 1864 the likelihood that many spies were gaining entrance within the Union lines under this guise was accepted as a part of the game of war and duly reported by military officers, often in the following casual form: "This morning one of our recruits deserted to the enemy; probably a spy." [4] And a provost marshal in commenting on a man who had come over from the Sixth Virginia Infantry said: "Informant's manner of coming over into our lines and his sang-froid give rise to suspicions that he was purposely sent in, to return again via Norfolk, such cases having occurred." And if sang-froid was an earmark of the spy, it must be admitted that this individual was stamped, for he stated that he had come over for the purpose of exchanging newspapers, that he had had no intention of staying when he started, but after getting a few points, "he thought he would stay." [5]

---

[1] *O. W. R.*, Ser. I, XXXVI, pt. III, 878.

[2] Major Porter wrote as early as June 14, 1861, from Chambersburg, Pennsylvania, "The deserters give various accounts, and I believe in some cases they have been sent here to deceive. They gained no information" (*O. W. R.*, Ser. I, II, 684).

[3] *Ibid.*, Ser. I, XVI, pt. I, 747, 751.

[4] *Ibid.*, Ser. I, XXXII, pt. III, 45.

[5] *Ibid.*, Ser. I, XLII, pt. III, 609.

Some of the fine points in the game are revealed in the ingenious suggestion of General D. H. Hill to a fellow Confederate officer: "B. and C. [the names are not revealed] tell me that our deserters are also suspected, and that the last two sent down are in irons. I wish, therefore, to arrange a plan with you for chasing the deserters and firing upon them until you run them into their lines. This would relieve all suspicions and enable me to stuff Foster to my heart's content." [1] This was the selfsame General Foster of the United States army of whom Hill had just declared, "It seems, then, a difficult task to put Foster on a wrong scent again." [2]

Sometimes the pretense of desertion was carried through to secure much needed equipment for the South and must be admitted as a clever ruse. General Maxey boasted as late as the winter of 1864 that "Yanks are frequently deceived by our men [bushwhackers], who come in and join and get guns, etc., and leave." [3] Sometimes it was resorted to in order to reap the double profit of a fat bounty and transportation South; this occurred when a prisoner of war in some Northern prison took the oath of allegiance, enlisted as a substitute for the sake of the bounty, though he knew clearly his intention of violating his new oath as soon as possible.[4]

But the South learned that the trick of "pulling the leg" of the foe was a game at which both could play, for if Southern deserters played the Union government for guns and clothing, the Northern bounty-jumpers played the Confederacy for mounts. A Union spy reports how a group of about thirty Northern deserters had joined a Confederate command, while on their way from confinement in Richmond at Castle Thunder to the Kentucky frontier, with the sole intention of being mounted, stealing the horses, and deserting.[5]

Occasionally the deception was due to the exigencies of a situation where the deserter was using his wits in any fashion to save his rascally neck. For instance, until the Union government had learned that the Confederacy was escorting Union deserters to the Kentucky border where they were turned loose to slip through the lines, the returning renegades secured simple entry by represent-

---

[1] O. W. R., Ser. I, XVIII, 1022.

[2] Ibid.

[3] Ibid., Ser. I, LIII, 965.

[4] Ibid., Ser. II, VII, 614. The South then paraded them as wishing to fight on her side but forced into the Union army (statement of Grant).

[5] Ibid., Ser. I, XLII, pt. III, 608–609.

ing themselves as deserters from the Confederate service. But after the Union learned to scrutinize each man who attempted to enter at that point, the simple trick of changing allegiance, as one faced North or South, failed.[1]

Occasionally there are to be found instances of double desertion, first from one side and then from the other, prompted not by a justifiable desire to return to the flag of one's real allegiance, however the means to achieve that end were execrated, but prompted apparently by utter depravity of character. A Confederate officer in describing his work in breaking up horse-thieving and plundering in West Virginia, reported the death of a deserter from their army, who had joined the Yankees, and deserted them to turn horse-thief and robber. His concluding words need no comment, that the man in question was "a great scoundrel."[2] Another man, a notorious bushwhacker, after originally belonging to the rebel army, deserted, was arrested by the United States, but allowed to enlist in the Eleventh Missouri Cavalry of the United States Army, which he accompanied only to Arkansas, where he deserted.[3] The reader will scarcely repose the confidence which General Jefferson Thompson did in two men who, according to their story, had been taken captive by the Northern army as Confederate prisoners of war and compelled to join the Federal army. He seemed to feel that he could rely confidently on information secured from them, but they had fallen into Thompson's hands while straggling from the Federals.[4]

Perhaps the palm for sleight-of-hand ease in shifting allegiance, must be awarded the captain who, originally a deserter from the Confederate army, became a captain of a company of Federal troops, then took advantage of General Breckinridge's proclamation of amnesty to return to the Confederacy, finally deserting from Yancy County, North Carolina, carrying with him some 250 men. This record puts four alternations of allegiance to his credit.[5]

Occasionally these tricksters received their just reward, for during Sheridan's Richmond raid, a guide, either a deserter or rebel in Union uniform, who had deliberately misled a Union party up

---

[1] *Ibid.*, Ser. IV, III, 863–864.
[2] *Ibid.*, Ser. I, XIX, pt. II, 631.
[3] *Ibid.*, Ser. I, XXXIV, pt. IV, 196. See also the position of Grant (*ibid.*, Ser. II, VI, 991).
[4] *Ibid.*, Ser. I, XLI, pt. III, 1013.
[5] *Ibid.*, Ser. I, XLIX, pt. I, 1034. For another turncoat, see Browne, *Four Years in Secessia*, p. 309.

to the very mouth of some Confederate guns, had his brains blown out by the leader of the party, who had suspected him of treachery from the first.[1]

Such shifts did not render any simpler the relations between the governments in regard to treatment of prisoners. The first and most natural ground of dispute would relate to men who had been conscripted for service, and had escaped to enter service on the other side. The United States consistently maintained the position that escape from conscription in the Confederate army could not be construed as desertion, where a soldier had never been sworn into the Confederate army. It insisted that such men, when taken captive in battle, should be treated as prisoners of war and not as deserters.[2] The Confederacy, on the other hand, felt obliged to be vigilant that men who had deserted their service should not escape the just penalty for that crime as prisoners of war. One officer answered tartly when approached by the Federals with regard to some executions, "I certainly do not feel called on to account to you for the disposition made of deserters from our service." [3]

This point led to a spirited exchange between Generals Pickett and Peck, involving even Grant and Johnston, when Peck protested against the execution of some North Carolinians of the Second United States North Carolina regiment and held eight Confederate officers of high rank at Fort Monroe as hostages for their safety. Pickett declared that if the latter could be proved to be deserters from the Federal army, Peck would be fully justified in treating them as the North Carolinians had been treated, but otherwise, should the Union officer retaliate by death for the execution of the deserters, he would "simply be guilty of murder." [4]

A phase of the subject which merits, at least, brief consideration is that of the relationship of desertion to our pension system. While the writer feels that any complete investigation of the degree to which deserters have crept upon our pension rolls would carry the study too far afield, it is clear that some recognition of the sub-

---

[1] *Battles and Leaders,* IV, 191.

[2] *O. W. R.,* Ser. I, XXXIV, pt. II, 530–531; Ser. II, VI, 991. See the way in which reports of capture of thirty-one North Carolina deserters was followed up by the Confederate officers (*ibid.,* Ser. I, XLVII, pt. II, 1406).

[3] *Ibid.,* Ser. II, VIII, 500–501.

[4] *Ibid.,* Ser. I, XXXIII, 867–870; Ser. II, VI, 994. For a similar case in Louisiana, see *ibib,* Ser. I, XLI, pt. II, 918.

ject is necessary in order to indicate one more of the many complexities of this involved subject. Desertion, a problem to the administrators of the war period, still claims time and consideration from the grateful legislators of the present day.

Not content with voting liberal pensions to all soldiers who had been honorably discharged, the legislators began to correct the war records of individuals. There existed in the eighties general legislation so liberal that most deserters ought to have been able to free themselves from the stigma of being "absent without official leave." But on March 2, 1889, Congress wrote on the statute books an "Act for the relief of certain volunteers and regular soldiers of the late war and the war with Mexico." It generously provides that a charge of desertion on the records of the adjutant general of the army may be expunged if it "shall be made to appear to the satisfaction of the Secretary of War" that the person so charged returned to his command within a reasonable time; that he had absented himself while suffering from wounds, injuries, or disease contracted in the line of duty; or that he had reënlisted in the army or navy within four months from the date of deserting.[1]

This mitigation from the rigors of war rules was passed on the plea that much of the desertion during the Civil War was due to mistreatment of the privates by the officers, or to the preference of the soldiers for serving in other companies or regiments than those to which they had been assigned.

But this act, it must be confessed, opened the door wide to the opportunity for falsification of records, if a pension-seeker had an elastic conscience. It would not be difficult, nearly a half-century after the close of the war, for a deserter to declare, without any very grave danger of detection, provided he was familiar with the military organization of 1865, that he had reënlisted. If he knew the name of some dead private of another regiment than his own, and if he could find one or two obliging friends who recalled "the fact" of his reënlistment, he could be assured of clearing his record and of drawing a pension.

The wisdom of Congress in allowing later service in the military ranks to efface an earlier act of desertion is questionable, aside from the temptation thus presented for falsification, as it fails to take note of the evils of bounty-jumping. There are thousands of cases on the records of a man enlisting for the period of the war in one com-

[1] *United States Statutes at Large,* XXV, chap. 390.

pany, serving for a few months, deserting, enlisting again a little later in another company under a fresh name for the sake of the bounties, and this time, possibly serving out his term. But he usually saw to it, under such circumstances, that when he was mustered out, it was under his real name. It is hard to follow the logic of Congress in decreeing that on the day such a man absconded he should be considered to have been "honorably discharged from the military service of the United States."

Although the law as originally passed required that applications for relief from the charge of desertion should be made before July 1, 1889, it was later extended for two years, and finally in 1895 all limitation of time was removed.

It is furthermore notorious that thousands of private bills have been introduced each session of Congress for the purpose of "relief" of deserters and soldiers dishonorably discharged and that hundreds of these cases have been rushed through during the last few hectic days of a session. In the session of 1910–1911 Congress devised the euphemistic phraseology which avoided all embarrassing reference to the old record and to an "order of dismissal by general courts-martial." Relief bills were made to read "that in the administration of the pension laws — — shall hereafter be held and considered to have been honorably discharged from the military service of the United States." [1] Congress in the last decade has improved upon that phraseology even, for now the word pension is omitted and the person who is to be considered "honorably discharged" is to share in any laws conferring rights, privileges, and benefits upon honorably discharged soldiers. [2]

Undoubtedly, the correcting of the record in many cases has been an act of mere justice. Many men, prevented by capture, by injuries, or by a shift of location of the camp from returning to their companies after a battle, found the word "deserter" entered unjustly after their names. Usually, it would appear that the interested parties by proper application to the War Department and by submission of evidence could clear their records. It is difficult, therefore, not to associate the thought of a pension with the belated zeal for correcting the record, when such relief bills are pressed fifty years and more after the invidious act occurred, especially since it is much harder for

---

[1] *Congressional Record,* 61st Cong., 2d sess., Sen. Resolution, No. 864.
[2] For an illustration see *United States Statutes at Large,* XLIV, pt. III. 417.

the government to prove the charge of desertion then than if the case had been opened only a few years after the war, when more uninterested witnesses would have been obtainable and when memories were fresher, to say nothing of the fact that legislators felt less temptation to take a generous view of a soldier's possible delinquencies.

Some of the presidents have used their veto power in an effort to prevent abuse of the pension system. President Grant, for instance, who presumably felt a special interest in cases of military discipline, vetoed four bills, intended to relieve deserters from the legal effect of their acts and to entitle them to pensions.[1] One of the bills was passed over his veto on the ground that the man was not a deserter.[2] To President Cleveland must be accorded fearlessness of the soldiers' vote, as he set his face steadily against the granting of excessive pensions. One of the most interesting of his many vetoes was one refusing the grant of a pension to a soldier wounded in attempting to desert![3]

The study made by Mr. William Bayard Hale of bills to alter the military records of soldiers during the session of 1910–1911, cases which he assures us were picked out at random, records several of manifest violence to justice in regard to desertion—injustice in regard to the tax-payers.[4] Probably the most conspicuous case which he cites is that of a man, whe returned on September 21, 1864, from confinement on the Dry Tortugas for eighteen months for the offense of desertion, where he had been branded on the left hip with a large letter *D*. On the date of his return from the islands his head was shaved in accordance with the sentence of the court-martial and he was drummed out of camp. But the act of Congress altered the record to show "honorable discharge" on that date.[5]

In order to determine whether the problem of Civil War desertions

[1] *Congressional Record,* 43d Cong., 2d sess., House Resolution, No. 4462; 44th Cong., 1st sess., House Resolutions, Nos., 83, 1337, 3367.

[2] *Ibid.,* House Resolutions, No. 1337, *Congressional Record,* 44th Cong., 1st sess., 4940, 5010–5011.

[3] Hale, "The Pension Carnival," *The World's Work,* XXI, 13977.

[4] A series of articles running through *The World's Work,* from October, 1910, to March, 1911 (XX and XXI). The writer was interested to follow a number of the cases cited by Mr. Hale and found that almost all the bills passed despite the exposure and a considerable public interest in the matter of the pension abuse. See *United States Statutes at Large,* XXXVI, pt. II, 1701, 1919, 1920, 1999.

[5] Hale, *op. cit.,* 14160. House Resolution, 61st Cong., 3d sess., No. 21646. *Sen. Reports,* 61st Cong., 2d sess., vol. A, No. 174.

is still existent as a problem to harass the present Congresses, the writer made a study of the measures to correct military records passed by the Sixty-ninth Congress, sitting during the years 1925–1927, the latest laws available for study at the time when this book was being written. In sixty-seven cases altered from dishonorable to honorable discharge, thirty-six corrected the records of Civil War Soldiers. Two veterans were literally reaching out from the grave to bless their dependents, for the charges, whatever they were which were staining their memories, were being blotted out after their death —probably to solace their widows.[1] Although the act in each case declared that "no pension, back pay, or bounty shall accrue *prior* to the passage of this act," it is legitimate to raise the query of the reason for this zeal in securing a clear record. The answer may possibly be found in a scrutiny of the pension rolls for the next few sessions of Congress.[2]

Time is thought to solve most problems, but the complexities of desertion resulting from the Civil War have not been untangled in more than sixty years.

[1] *United States Statutes at Large,* XLIV, pt. III, 1811, 1461.
[2] Of course, it is not necessarily true that all of these thirty-six cases involved dishonorable discharge because of desertion.

CHAPTER XVI

Effects of Northern Desertion

The reader who has followed this account of the defections in the Union army has been brought, long before this, to the conclusion that the amount of desertion was appallingly great. He needs only to be reminded of Grant's estimate that for every eight bounties paid, his army was benefited by the services of one good soldier, or Rosecrans's calculation that as early as 1862 the government paid one hundred men to get the services of seventy-five or eighty. In other words, the strength of the army would have steadily diminished except for constant fresh enlistments. The bald number of desertions for the period of the war is likely to stagger the lay reader.

The conclusion to which one is brought by a study of the desertion in the volunteer army for the entire war period as compared with the regular troops is most surprising as it reveals a larger proportion where it would not be expected—in the regular army. In that branch of the service it reached the high rate of 244.25 per thousand, according to the provost marshal general, while it was but 62.51 in the volunteers. One is forced to the inference that the men who enlisted in the regular service were far inferior in character to the troops furnished by the States. But local pride and awakened patriotism poured its best into the volunteer organizations. When that was exhausted, the draft dragged in an inferior class into the volunteer army.

Secondly, the conclusion seems just and accurate that desertion was swelled by the foreigner and bounty-jumper from the large cities in the East, if the comparative statistics of the provost marshal general are to be relied upon, which show a far higher ratio for the Eastern States with their large urban population, in which the foreign population was already a large factor, than for the Western States where a large native-born proportion prevailed.

The student of this subject is inevitably driven to the firm conviction that the bounty system, as practised by the United States in the Civil War, was thoroughly vicious. With the threat of a draft always over their heads, local officials did not bother to reason the policy through and to foresee that the generous cash bounties offered as bait for enlistments, offered encouragement also to repeated desertion for such "easy money." They were interested only in the fact that bounties in hand secured recruits, while to the central government was left all the problems resulting from their ill-directed zeal, such as the recovery of the deserters. The larger the sum the recruit received, the more easily did he take his departure. When, on the other hand, the State authorities thought wisely to remove the temptation to desert by paying the bounties in installments, the inducement to enlist was also diminished as only bounties paid in advance were attractive to the professional enlister.

That the creation of the office of provost marshal general in 1862 did check desertion and did return many deserters is irrefutable. It cannot be successfully asserted that the number of deserters was markedly reduced in 1864 from that reached in 1863, but it is clear that with the lower character of drafted men the number would have been far greater, but for the deterring influence of the activity of the provost everywhere felt and seen in the army and in the cities of the North. As recorded earlier, the bureau claimed credit for returning 75,000 deserters to the army.

Desertion operated to reduce the army in a double fashion. It not only subtracted a given number of men from the ranks but it worked to check enlistments, especially before the application of the draft when it was desirable that no influence should dampen the ardor of possible volunteers. Illegal absentees, to palliate their own crime, told wildly exaggerated stories of the unnecessary hardships and sufferings of campaign life, of the barbarities practised upon them by their officers, and of the carnage of the battle-field. These tales gained credence and, in the opinion of the provosts, were among the most serious obstacles to recruiting.[1]

Desertion was very costly to the United States, from a monetary point of view. There is first to be taken into account the cost of the arms, clothing, and equipment with which the soldier disappeared. If he went over to the enemy, he sold his arms to the Confederate authorities,[2] thus supplying them with the greatly needed means to

[1] O. W. R., Ser. III, V, 676, 755.
[2] Colonel Ford reported from Houston, Texas, that he had agents busy buying arms from the Yankee deserters (O. W. R., Ser. I, LIII, 994).

continue the war; if he tried to play a lone hand in order to effect
his escape North, he frequently sold his clothing and arms to the
needy Confederate citizens; but even if he threw away his arms,
buried his clothing after he had disguised himself in civilian garments, or hid them in his own cellar, they represented so much
material and cash withdrawn from the Federal treasury as waste. If,
as Draper estimated in December, 1862, the deserters then absent had
cost the government $10,000,000 without reference to bounties,[1]
they must have cost more than twice as much by the close of the war,
due to the heavy expense of the bureau.

When the government embarked on the policy of an aggressive
pursuit of the renegades by launching the system of provosts, in
the fall of 1862, it was fastening another heavy burden on the
shoulders of the tax-payers. The quartermaster's report for the
year ending June 30, 1864, shows $157,031 paid in bounties alone for
the apprehension of deserters, and for the final months of the war,
November, 1864, to April 1865, $12,158 for the same purpose.[2] The
total expense for the operations of the bureau in arresting deserters
cannot be computed as distinct from its other activities of enrolling
recruits, and so on, but it is clear that it must have been a heavy item.[3]
Probably Senator Wilson was correct in his opinion that the expense
incurred was justified by the results.[4]

The experience of the bureau proved indisputably that the reward
for apprehending deserters must be sufficiently high to prove attractive and remunerative to those engaging in it. When the sum was
kept at the negligible amount of $5, few deserters were arrested, and
the necessary incidental expenses which were not included in the fee
when it was kept at the lower figure, generally swelled the amount to

[1] *Ibid.*, Ser. III, II, 940.
[2] *Ibid.*, Ser. III, IV, 876. Although the report for 1865 includes the period
up to November 1, 1865, the figures are accurate for the war period, as practically no arrests were made after April.
[3] The provost marshal for Illinois, James Oakes, estimated the expense
of operation in his district for each man placed in the army, including deserters
and drafted men, at an average cost per man of $13.46. As it certainly cost as
much to arrest and return a deserter as to draft and enroll a new man, some
slight conception of the cost of desertion may be arrived at by multiplying
the cost per man by the total number of deserters returned, 81,000. But even
the above estimate included only the items connected with the provost marshal's office and were exclusive of the cost of transportation. If all the items
were included, the average cost per man would be greatly increased (*House Ex.
Doc.*, 39th Cong., 1st sess., No. 1, vol. IV, pt. 2, 22).
[4] *Congressional Globe*, 38th Cong., 1st sess., pt. II, 1249.

more than the larger sum of $30 which was later paid, not to mention the clerical cost of examining expense vouchers. Coupled as the arrest always was with the possibility of the man proving not to be a deserter, and with the risk attending capture, men of the right kind would not make arrests for a negligible reward.[1] And the higher amount would naturally prove more of a restraint on the would-be deserter, as it was deducted from his pay, if he were apprehended.

As in the South, the defection cost the use of some loyal men to intercept the deserters. We find an officer writing to Sheridan that he was obliged to send a battalion of the Eighth Illinois Cavalry to Fort Tobacco, Maryland, to intercept deserters from the Army of the Potomac; and that he already had a battalion on duty picketing the upper Potomac.[2] We know that bodies of cavalry and details were available for the various provosts in their searches and seizures of skulkers in the North. Soldiers serving in that capacity were not available to fight the Confederates.

When all factors are duly weighed, it is apparent that the one action which really availed to reduce desertion was the greater severity of the courts-martial in imposing the death penalty and of the officers in executing the sentence. The real deterrent manifest in the fall of 1864 and in 1865 was the greater certainty that the sin would bring the ultimate penalty of death.

Here should be discussed the question of the wisdom or folly of the clemency of the government toward the crime of desertion. It was the opinion of Provost Marshal General Fry that the government was entirely at fault in not promptly punishing deserters severely. He held that the country was enthusiastically supporting the war, and that it would have assented to whatever stringent measures seemed necessary to maintain the integrity of the army and to suppress desertion; that it understood and expected an inflexible war policy and the remorseless execution of deserters. The government delayed until such swarms of deserters thronged every State that it was too late to avert the calamity. All could not be shot and so none were shot—and the evil increased. But it is necessary to recall that such severe measures as execution for desertion could not justly have been applied to high-minded patriots not yet adjusted to, or comprehending the necessity of, military discipline; by the fall of

---

[1] *O. W. R.*, Ser. III, V, 754, 834. One provost advocated a reward of $100, the agent then to bear all expenses (*ibid.*).

[2] *Ibid.*, Ser. I, XLIII, pt. II, 63-64.

1862 when it was recognized for the serious evil it was, thousands and thousands of officers and privates were absent. Lincoln was exactly right when he exclaimed to Miss Livermore's query of why the law was not being enforced, "Because you cannot order men shot by dozens and twenties. People won't stand it, and they ought not stand it." [1] He probably understood the temper of the country when he told her that if he took to shooting men by the score for desertion, he would have "such a hullabaloo" about his ears as he had not yet evoked. [2]

It is hard for us to-day to realize how much disunion and division of sentiment there was in the North during the war. Lincoln was obliged to guide and lead the people gently, never getting out of touch with the masses, and it is the judgment of the writer that severity in regard to desertion to the point of the death penalty could not have been resorted to in the early years of the war, that it was only possible to a large degree by 1864 because the nation by means of four years of war and by the revelation of disloyal secret organizations had become educated to the inevitability of war rigor in time of war. By promptly inflicting shooting for unauthorized, possibly temporary, absence, Lincoln could easily have become completely alienated from the people. On the other hand, if the war had lasted a few years longer, the government, steadily growing stronger, might really have been able to suppress desertion by pursuing a policy of ruthless execution, though the method had by no means attained success by the time the war closed.

One need have no hesitation in drawing the conclusion that the long delays between arrest and trial afforded the reckless and often skilled deserter too great opportunity for escape. For desperate and proved offenders, immediate trial and swift execution would have been justice and would have left a salutary influence on their comrades in arms.

It is obvious that absenteeism must have cost the North victories. Sherman frankly states that the absence of 70,000 men almost lost the battle of Shiloh to the Union. [3]

---

[1] Livermore, *My Story of the War,* p. 559.

[2] *Ibid.*

[3] "This cause nearly defeated us at Shiloh, when 57,000 were absent from their regiment without leave. . . . This abuse has led to may catastrophes, and you can't pick up a paper without some order of the President and Secretary of War on the subject" (July 31, 1862. *Sherman's Home Letters,* p. 232).

As on the Southern side, one finds but a few points to be placed on the credit side of the ledger for desertion; there is but one in fact, and that only for the disease in its incipient stage of straggling. Better flankers than these temporary absentees, we are told by one writer, could not be found, for, spreading out from the marching column, they were the first to scent danger, and the last to leave the field. And, wandering off by themselves, small parties of them without officers would join together to resist a squad of Confederate cavalry, or to make an unpremeditated attack on the small body of the enemy suddenly discovered in their path, in which encounters they usually came off victors.[1]

But it could not be pretended, obviously, that this one credit offset in any appreciable way the debits to be charged against the evil practice of irregular absence from the ranks.

[1] Nichols, *The Story of the Great March*, p. 243.

CHAPTER XVII

CONCLUSION

COMPARISON OF DESERTION IN THE TWO SECTIONS

It may be well to begin our conclusions with a statement of a fact which is all but completely obscured by the emphasis placed in this study on the worst, if happily the comparatively small, element in both armies. Both sides have just cause to be proud of the vast majority of the men engaged in the war between the States. Testimonies of their remarkable daring and coolness under fire, the dependence which could be placed upon them in emergencies, their obedience to orders in an engagement, the stoicism with which they endured the hardships incident to a difficult terrain and climate without murmur are legion and are taken for granted by the writer. Likewise the sustained enthusiasm and dogged determination of the majority of the civilian population to support the war, whether to win independence from an oppressive, centralized government or to sustain the integrity of the Union, need no comment or eulogy.

In the next place, the reader should be reminded that desertion neither made its appearance in the world with the Civil War nor vanished with it. It existed as a problem in the army of the Unted States before 1861 as the abolition of flogging as a cure in 1860 sufficiently attests; and it failed to have found a cure by 1865, for we find the provosts gravely discussing it in 1866 and President Johnson again interposing with an offer of pardon. It has tormented other nations in other periods. Its existence as a thorn in the flesh for Napoleon has already been commented on; it is a notorious fact that the number of deserters from Wellington's army in Spain and Portugal, who deliberately abandoned the British Jack and wandered about the alien country, was by no means inconsiderable; while the behavior of the German and French regular soldiers in the Franco-Prussian War of 1870, in dashing back in panic through the village of Gambetta, but furnishes another instance of departure in practice from the theory of military tradition.

A further factor, which the reader should keep in mind in order not to despise the subject of this treatise, is the change in attitude on the part of the civilian mind. While the officers of the regular army and those trained in the West Point tradition execrated the evil as a crime, the layman seems to have condoned it as excusable when the hardships of war proved more than human flesh could be expected to bear. But to-day the term *deserter* is one of reproach and disgrace on the lips of every one and the average layman learns with surprise and some doubt that the penalty for desertion is not always death, without alternative. Still human nature continues in the flesh weak and faulty and desertion has not even yet vanished from the face of the globe; probably it will become obsolete only when wars have ceased to exist. The writer has been told by an American officer who served in France during the World War that it was a rare morning that he was not awakened at daybreak by a single salvo of guns from the British camp which announced that desertion was still execrated in the British army and that that execration was being emphasized to some unfortunates.

A close comparison of the losses in both armies due to desertion alone yields some interesting facts. If we accept Livermore's figures of the number of enlistments in the Union armies as 1,556,678 with Fry's estimate of 200,000 desertions as compared with 1,082,119 services in the Confederate armies and 104,000 desertions, the proportion of desertion is even greater in the Union than in the Confederate army. It stands one desertion to each seven enlistments in the Northern army as compared with one to nine in the Confederate army. In both, however, it was obviously a grave and serious evil, threatening to undermine the armies. The fundamental difference lay in the fact that whereas it was growing worse in the Confederate ranks so that by 1865 that army was visibly melting away, the condition seemed to be improving in the Northern armies where the authorities were beginning to get a grip on the evil, as that section grew in consciousness of its strength.

The loss of material equipment carried off by the absconding soldiers in the form of clothing and arms represented a loss to each side, but in the balance it was more telling against the Confederacy because it could less well afford the loss and because it was far more difficult for it to replace the guns and uniforms with the tightening blockade.

The greater wealth of the Union produced another evil from which the Confederacy was free, because of its very poverty—the vicious bounty system. As noted before, a Union soldier might cost the governments, national, state, and local, from first to last, up to $800. The bounty, intended as an inducement to enlistment, became in truth an inducement to desertion, as so lucrative a trade yielded its largest profits by being assiduously applied, and as it furnished the cash to facilitate departure. In general, those States which gave the most liberal local bounties were marked by the largest proportion of deserters.

The system developed one feature peculiar to the North—the bounty-broker, for which, happily for the South, it had no equivalent, the men who monopolized the business of seeking out and presenting volunteers and substitutes and who thereby pocketed handsome profits on the transaction at the expense in the end of Uncle Sam, who received shoddy goods or none at all.

Both sides were too lenient in dealing with defection in the beginning; and this statement is made with full recognition of the fact that probably neither could have pursued a different policy under existing conditions, even if they had seen clearly from the very first the compelling necessity of a different course.

Both tried to coax instead of to drive the deserters back into the ranks and with similar results—indifferent success. Lincoln put forth two offers of general pardon, those of 1863 and of 1865; the Confederates offered what amounted to three general amnesties, the executive offer of August, 1863, that of 1864 put out by the two chief commanders in the field, and, finally, Lee's amnesty upon assuming the post of general-in-chief of the armies. But the North was happier in the phraseology in which the pardon was couched, for it seemed less of a prayer to soldiers to return and more of a threat to return or pay the penalty. In other words, the North saved its face better.

Another difference lay in the number of appeals. The North seemed not to need to learn that soldiers were not to be lured back to hardships which they had forsaken by fair words, by flattery, and by appeals to their honor, whereas the South was prolific in perfervid oratory from Davis, from the military commanders, from the governors, and even from private citizens who flattered themselves that they wielded an influence.

The penalties were, naturally, with people of the same race and bred in the same West Point traditions, similar, except that the

Confederates were much more ingenious with their barrel-jackets, gagging, and bucking, probably because they were more loath to lose the men by inflicting the full rigor of the law—men were too scarce and precious. But in the end both had to come to exacting the death penalty. The chief difference was that the Federal authorities grew steadily more severe, inflicted the death sentence almost daily and with greater consistency so that although the evil had by no means ceased, the signs were pointing toward extermination. If the war had lasted a few years longer, desertion might have been largely harried out of the Union army.

A like-minded people devised similar agencies to cope with the problem: the South a Conscript Bureau, the north a Provost Marshal General's Bureau, each with a division or branch for deserters, but the latter was much more widely and efficiently organized and, hence, more effective. Both detailed men from the army to gather in absentees to aid the bureau agents, but the drain on the Union army was far less than on the Confederate, where such prominent generals as Pillow, Sam Jones, Forrest, and Polk took over for periods of time the task of "driving" the country for renegades. The pursuit also was less unrelenting, less bitter in the North. Though deserters were besieged in a log fortress in Indiana and pursued to their hiding-places in the mountains of Pennsylvania, there was no cordon drawn as if hunting game nor tracking of soldiers with bloodhounds as was done in the swamps of Florida. There was, in consequence, very little in the North of that intensely bitter feeling which persistent harrying of the deserter with troops and dogs inflamed in the heart of the Florida cracker or the North Carolina mountaineer, which held over into peace-time and led to more than one murder of an ex-home guardsman or Confederate officer, which the murderer regarded as praiseworthy vengeance.

The gain to be secured by encouraging desertion from the ranks of its foe occurred to the leaders of both sides. The North issued its General Orders No. 65, promising Confederate deserters pay for their equipment and immunity from enforced military service against their former compatriots; the South promptly retaliated with its General Orders No. 64, offering to assist prospective deserters in their journey back to their own homes in the North.

The offer of each government to purchase arms from the deserters was prompted by a double motive: to benefit itself and to injure the foe, and worked both ways. If the North spent much money on Confederate arms, it was well-invested. On the whole the North probably profited the more from this traffic, as the heavier proportional surrender to that side enabled it to rake in more of the precious guns and it could better afford the expenditure. Both lost in the subtraction of the arms and equipment carried off by their respective deserters.

On the whole, the treatment accorded the enemy deserter differed. Whereas the Union soon decided to parole deserters on the oath of allegiance, enlisting them only for Indian service in the Northwest, the Confederacy held Federal deserters practically as prisoners of war until it conceived the brilliant plan of facilitating passage through the Confederacy to the Federal line and of shipping foreign deserters to their home lands, thus solving the problem of getting deserters but of not having to feed them.

The demoralization of society marks a real difference between the two sections, due, of course, in part to the fact that the Confederacy was the theatre of war, but due also partly to the presence of such a vast horde of deserters in a relatively small population. Nowhere in the North was there such a *deserter-country* as existed in Alabama, Mississippi, and North Carolina, for Cambria and Sckulykill Counties of Pennsylvania are interesting only as affording a distant parallel; and 200,000 absentees, to take the largest possible estimate, scattered over an area of over two million square miles, was almost lost in a population of 23,000,000. Where the defiant renegades had ruffled the surface of society in Indiana and Iowa during the war, and where the returning deserters, slipping back over the Canadian border into Maine, Minnesota, and New Hampshire during the summer of 1865, troubled an orderly society by some turbulence, the ruffianly bands in the South, about one hundred thousand in a population of nine millions, which had been indulging for nearly two years in robbery, arson, and murder, threatened the very foundations of society. Whereas the disturbances quieted down almost at once in the Northern section, it is doubtful whether, even without Reconstruction, society in the old Confederacy would have become orderly at once and whether a Ku Klux Klan would not have manifested itself in some form.

To sum up the question, it may perhaps be said that though Confederate desertion was bad, appallingly so, it was offset by the desertion in the Union ranks. Taking for granted in the present state of our historical information the outcome, the fact that the South must have inevitably had to yield to superior resources and wealth, the Northern desertion is the factor the more to be deplored, as it lengthened the war, by distracting energies and men to struggle with this problem in the persons of the provost marshals and soldiers who might otherwise have been in the field; it added to the already enormous burden of taxation; while the tales of the Union deserters, added to the mere fact of their abandoning the cause, however unrepresentative these bounty-jumpers were of the men who were winning the war, kept up a fictitious courage and hope in the breasts of devoted Confederate leaders for the new republic, which only a few of the more clear-visioned among them divined was to prove a "Lost Cause."

APPENDIX

TABLE I
NUMBER OF DESERTERS FROM THE CONFEDERATE ARMY BY STATES

	Officers	*Men*
Maryland		28
Virginia	84	12,071
North Carolina	428	23,694
South Carolina	36	3,579
Georgia	79	6,797
Florida	8	2,211
Alabama	5	1,578
Mississippi	56	11,604
Louisiana	24	4,517
Texas	9	4,655
Arkansas	66	10,029
Missouri	45	4,365
Tennessee	153	12,155
Kentucky	16	3,466
Arizona		16
Indian Territory		154
Regular Army	5	1,274
Jeff. Davis Legion	14	1,207
Total	1,028	103,400 [1]

[1] *House Ex. Doc.,* Cong., 1st sess., No. 1, IV, pt. I, 141.

TABLE II

DESERTERS FROM THE CONFEDERACY RETURNED TO THE ARMIES

Virginia	8,596	
North Carolina	8,832	
South Carolina	2,514	(Since September, 1862)
Georgia	5,173	
Alabama	5,055	(Since February, 1864)
Mississippi	2,031	(Since February, 1864)
Florida	220	
East Louisiana	75	(Since August, 1864)
East Tennessee	560	(Since November, 1863)
Total	21,056	(Incorrectly added) [1]

[1] *House Ex. Doc.*, 39th Cong., 1st sess., No. 1, IV, pt. I, 139.

APPENDIX 233

Table III

Deserters from the Union Armies Reported by Regimental Commanders by Months

1863

April	4,044
May	2,646
June	3,956
July	5,540
August	5,447
September	5,469
October	4,391
November	3,376
December	3,427

1864

January	6,916
February	5,004
March	6,045
April	7,072
May	5,371
June	6,827
July	6,422
August	8,776
September	8,780
October	10,692
November	10,673
December	8,162

1865

January	6,753
February	6,404
March	5,621
April	7,019
Total	278,644 [1]

[1]*House Ex. Doc.*, 39th Congress, 1st sess., No. 1, IV, pt. I, 232–235.

TABLE IV

DESERTIONS FROM THE UNION ARMY BY STATES

United States Regulars and Volunteers	21,158
United States Veteran Reserve Corps	2,538
United States Colored Troops	8,607
United States Military Posts	9,561
United States Recruiting Stations	2,967
United States Draft Rendezvous	6,450
United States General Hospitals	33,430
United States Provost Marshal Headquarters	3,565
Maine	2,370
New Hampshire	3,648
Vermont	1,578
Massachusetts	7,352
Rhode Island	1,384
Connecticut	4,720
New York	44,913
New Jersey	8,468
Pennsylvania	24,050
Delaware	1,384
Maryland	5,328
District of Columbia	912
West Virginia	1,982
Ohio	18,354
Kentucky	7,227
Indiana	8,927
Illinois	16,083
Missouri	5,743
Iowa	2,627
Michigan	6,525
Wisconsin	3,415
Minnesota	576
Oregon	112
Washington Territory	378
California	1,855
Kansas	1,922
Nebraska	308
Colorado	219
Tennesse	3,690
Arkansas	2,245
North Carolina	142

South Carolina	209
Alabama	325
Mississippi	528
Florida	90
Louisiana	426
Texas	453
Total	278,044 [1]

[1] *House Ex. Doc.*, 39th Cong., 1st sess., No. 1, IV, pt. I, 234–235.

TABLE V

NUMBER OF DESERTERS FROM UNION ARMIES ARRESTED BY MONTHS

1863

May	580
June	2,364
July	3,597
August	4,983
September	5,002
October	4,842
November	3,570
December	3,221

1864

January	2,783
February	2,963
March	3,633
April	3,653
May	3,106
June	2,667
July	2,850
August	3,055
September	2,927
October	3,191
November	3,353
December	3,824

1865

January	2,979
February	2,394
March	2,075
April	1,173
Total	77,181 [1]

[1] *House Ex. Doc.*, 39th Cong., 1st sess., No. 1, IV, pt. I, 236–237.

BIBLIOGRAPHY

Public Documents

Articles of War for the Armies of the Confederacy (Richmond, Virginia, 1861).

Articles of War for the Armies of the United States (Washington).

Congressional Globe.

    The debates in Congress touched the subject very seldom.

House Executive Documents. Thirty-ninth Congress, First Session, Document No. 1, "Appendix to Report of Secretary of War."

    The report of the provost marshal general is found here in full.

Journal of the Senate of the Confederate States. Found in *United States Senate Documents,* Fifty-eighth Congress, Second Session, XVII.

    Valuable for showing the attitude of the legislators.

Confederate Statutes at Large (Richmond, Virginia, 1861–1864).

Statutes at Large of the United States (Washington).

The War of the Rebellion. A Compilation of the Records of the Union and Confederate Armies. (Referred to in the notes as *Official War Records,* or *O. W. R.*)

    This monumental compilation of the reports and correspondence of the military leaders directing the war, both Union and Confederate, has been invaluable for this study, and has been by far the chief source. Almost every volume of each of the four series has yielded some grist for the mill.

State Documents

Acts of the Assembly of Alabama, 1862, 1863.

Acts of the Assembly of Arkansas, 1862.

Acts of the Assembly of Georgia, 1863.

Acts of Louisiana, Special Session, 1863.

Laws of the Assembly of Mississippi, 1862.

Public Laws of North Carolina, 1864, 1864–1865.
Acts of the General Assembly of South Carolina, 1863.
Laws of the Thirty-fourth Assembly of Tennessee.
General Laws of the Ninth and Tenth Legislatures of Texas, 1863.
Laws of Virginia, 1863, 1864.

> The legislation of the Southern States is naturally valuable in revealing the sincerity of effort made locally to curb the evil. The printing of the session laws seems to have been so hastily and carelessly done that it is difficult to find identical copies for any given year in the libraries of the country.

Non-official Collections of Sources

American Annual Cyclopedia, 1861–1865, ed. W. T. Tenney.

> An admirable digest. Valuable, though not abundant, material on this subject is to be found scattered through these volumes. (After 1875 *Appleton's Annual Cyclopedia.*)

Battles and Leaders of the Civil War, ed. R. U. Johnson and C. Clough Buel (New York, 1887–1888), 4 vols.

> Papers of soldiers of all classes.

A Cycle of Adams Letters, ed. Worthington C. Ford (Boston and New York, 1920).

Hart, Albert Bushnell, *American History Told by Contemporaries* (New York, 1918), Volume IV.

Lee's Dispatches, ed. W. Jones DeRenne (New York, 1915).

> Unpublished letters of General Robert E. Lee to Jefferson Davis and to the War Department of the Confederate States of America.

Personal Narratives of Events in the War of the Rebellion, by Rhode Island soldiers and sailors (Providence: Rhode Island Historical Society, 1878).

Soldiers' Letters, ed. Lydia Minturn Post (New York, 1865).

Underwood, J. L., *The Women of the Confederacy* (New York, 1906).

Newspapers

Baltimore American and Commercial Advertiser.
The Sun (Baltimore).
Boston Daily Evening Transcript, 1865.

Charleston Daily Courier, 1863.
Chicago Tribune, 1862.
The Daily Sun (Columbus, Georgia), 1862.
The Detroit Free Press, 1863.
Daily Illinois State Journal (Springfield, Illinois).
Louisville Daily Democrat, 1862, 1863.
New York Daily Tribune, 1864.
The New York Herald, 1864.
Raleigh *Daily Progress,* 1863–1865.
North Carolina Standard, 1863–1865.
Richmond Enquirer, 1863.
Daily Richmond Examiner, 1863.
Richmond Whig, 1863.
The Morning News (Savannah, Georgia), 1862.

The material in the newspapers is naturally scattered and less abundant than might be hoped, no doubt because of the effort of both sides to conceal from the enemy knowledge of the degree of the evil.

Military Reminiscences and Personal Experiences

NORTHERN PARTICIPANTS.
Browne, Junius Henri, *Four Years in Secessia* (Hartford, 1865).
Dana, Charles A., *Recollections of the Civil War* (New York, 1913).
Goss, Warren Lee, *Recollections of a Private* (New York, 1890).
McClellan, George B., *McClellan's Own Story* (New York, 1887).
McElroy, John, *Andersonville* (Toledo, Ohio, 1879).
Meade, George G., *The Life and Letters of General George Gordon Meade* (New York, 1913).
Nichols, George Ward, *The Story of the Great March* (New York, 1866).
Noyes, George F., *The Bivouac and the Battle Field* (New York, 1863).
Paris, Comte de (Louis Philippe d'Orleans), *History of the Civil War in America* (Philadelphia, 1876).
Schurz, Carl, *Reminiscences* (New York, 1917).
Schurz, Carl, *Speeches, Correspondence and Political Papers* (New York, 1913–1917).
Home letters of General Sherman, ed. by M. A. De Wolfe Howe (New York, 1909).

240   DESERTION DURING THE CIVIL WAR

The Sherman Letters (New York, 1894).

Sheridan, P. H., *Personal Memoirs* (New York, 1888).

Trobriand, Philip Régis de, *Quatre ans de campagnes à l'armée du Potomac* (Paris, 1867–1868).

Wallace, Lew, *An Autobiography* (New York, 1906).

Wilkeson, Frank, *Recollection of a Private Soldier* (New York, 1887).

SOUTHERN PARTICIPANTS.

Barron, S. B., *The Lone Star Defenders* (New York, 1908).

Borcke, J. H. Heros von, *Memoirs of the Confederate War for Independence* (Philadelphia, 1867).

Casler, J. O., *Four Years in the Stonewall Brigade* (Dallas, 1906).

Cooke, John Esten, *Wearing of the Gray* (New York, 1865).

Eggleston, George Cary, *A Rebel's Recollections* (New York, 1889).

Ellis, E. S., *The Camp Fires of General Lee* (Philadelphia, 1886).

Gilmore, Harry, *Four Years in the Saddle* (New York, 1866).

Headley, John W., *Confederate Operations in Canada and New York* (New York, 1906).

Hood, J. B., *Advance and Retreat* (New Orleans, 1880).

Johnston, J. E., *Narrative of Military Operations* (New York, 1874).

Longstreet, James D., *From Manassas to Appomattox* (Philadelphia, 1903).

Maury, Dabney H., *Recollections of a Virginian* (New York, 1894).

McCarthy, Carlton, *Detailed Minutiæ of Soldier Life in the Army of Northern Virginia* (Richmond, Virginia, 1882).

Scott, John, *Partisan Life with Colonel John S. Mosby* (New York, 1867).

Sorrel, G. M., *Recollections of a Confederate Staff Officer* (New York, 1905).

Williamson, James J., *Mosby's Rangers* (New York, 1909).

Wise, George, *History of the Seventeenth Virginia Infantry* (Baltimore, 1870).

Wise, John S., *The End of an Era* (Boston and New York, 1899).

This group of personal memoirs detailing personal experiences proved valuable as much for gaining an impression of the atmosphere which bred desertion as for the items of specific information.

Civil Biographies and Reminiscences

Avary, M. L., *A Virginia Girl in the Civil War* (New York, 1903).

Campbell, J. A., *Reminiscences* (Baltimore, 1887).

Gay, May A. H., *Life in Dixie during the War* (Atlanta, 1894).

Henderson, G. F. R., *Stonewall Jackson and the American Civil War* (London, 1898).

Jones, J. B., *A Rebel War Clerk's Diary* (Philadelphia, 1866).

DeLeon, T. C., *Four Years in Rebel Capitals* (Mobile, 1890).

Livermore, Mary A., *My Story of the War* (Hartford, 1889).

Welles, Gideon, *Diary of Gideon Welles* (Boston and New York, 1911).

North, Thomas, *Five Years in Texas* (Cincinnati, 1871).

Pollard, E. A., *Life of Jefferson Davis* (Philadelphia, 1869).

The works in this class yielded only isolated fragments of information, but helped in the study by revealing the psychology of the civilian population.

Secondary Sources

Arthur, John Preston, *Western North Carolina* (Raleigh, 1914).

Curry, J. L. M., *Civil History of the Confederate States* (Richmond, Virginia, 1906).

Davis, William W., *The Civil War and Reconstruction in Florida* (New York, 1913).

Fleming, Walter L., *Civil War and Reconstruction in Alabama* (New York, 1905).

Jones, J. W., "The Morale of the Confederate Armies," *Confederate Military History* (Atlanta, 1899,) XII.

Classified here by virtue of the nature of the book, rather than according to the character of the article.

Mason, Edward Campbell, *The Veto Power* (Boston, 1890).

Moore, J. W., *History of North Carolina* (Raleigh, 1890).

Moore, Albert B., *Conscription and Conflict in the Confederacy* (New York, 1924).

Owsley, F. L., *States Rights in the Confederacy* (Chicago, 1925).

Polk, W. M., *Leonidas Polk* (New York, 1915).

Pollard, E. A., *Life of Jefferson Davis* (Philadelphia, 1869).

Rhodes, James Ford, *History of the United States from the Compromise of 1850* (New York, 1907), V.

——*History of the Civil War* (New York, 1917).

Schwab, J. C., *The Confederate States of America* (New York, 1901).

Stephenson, N. W., *Day of the Confederacy* (New Haven, 1919).

Wyeth, John A., *Life of General Nathan Bedford Forrest* (New York, 1899).

Statistical

Fox, W. F., *Regimental Losses in the American Civil War* (Albany, 1889).

Livermore, Thomas L., *Numbers and Losses During the American Civil War* (New York, 1900).

Probably the most authoritative work on the phase of numbers engaged on both sides in the war.

Phisterer, Frederick, *Statistical Record* (New York, 1883).

Magazine Articles

Adams, Charles Francis, "Pensions—Worse and More of Them," *World's Work* (New York, 1911–1912).

Dodge, David, "Cave Dwellers of the Confederacy," *Atlantic Monthly,* LXVII (Boston, 1891).

Greenleaf, Major C. R., "Recognition of Deserters," *Journal of the Military Service Institution* (November, 1889).

The only file of this periodical which the writer has been able to locate is in the United States Naval Academy at Annapolis.

Hale, William Bayard, "The Pension Carnival," *The World's Work,* XX–XXI (New York, 1910–1911).

Prentice, W. R., "On the Dry Tortugas," *McClure's Magazine,* XVIII (April, 1902).

Tarbell, Ida, "The American Woman," *American Magazine,* LXIX, (April, 1910).

INDEX

INDEX

A

Adams, Charles Francis, 160

Alabama, 3, 72, 78, 80, 82, 83; troops of, 14; deserters in mountains, 24, 25; statistics on deserters, 26; plot in Clanton's Brigade, 27; Pillow's comment about soldiers of, 31; desertion from troops of, 32; haunts of deserters in, 62, 63; guerillas in, 68; estimate of number of deserters in, 71; deserters jailed, 96; secret societies in, 100; governors' conference, 112; State legislature, 113; no relief measures for soldiers' families, 115; Union deserters in, 200, 201

Allen, Gen., 71

Amacker, Capt., 81

Amnesty, offers of, 46, 49, 213, 227

Anderson, Gen., 87

Andersonville, 184, 187

Andrew, Gov., of Mass., on pardons, 171

Antietam, Battle of, 144

Arkansas, 152, 153, 194; desertions from troops of, 26; haunts of deserters in, 62; success in gathering deserters in, 89, 90; State legislature, 113; provisions for families, 115; Union deserters in, 199, 200

Armisted, Gen., 25

Arms, Confederate lack of, 10; Union lack of, 130

Army of Potomac, 222; hardships, 131, 132, 145, 146, officers absent without leave, 147; desertions from, 150; abuse of sick leave, 157; death penalty, 181, 182

Arrest of deserters, 52-54

Articles of War, 56

Artillery; rounding up deserters, 78, 81

Atlanta, fall of, contributed to Confederate desertion, 32

B

Barrel-shirt, 57

Beauregard, Gen., 29, 33, 188, 189, 193, 211

Bee, Gen. H. P., 64, 65, 195

Betrayal of Lee's plan before Wilderness Campaign, 103, 104

Bloodhounds, 83, 89

Bond as security for fidelity, 92, 93

Bonham, Gov., of South Carolina, 106, 108

Bounties, 139, 141, 216, 220, 227

Bounty-broker, 227

Bounty-jumpers, 139, 141, 142, 160, 184, 219, 230

Boykin, 54

Boyle, Gen., 211

Bragg, Gen., 101, 104, 145

Bragg's Army, 34, 36, 47, 102, 103; desertions from, 23; shooting of deserters, 31

Branding, 58

Breckenridge, Gen., 24, 28, 138, 191; proclamation of amnesty, 213

Brown, Gov. of Georgia, 106, 109, 110, 112, 116

Bucking, 57

Buckingham, Gen., on prevention of desertion, 173

Buell, Gen., 145, 168

Burleson, Lt. Col., 44

Burnside, Gen., 131, 144, 194

Bushwhackers, 3, 119

Butler, Gen., 194, 196

C

Camp Chase, Columbus, for prisoners of war, 93, 94

Campbell, Secretary of War, 29, 48

Canada: asylum for deserters, 202

Capers, Col., 83

Castle Lightning, 184

Causes of defection, Confederate: elective principle, 16; want of active service, 17; speculation and extortion, 17; peculation, 17; discrimination by brokers, 17; weariness and hopelessness, 18; threats of invasion of home, 18; lack of discipline, 18; immunity to deserters from Washington, 19; civilian public opinion, 19

245

J

Jackson, Stonewall, 59, 193
Jayhawkers, 63, 66
Johnson, Andrew, 170
Johnson, Gen., 29, 41
Johnston, Gen., 8, 32, 34, 40, 53, 56, 63, 102, 104, 194, 195
Jones, Gen., 16, 34, 90
Jones, Gen. Sam., 228
Jones, War Clerk, estimate of desertion, 29

K

Kasion, 3
Kentucky, 199, 200; Confederate recruits from, 5; troops of, 16; desertions from troops of, 23; haunts of deserters in, 63; Union, complaint of non-payment of troops in, 132; desertions from troops in, 152; deserters sent to, 191; spies, 212
Knights of the Golden Circle, 100, 204, 205, 208
Ku Klux Klan, 122, 229

L

Law to relieve the army of disqualified, disabled and incompetent officers, 34
Laws dealing with deserters, 114
Lawrence, Gen., 25
Lee, Gen., 8, 12, 15, 16, 19, 24, 25, 28, 32, 34, 43, 46, 47, 48, 50, 52, 54, 55, 56, 79, 88, 89, 91, 120, 146, 189, 190, 194, 196, 227
Letcher, Gov., of Virginia, 16, 108
Libby Prison, 184
Lincoln: proclamation of Pardon and Amnesty, 95, 144; statistics, 150, 151; clemency of, 169, 170; policy on punishment for desertion, 223; pardons, 227
Lockhart, 89
Longstreet, Gen., 8, 9, 55, 77, 101, 103, 104; desertion of his men, 22; complaint of Georgia troops, 32
Louisiana: sufferings of troops, 7; complaint by Lee, 56; haunts of deserters, 62; guerillas, 68, 70, 71; force needed to hunt deserters in, 78, 79; Ninth cavalry, 81; provision for soldiers' families, 115; Union deserters in, 199

M

McClellan, Gen., 143, 144, 147, 194, 195, 204; table of desertions, 150; abuse of sick leaves, 157
McCulloch, 78, 79

McCullough, Gen., 76, 77, 84, 85
Magruder, Gen., 79, 80
Mahone, Gen., 32
Maine overrun with deserters, 207
Marmaduke, Gen., loss of men by, 31
Maryland: stragglers in, 43; haunts of deserters in, 64; statistics of Union deserters, 152
Massachusetts: bounties, 140
Maury, Col., 82
Maury, Gen., 59
Maxey, Gen., 212
Meade, Gen., 129, 135, 138, 144, 181
Meridian: surrender of Gen. Dick Taylor in, 30
Mexicans: in Confederate service, 5; H. P. Bee on conscription of, 5; in Union army, 139, 191, 192
Mexico: haunts of deserters in, 63, 64; draft dodgers, 203
Militia, State, 54, 80
Milroy, Gen., lack of discipline, 136
Milton, Gov., of Fla., 70, 85, 88, 116
Mines, labor in, 185
Minnesota draft dodgers, 207
Missionary Ridge, 35, 103, 120
Mississippi, 3, 14, 32, 153, 200; statistics of desertions, 26, 32; haunts of deserters, 62; guerillas, 68, 70-72, 75, 76; success in gathering deserters, 89, 90; State reserves, 112; governors' conference, 112; State legislature, 112; provisions for families, 115; loss of morale, 122
Missouri, 199, 200; Price's campaigns' contribution to desertion, 32; guerillas in, 71; treatment of Confederate deserters by North, 92; Union defections, 128; complaint of non-payment of troops in, 132
Mobberly, Union deserters with, 199
Moore, Gov., of Louisiana, 108
Morgan, Gov., of New York, 157
Morgan, 32, 46, 56; character of his men, 5; as police force, 119
Morton, Gov., of Indiana, 169
Mosby, 15, 118, 191; as police force, 119; Union deserters with, 199
Mossback, 3
Moxey, Gen., 26
Mud march of Burnside, 131
Mugging, 184
Murfreesborough, 104

N

Nashville: deserters received at, 23
Negroes: desertion of, 36; law to enlist and arm, 46
New Hampshire: bounties, 140; in